GOVERNING TOGETHER

Also by Jean Blondel

CABINETS IN WESTERN EUROPE
  (*editor with Ferdinand Müller-Rommel*)
COMPARATIVE GOVERNMENT
COMPARATIVE LEGISLATURES
THE DISCIPLINE OF POLITICS
GOVERNMENT MINISTERS IN THE CONTEMPORARY
  WORLD
THE ORGANIZATION OF GOVERNMENTS
POLITICAL LEADERSHIP
POLITICAL PARTIES
THE PROFESSION OF GOVERNMENT MINISTER IN
  WESTERN EUROPE (*editor with Jean-Louis Thiébault*)
VOTERS, PARTIES AND LEADERS
WORLD LEADERS

Also by Ferdinand Müller-Rommel

CABINETS IN WESTERN EUROPE (*editor with Jean Blondel*)
EMPIRISCHE POLITIKWISSENSCHAFT (*with Manfred Schmidt*)
GRUNE PARTEIEN IN WESTEUROPA
INNERPARTEILICHE GRUPPIERUNGEN IN DER SPD
NEW POLITICS IN WESTERN EUROPE
VERGLEICHENDE POLITIKWISSENSCHAFT
  (*with Dirk Berg-Schlosser*)

Governing Together

The Extent and Limits of Joint Decision-Making in Western European Cabinets

Edited by

Jean Blondel
Professor of Political Science
European University Institute, Florence, Italy

and

Ferdinand Müller-Rommel
Professor of Political Science
University of Lüneburg, Germany

St. Martin's Press

First published in Great Britain 1993 by
THE MACMILLAN PRESS LTD
Houndmills, Basingstoke, Hampshire RG21 2XS
and London
Companies and representatives
throughout the world

A catalogue record for this book is available
from the British Library.

ISBN 0-333-55656-9

Printed in Great Britain by
Ipswich Book Co Ltd
Ipswich, Suffolk

First published in the United States of America 1993 by
Scholarly and Reference Division,
ST. MARTIN'S PRESS, INC.,
175 Fifth Avenue,
New York, N.Y. 10010

ISBN 0-312-09990-8

Library of Congress Cataloging-in-Publication Data
Governing together : the extent and limits of joint decision-making in
Western European cabinets / edited by Jean Blondel and Ferdinand
Müller-Rommel.
p. cm.
Includes bibliographical references and index.
ISBN 0-312-09990-8
1. Cabinet system—Europe. 2. Public administration—Europe-
-Decision making. I. Blondel, Jean, 1929- . II. Müller-Rommel,
Ferdinand.
JN94.A63G68   1993
351.004'094—dc20   93-17276
                                                                CIP

Contents

Contents

9 The Role and Position of Ministers of Finance
   Torbjörn Larsson   207

10 Prime Ministers and Cabinet Decision-making Processes
   Wolfgang C. Müller, Wilfred Philipp and Peter Gerlich   223

Part IV   Conclusions: Achievements, Problems and Reforms

11 Decision-Making, Policy Content and Conflict
   Resolution in Western European Cabinets
   Jaakko Nousiainen   259

12 Evaluating Cabinet Decision-Making
   Svein Eriksen   283

13 Conclusion
   Jaakko Nousiainen and Jean Blondel   301

Appendix I: The Ministerial Survey   308
Appendix II: The Newspaper Survey   316
Bibliography   319
Index   332

Preface

By the closing years of the twentieth century, one can say without fear of contradiction that cabinet government has been a great success. This success was not planned, however, and cynics might perhaps note that this is possibly the real reason for the success of the cabinet formula. The truth is that cabinet government emerged by accident and spread by accident. It emerged by accident in the eighteenth century in Britain and Sweden: one can describe how it emerged, but it is more difficult to say why it did, especially since this form of rule did not correspond to any pre-existing theory. Cabinet government then spread by accident, but in a slow, tortuous, and often painful manner, to almost the whole of Western Europe. Before the Second World War, this system seemed on the verge of perishing as it appeared unable to provide the leadership and the basic strength required if national executives were to be effective politically, socially, and economically; yet half a century later, cabinet government is thriving.

New worries have been voiced, though, as it has been noted that the system seemed to survive only by losing much of its specificity. Cabinet government has often been described as government by a committee of equals. This appears to be questionable for the following reasons: many ministers are so burdened that they concentrate on their departments; many decisions are taken by smaller groups that by-pass the full cabinet; and, above all, prime ministers have become near-'presidential', at least in some countries.

These assertions are controversial, but they are intriguing enough to warrant a comparative inquiry into the state of cabinet government across Western Europe at the end of the twentieth century. This is the aim of this volume, which is comparative in that it analyses national cabinets in twelve Western European countries on the basis of a common framework and a set of identical interviews of cabinet ministers, mainly ex-ministers, in these countries. It is also comparative in that each chapter is devoted to a particular aspect of the life of national cabinets, such as the rules under which these operate, the part played by parties, the role of individual ministers and of prime ministers, and, above all, the extent to which the single-party or coalition structure of the government affects the decision-making process.

Governing Together is thus a truly collective and collegial effort. Such an undertaking would not have been possible without a dedicated team of scholars, some of whom were so disinterested that they were not directly involved with the drafting of any of the chapters of the finished product. We wish therefore to record our particular thanks to all the members of the team, whether they are those who appear in the volume as authors (R. B. Andeweg, M. Burch, L. de Winter, S. Eriksen, A.-P. Frognier, P. Gerlich, T. Larsson, W. C. Müller, J. Nousiainen, W. Philipp, and J.-L. Thiébault), or those who undertook, as did the rest of the team, the task of interviewing ministers in their country and of supervising the collection of other data, in particular from periodicals (M. Cotta and P. A. Isernia for Italy, B. Farrell for Ireland, and T. L. Schou for Denmark). We wish to record our warmest thanks to the more than four hundred ministers, across the twelve countries covered in the study, who were willing to answer the questions put to them and who did so in the most straightforward and frankest manner.

We are most grateful to the European University Institute for the intellectual and financial support that was given to us throughout the period of gestation of this study and in particular to the presidents of the Institute, W. Maihofer and E. Noel, who were willing to devote substantial time to advise and to help. We wish to thank the University of Lüneburg and the *Deutsche Forschungsgemeinschaft* as well as the University of Lille-II and the French *Conseil National de la Recherche Scientifique* for their generous support. Last but not least, we wish to thank Robert Danziger for his advice on computing problems, Clare Tame and Laurence Morel who helped so magnificently in preparing, coding, and analysing the data, and Maureen Lechleitner who patiently typed many parts of this work, and in particular the tables.

This has been an exciting enterprise of collaboration which led to many friendships and is also resulting in further joint work. We hope that this volume will achieve its main aims – namely, to provide students of politics and practitioners with information on the extent to which cabinets still 'govern together' and to make better known a form of government of which Western European countries – and to begin with Britain and Sweden – can truly be proud.

Florence and Lüneburg   JEAN BLONDEL
FERDINAND MÜLLER ROMMEL

Notes on the Contributors

Rudi Andeweg is Professor of Political Science at the University of Leiden.

Jean Blondel is Professor of Political Science at the European University Institute, Florence.

Martin Burch is Senior Lecturer in Government at the University of Manchester.

Lieven de Winter is Assistant in the Department of Political Science at the University of Louvain-la-Neuve.

Svein Eriksen is Assistant County Governor, Westfold County, Norway.

André-Paul Frognier is Professor of Political Science at the University of Louvain-la-Neuve.

Peter Gerlich is Professor of Political Science at the University of Vienna.

Torbjörn Larsson is at the University of Stockholm.

Wolfgang C. Müller is Lecturer in Political Science at the University of Vienna.

Ferdinand Müller-Rommel is Professor of Political Science at the University of Lüneburg.

Jaakko Nousiainen is Professor of Political Science at the University of Turku.

Wilfried Philipp is Lecturer in Economics at the University of Vienna.

Jean-Louis Thiébault is Professor of Political Science at the University of Amiens.

1 Introduction

Jean Blondel and
Ferdinand Müller-Rommel

This book is about the characteristics of decision-making processes in Western European governments. It is also about the limits to the collective and collegial nature of these governments, limits that are set in particular by the requirements of efficiency. The problem posed by these limits is at the very root of the functioning of cabinet systems and it touches on a feature that is almost unique to these executives. For practically no other national executive (in fact no other executive except that of Switzerland) requires that governmental decisions be taken by ministers as a group. Clearly dictatorial or even authoritarian systems do not have such a requirement, as they rely primarily on the power of one man or at most on a very small inner group. Nor does the requirement of group decision-making exist in the presidential system, which is the other main form of liberal rule besides parliamentary government; in presidential government, the 'buck' can be passed, so to speak, to the chief executive, who appoints the ministers, these being in turn responsible to the president alone, who also allocates among them the tasks that they will have to undertake. In cabinet government, on the other hand, both in theory and to a large extent in practice, ministers and prime ministers form part of a common enterprise in which they have a share.

Cabinet government is unique because it is collective and collegial. This unique characteristic stems, first and foremost, from the fact that links have to be maintained between executive and legislature. Although most parliaments may not be, or are no longer, in a position to exercise truly their lawmaking function, they continue to affect markedly the nature of the government by way of the condition that that government needs the confidence of parliament to remain in office. This explains in large part why so many ministers are drawn from the legislature;[1] this explains also, indirectly at least, the fact that the government has to act together. Since the cabinet may fall as a group, it tends naturally to be constituted as a group; since it is constituted as a group, it tends to act as a group throughout its existence.

1

Yet, as we noted earlier, governing together does not seem to be well adapted to the pace of the contemporary world. If applied to the letter, the requirement would indeed call for the involvement of all the ministers on all matters, ranging from the initiation of the most important policies to the detailed implementation of the most trivial: this is obviously not realistic. Thus cabinet government can function effectively only if it abandons to an extent its basic principle of organisation. There is therefore a dilemma and a balance has to be struck: it may be efficient for ministers not to govern together; but, as they are collectively responsible to parliament, joint decision-making cannot be altogether abandoned. The requirement may be 'bent' to an extent, but some important element has to remain. What needs to be examined is the nature of the trade-off between the two opposite principles on the basis of which governments are organised in cabinet systems.

This means, first, investigating the many ways in which joint action by government ministers can be and indeed is reduced and, in the process, classifying these mechanisms in terms of broad dimensions. As a matter of fact, a number of dimensions help to provide such a classification. They form the framework within which the various types of cabinet decision-making that exist in the contemporary world can be analysed: they will be presented and discussed in the following chapter.

There are also diverse origins to the limitations on the extent to which parliamentary cabinets govern together. They, too, fall into two broad categories. On the one hand, rules, habits, or practices have been introduced or happen to have emerged here and there as they have been found to speed up or simplify the decision-making process. For instance, the power to take decisions on behalf of the government in the sphere of jurisdiction of individual departments is often delegated to the ministers concerned: this reduces *ipso facto* the number of decisions that go to the whole cabinet. For instance, too, ministers may often wish not to be involved in matters that are not within the field of their department: decisions may therefore be taken by others by default, as a result of the self-denying ordinance of these cabinet members. Above all, prime ministers can and often do play a very large part in shaping the decisions taken, to the extent that some types of governments have been described, perhaps with some exaggeration, as prime ministerial governments.[2]

Restrictions on joint governmental action also have another origin, though, for they result indirectly from the second most important characteristic of cabinet government (alongside the fact that it is based on the idea of deciding together), namely, the role of parties in the overall structure and behaviour of the executive. Cabinet government has been advisedly referred to as party government; it does not function without parties in the contemporary world because, as a matter of fact, it cannot function adequately without parties.[3] This is not just because parties provide a crucial link between executive and legislature, a link that has of course to exist if the system is to operate at all; it is also because parties have a direct effect on the ease with which decisions can be taken jointly by ministers. If cabinets were a microcosm of the nation, if they were a microcosm of parliament even, almost any question would give rise to debate: the decision-making process would be extremely slow; that this is not so is largely a result of the fact that ministers are members of the same party or members of parties that have agreed to work together to implement certain policies. As a result, large numbers of measures can be adopted with no or little discussion, for there is on these a common viewpoint. Parties provide the framework within which, and the instrument by which an understanding emerges among cabinet members even before any meeting takes place. This is why cabinet government cannot operate well without party; indeed, when parties are weak and/or very numerous, as in France before 1958, the cabinet system is so handicapped that it can collapse altogether.

Yet, while cabinet government is party government, the party structure of these cabinets varies markedly. Some are composed of members of one party only, a party which may or may not enjoy an overall majority in parliament; others are coalitions and may be based on two, three, or more parties, which may or may not be equal in strength. Ostensibly at least, this structural difference would appear to affect markedly the character of the government. Single-party cabinets are composed of men and women who fight election campaigns together and can be assumed to have much in common; coalitions bring together politicians who have been opposed to each other in the past and are likely to oppose each other again in the future. Not surprisingly, the distinction is widely regarded as a major discriminating element and, arguably, as *the* major discriminating element among parliamentary cabinets.

It has indeed sometimes been suggested in recent decades that the difference relates to two distinct types of political cultures, the culture of 'adversary' politics where government confronts opposition, as in Britain and many Commonwealth countries, and the culture of consensus and 'consociational' politics which many coalition govern-

ments of the Continent appear to embody.[4] Whether there is such a
sharp contrast in practice needs therefore to be assessed and this
assessment is one of the main purposes of this study, the specific
questions being to what extent decision-making processes differ in
single-party governments from the way they are in coalitions, and how
far the extent to which cabinet ministers govern together is affected by
this difference. However, since, as we noted, various rules and practices
also affect (by design or by accident) this joint decision-making
process, the interplay between these rules and practices and the single-
party/coalition distinction needs also to be closely examined.

THE DISTINCTION BETWEEN SINGLE-PARTY AND COALITION CABINETS – ORIGINS AND CONSEQUENCES ON THE NATURE OF GOVERNMENT

Ostensibly at least, the distinction between single-party government
and coalition government would seem to have a significant effect on
the characteristics of cabinets: in some respects at least it is indeed the
summa divisio among cabinets. It has been regarded as such by many
observers and practitioners for a number of decades, principally on the
grounds that single-party governments were considered to be markedly
more stable than coalitions: the point having been shown not to be
valid or at most to be valid to a very limited extent only, this debate has
come to an end.[5] Perhaps as a result, by an interesting twist, major
virtues have now been found in coalition governments. Far from being
regarded as 'aberrations' or 'pathological' developments, they have
started to be admired for the self-restraint that they require on the part
of their members. They may indeed arguably be viewed as a more
sophisticated form of cabinet arrangement than single-party
governments, since they require complex written and unwritten
agreements among the partners. This complexity may also account
for some of the difficulties experienced by coalitions in the past: time
was needed for practices to be fully elaborated and for these practices
to be well understood and accepted.

The development of coalition governments in cabinet systems

The concept of coalition government emerged only gradually in cabinet
systems. Even the fundamental part played by parties for the smooth
operation of these systems was not immediately obvious, to a large

extent because cabinets were appointed at first by, and primarily responsible to, the chief executive who, being a monarch, was outside and somewhat above the political system. Moreover, even where governments were closely associated with a party (as with the Whigs or Tories in Britain), that party may well not always have commanded an overall majority in parliament; it was also typically rather loosely organised and therefore not sufficiently disciplined to provide the government with solid support for its bills and its budgetary requirements. Prime ministers had therefore to use a panoply of means, from threats to blandishment and favours, to ensure the passage of their requests on the statute book.

Thus what tends to be regarded at present as unusual – minority governments – was in some sense the rule in the early period of cabinet government. This occurred for instance in Britain as late as the early part of the twentieth century: the governments elected at the two 1910 elections did not have a 'majority' in the contemporary sense of the word. Furthermore, minority governments continued to prevail beyond the early part of the century even when parties became more cohesive and independents tended to be squeezed out, as new parties began to emerge and complicate the political scene (social democratic or Labour parties, for instance): thus Britain was ruled by minority governments in 1924 and in 1929–31. The minority governments that are periodically formed, in Scandinavia in particular, are therefore the continuation of an established practice rather than a new phenomenon.[6] As a matter of fact, single-party (and to a lesser extent coalition) minority governments remain a feature of political life in some other countries, albeit a somewhat minor one.[7]

A common method used by cabinets and in particular by their prime ministers to find majorities in parliament consisted of exercising various forms of manipulation. The idea and reality of coalitions developed in this context, but the experiments were at first limited in time and scope. Indeed, coalitions are not regarded as being a normal feature of presidential systems; this is particularly the case in the United States where politicians of both the executive and legislative branches are periodically concerned with the build-up of specific alliances designed to help the passage of a bill or of, at most, a package of measures.[8] This is consistent with the nature of the presidential system, since the government does not depend in this case on a majority of the legislature to remain in existence; yet the executive does need to see at least some of its proposals endorsed by the Congress: in particular, a budget has to be adopted. The behaviour of contemporary presidential executives is thus often likely to be akin to that of cabinet systems in the past and follows the model of the single-party minority government: in this case, coalitions continue to display an essentially temporary and even shaky character.

Meanwhile, the nature of the concept of coalition did change in cabinet systems. As a result of the gradually tighter hold of parties on legislatures and on legislators, governments found it increasingly difficult, and indeed in many cases impossible, to resort to manipulation; they were confronted with solid parliamentary parties with which they had to negotiate. The tables were turned as the parliamentary parties, rather than the executive, became the more powerful element: no one outside parliamentary and party leaders could exercise significant influence any longer; in particular, the head of State ceased to play a key part in the process: his or her role was confined to the selection of the prime minister and even this power tended to become formal or aimed somewhat technically at discovering the politician most likely to be able to build a government.[9] The parties were the government-makers. Meanwhile, in countries where, election after election, no outright majority came out at the polls, parties had to recognise that, if political life was to function, agreements had to be struck among them. Occasionally these were signed before the election, if it was thought that seats would be gained in this way; sometimes these alliances also included an undertaking that the parties concerned would collaborate to form the government if they obtained an overall majority. More often, agreements were ironed out when the Chamber reconvened.[10]

The idea that coalitions were a normal feature of cabinet government, indeed in some cases even a permanent one, emerged in the process. What began as a political necessity came in some cases to be regarded as a valuable change in the character of cabinets. Since no party could win outright and opponents could therefore not be thoroughly 'beaten', there could not be a well-defined alignment between government and opposition; the system could not have an entirely 'adversary' character: it had to be based on some form of 'accommodation'.[11] Coalitions could thus be regarded as a more mature and sophisticated form of governmental arrangement in which there would be efforts at reciprocal understanding. This approach to the nature of government is specific to cabinet systems and indeed to some of them only: it does not need to emerge in presidential systems, as we noted earlier, since in these the executive does not depend on the legislature for its existence;[12] nor did the idea take roots in those cabinet systems, mostly from the Commonwealth, in which one party could normally expect to obtain an absolute majority of seats. On the other hand, in some countries of the Continent where governments tend to be coalitions, 'consociational' politics came to be regarded not just as the norm, but as a preferable form of government.

Not all coalition governments are based on 'accommodation', though. The link between the practical need for a coalition and the ideological rationalisation in terms of 'accommodation' often does not exist. In some countries, coalitions are based on a well-defined division between a 'bourgeois' block and a 'workers' block: this tends to be the case in Sweden, Norway, or France: there is then 'adversary' politics between the 'blocks'. Moreover, coalition governments that begin in a spirit of good feelings may become conflictual after a period, as the partners find that they disagree on an increasing number of issues. Conversely, in 'adversary' systems such as Britain or other Commonwealth countries, the political parties do not always oppose one another. Indeed, when a major crisis occurs, in particular in times of war, consensus prevails and a coalition may even be set up, at least if the armed conflict is prolonged: this was the case in Britain from 1916 during the First World War and from 1940 during the Second World War. Yet the practice remains exceptional. On the contrary, in polities where coalitions are regarded as normal – and indeed are normal, especially where a major party (a 'pivot') changes its partners from time to time or where very large coalitions are occasionally set up, collaboration between the parties has to take place more openly: a future coalition might include any or almost any of the parties represented in parliament.

Thus, at least at the polar extremes of the distinction between single-party governments and coalitions, the character of the cabinet is likely to be affected. Cabinets composed of members of one party and facing the clear opposition of another party with which there is no question of building a coalition will tend to have the character of *teams* aiming at working together to ensure that the other party does not win the next election; where coalitions are the norm, on the other hand, the government can perhaps be better described as a *board of management* entrusted for a period by its 'godfathers' (the parties in the coalition) with the mission of conducting jointly the affairs of the State. There will of course be some fighting against the opposition parties, especially if the coalition is small or 'minimum winning';[13] but these opposition parties, or at least some of them, may be coalition partners in the next government and indeed may well have been coalition partners in the past. Compromise is therefore more likely to prevail; in some extreme cases, the boundary between government and opposition may become vague and blurred. Although the distinction between single-party governments and coalitions is thus only partly coextensive with the contrast between 'adversary' and 'consociational' politics, the two elements may well combine to affect jointly the characteristics of many cabinets.

SINGLE-PARTY GOVERNMENTS, COALITIONS AND THE GOVERNMENTAL COMPACT

What the 'consociational' ideology suggests is that parties need to an extent to respect each others' views if the system is to function at all. This is why there has to be some degree of give and take if coalitions are to be effective. The question has therefore a clear and practical dimension. Ostensibly at least, single-party cabinets would seem better able to handle governmental issues as their members are more likely to be united over a wide range of issues; conversely, the problems posed by the elaboration of a common programme appear likely to be large in coalitions.

The scope of cabinet decision-making in single-party government

In single-party governments, ministers can be presumed to be and indeed to a large extent are, in agreement on basic party policies. Consequently, there should be no or very little conflict over at least the broad governmental goals: these may not even give rise to much discussion. Disagreements will tend to occur, if they occur at all, on the implementation of policies and on problems that emerge unexpectedly.

The governmental agenda is all the more non-controversial within the cabinet in that it is likely to be based on the electoral programme: this provides a further brake against potential conflicts, since ministers will either spontaneously agree to the programme or at least recognise that they are bound by it. Circumstances may force the government to change policies, admittedly; but such a move will be attacked, including in the cabinet meeting. Modifications are more likely to occur insidiously and by small steps than in a clear and obvious manner, unless it can be claimed with some justification that unforeseen developments, especially abroad, are the cause of the 'U-turn'.

Admittedly, this picture of broad consensus does not always characterise single-party government. Where there are deep ideological divisions within the governing party, a state of affairs that cannot be ruled out since the party is electorally large – as it would not, otherwise, have won the election outright – these are sometimes reflected at the level of the cabinet: British governments have thus been divided in this way. Moreover, disagreements on the implementation of policies may grow over time and even come to have ideological undertones. When this occurs, efforts have to be made to resolve the conflicts internally and to give the impression that unity prevails, for otherwise not just the life of the government may be jeopardised, but the electoral future of the party. On the whole, however, outright conflict is likely to be relatively rare: single-party cabinets seem able to handle large numbers of matters on the basis of pre-existing agreements among ministers. Only in extreme cases can they not do so; the party then is in real trouble and may even be on the verge of splitting.

The scope of cabinet decision-making in coalitions

The situation appears *prima facie* different in coalitions, as these seem to have a greater potential for conflict than single-party governments: the coalition partners are likely to differ on many policy points, even if one can expect them to have at least some common orientations, especially when the ideological span covered by the parties is small. Furthermore, the parties run for election against one another and they have to emphasise their differences at the polls. These matters are likely to constitute stumbling blocks in the government formation process: the basis for a common understanding may be rendered more difficult as a result.

Such an understanding is typically achieved in the course of a period, often protracted, during which areas of potential conflict are gradually reduced and ultimately eliminated in order to elaborate a common governmental programme, which is often worked out in considerable detail in the form of the coalition agreements that have been referred to earlier. If the conflictual issues cannot be settled, the negotiations between the partners break up and a different coalition has to be set up. Once the agreement is concluded, however, governmental life may be relatively smooth, in many cases not so much because harmony prevails, but because the scope of governmental action tends to be markedly constrained by the coalition agreement.[14]

Therefore coalition cabinets often have less freedom of manoeuvre than single-party governments: not so many matters are left open. Moreover, even if a conflict does occur none the less, either because of some unforeseen problem or because questions were not handled satisfactorily in the coalition agreement, the cabinet may not be in a position to resolve the issue. This will have to be settled at the level of the leadership of the coalition parties: if an acceptable arrangement is found, the government is able to carry on, although its credibility is probably somewhat reduced. If the party leaders cannot agree, the government falls and a new coalition has to be formed, perhaps after lengthy discussions and elections have taken place.

Some coalition governments may not be very conflictual, but this may be when the cabinet is not the true deciding body on key policy matters. Such coalition governments must be regarded as having a rather narrow brief and as operating more at an 'administrative' level than at a 'high policy' level: they cannot be said to be truly 'central' to decision-making. Delicate issues may simply not be raised, for fear that they might generate conflicts, the government being primarily concerned to implement what has been decided during the process of cabinet formation. Parties are thus truly crucial agents in making cabinet government function; but they are agents that exercise their function in diverse ways, depending on where the government is located on the dimension ranging from the united single-party team to the highly 'consociational' coalition board.

THE LIMITATIONS ON THE DIRECT EFFECT OF THE DISTINCTION BETWEEN SINGLE-PARTY AND COALITION GOVERNMENTS

Cabinet differences or country differences?

Yet, as we have already noted, other elements are likely to exercise an influence on cabinet decision processes; the interplay between these elements and the single-party/coalition distinction is likely to reduce at least the direct impact of that distinction.

Many differences seem to be on a country basis. To begin with, single-party cabinets and coalition cabinets can, and indeed frequently do, follow each other in the same country: in Ireland, Denmark, and Norway, for instance, there have been periodic oscillations from one type to the other; in Austria, a long period of single-party rule (seventeen years) occurred between two periods of coalitions (to 1966 and from 1983). Although the 'culture' of government is often different in single-party cabinets from that in coalitions, this is probably not altogether the case in the cabinets of those countries that have experienced successively both types of party arrangements. Thus the ideology of 'adversary' politics may prevail even when there is a coalition government, for this coalition may be viewed as temporary or there may be strong opposition between two blocks, especially when there are oscillations from one type of party structure of the cabinet to the other, as in Ireland or Norway. Conversely, consociationalism may at least to an extent prevail even when one party runs the government alone, either because it is a minority government, as is often the case in Denmark and sometimes occurs in Italy, or when there is a single-party majority or near-majority government, as in Austria. There is thus an interplay between the 'values' and the 'structural instruments', so to speak: the 'values' that prevail in a single-party government structure or, conversely, in a coalition government arrangement, may well remain the same although the cabinet moves from one type to the other: the effect of the single-party/coalition distinction on decision-making processes is likely to be reduced as a result.

Internal party characteristics

Internal party characteristics also play a part; these characteristics are indeed often shared by many or all the parties in a given country. For example, single-party governments are likely to behave differently if the party in power is highly factionalised or if it is, on the contrary, very united, as disagreements among ministers will recur more frequently when a party has well-defined 'wings': such single-party governments are probably in practice fairly close to being coalitions in all but name. This characteristic often marks several parties in a country: there is more internal party factionalism in some countries than in others – in Japan or Italy, for instance, than in Sweden or even Britain. Cabinet decision-making processes may also be affected by the ideological character of the party or parties in power: social-democratic parties seem generally less united than parties of the Right, for instance. Thus a number of internal party characteristics are likely to affect governmental behavioural patterns and to modify in a number of ways the impact of the distinction between single-party and coalition cabinets.[15]

Rules and practices designed to streamline decision-making; their relationship to the party structure of cabinets

Yet what is usually regarded as most affecting patterns of collective decision-making in cabinets are the arrangements and practices that are introduced in order to render governmental processes more efficient; these rules and practices tend also to affect decision-making in all the cabinets of a country as they are unlikely to be altered, at any rate markedly, even when there are oscillations from one form of party structure of the cabinet to another. Moreover, the rules about cabinet arrangements are sometimes imitated across countries, if they are felt to help decision-making processes in the country of origin. On the other hand, these rules and practices are related in some manner to the single-party or coalition character of the cabinet, if only because they sometimes exist to help modify the 'natural' effects of single-party or of coalition behaviour in the cabinet. There are thus many links between rules and practices of cabinets, on the one hand, and the single-party/ coalition distinction, but these links are difficult to disentangle.

Procedural arrangements

These rules and practices are of several types. There are, first, procedural devices designed to speed up cabinet deliberations and make the machinery of government more efficient; the role of the cabinet meeting is consequently reduced in the process. The setting up of a cabinet secretariat and of a prime minister's office, the introduction of measures designed to streamline discussions, or the power given to the prime minister to curtail debate are all arrangements that ensure that the cabinet becomes less of a forum for true joint decision-making. This is inevitable: two or three hours of meeting every week do not give enough time to enable a group of between fifteen and twenty or more ministers to give full attention to the many questions on the agenda.

Yet the cabinet meeting is in most countries the only occasion that is attended by all ministers (Swedish 'lunches' and Finnish 'dinners' being apparently the only other examples).[16] Real debates occur therefore in smaller groups, either formally constituted (committees, for instance) or informally called together – typically when two or three members see each other, one of them being, in many cases at least, the prime minister. Thus, while sub-group discussions are likely to be frequent, true debates of the full cabinet are relatively rare. Cabinet government may give opportunities to a few members to discuss thoroughly the problems that particularly concern them; it seems no longer able to provide all ministers with an opportunity to debate most questions jointly. An important element of joint decision-making has consequently been undermined.

One might expect such developments to occur broadly along the same lines in single-party governments and in coalitions: a reduction in collective or even collegial activities is likely to take place everywhere: indeed the complexity of the issues and, therefore, the size and degree of homogeneity of the country may play a large part. However, different arrangements may well be used in different types of cabinet structure: it seems plausible that single-party cabinets might resort more often to 'authoritarian' means of controlling discussions within the meeting itself, while coalition governments may rely more heavily on consensual arrangements.

The extent of involvement of ministers

For cabinet members to govern together, it is not sufficient that there be occasions when ministers can discuss issues as a group; there has also to be a will on the part of all government members to participate in the discussion of these issues. Yet this will may not always be present; indeed it is likely to be absent in many circumstances. Specifically, 'generalist' ministers are more likely to want to be involved than 'specialists'; similarly, ministers who move from one department to another are more likely to want to be involved in the affairs of other departments than ministers who remain in one post; the same difference will be found between ministers who are well briefed by a large staff and those who are not. Above all, the behaviour of ministers is also likely to be affected by the belief that they will have a better chance of seeing their proposals adopted by the cabinet if they concentrate on the affairs of their department: this belief seems rather widespread. On the one hand, ministers are more likely to be left alone if they do not discuss, criticise or raise points about matters that concern other departments. On the other, even if they are or want to be 'generalists', ministers are close to their departments: they are in their office throughout their working day and are members of the cabinet only episodically. It is therefore the department rather than the cabinet that is likely to be their main reference point.

One might expect the origins of ministers to vary from country to country;[17] but one might also expect the single-party/coalition distinction to play a part, though perhaps more in countries where the government is always or nearly always of the single party or of the coalition type than when it oscillates from one form to the other. One might therefore for instance hypothesise that there may be more 'generalists' in single-party governments and more specialists in coalition governments: in the latter, there might often have to be a balance between party political experience (which will tend to characterise the party leaders) and a rather technical background. Such a balance is not found – or indeed even sought – in single-party governments, perhaps because the concept of the team prevails and a division between two types of ministers is therefore less likely to emerge.

The impact of leadership

One way of streamlining decision-making is to give substantial powers to leaders and to ensure that these effectively control both the agenda and the direction of the debate. Although, in theory, prime ministers in parliamentary governments are regarded as merely 'first among equals', they are in practice appreciably more influential. Yet there are marked variations in the role of these prime ministers; moreover, leadership extends sometimes beyond the prime minister, either if an inner cabinet exists or because another minister – often the minister of finance – plays a major part. There can therefore be cases of 'dual' or oligarchical leadership alongside more widely known examples of prime ministerial leadership.

The effective part played by prime ministers and other leaders is likely to depend in large part on the personalities of the politicians concerned: some prime ministers want to be very active, while others are less ambitious. One aspect of this role is substantive: it is concerned with the desire of the head of the government to see some policies adopted and implemented; another aspect is procedural and relates to the desire of the prime minister to see the business of government proceed smoothly. These two goals – a peaceful cabinet life and the desire to put forward policies – correspond to two different roles of prime ministers, those of *arbitrator* and of *activist*, consensus-seeking and forcing issues. They are complementary to an extent, in that the prime minister will wish to be a consensus-seeker with respect to matters in which he or she is not primarily interested, and be forceful regarding those with which he or she is really concerned; the more the prime minister can smooth problems arising among ministers, as a consensus-seeker, the more he or she can have time and opportunity to be forceful.

While circumstances, time, and personality obviously play a part in determining the consensual or forceful character of a prime minister, the party structure of the cabinet seems *prima facie* to have a major role also. Prime ministers of single-party governments would seem to have greater opportunities to be truly forceful; in coalitions, prime ministers seem more often constrained to being consensus-seekers. By and large, too, in single-party governments, the prime minister seems more likely to be able to exercise leadership alone or at most with one colleague (often the minister of finance); in coalitions, other ministers are likely to have a share in leadership.

THE NATURE AND CHARACTERISTICS OF THIS STUDY

This work is therefore a study of the interplay of one major independent variable – the single-party or coalition character of the cabinet – with a number of structural and customary arrangements in governments, and of the combined effect of these factors on decision-making processes in Western European parliamentary cabinets. It is based on a fully comparative analysis of cabinet decision-making processes in twelve Western European countries: Britain, Ireland, France, Belgium, the Netherlands, Germany, Denmark, Norway, Sweden, Finland, Austria, and Italy. As the study is comparative, it can examine systematically problems that so far have tended to be considered on a country basis and thus have not been fully explored.

Of course, the numerous single-country studies that have appeared have helped gradually to build a global picture.[18] In Britain, for instance, the basic work by Mackintosh traced the historical origins of the current cabinet processes;[19] the many works that have been written since, both directly on the cabinet and, more indirectly, on the role of the prime minister, have contributed to the generally held view that British cabinets have tended to be, to say the least, markedly controlled by their leaders, though it is also recognised that ordinary ministers can and do have ways of exercising collective pressure.[20]

In France and Finland, much of the literature has tended to concentrate either on the constitutional and political powers of the president or on the relationship, often conflictual, between president and prime minister.[21] Only recently have French political scientists shown a marked interest in the cabinet and in the administrative machinery that supports it.[22]

In Germany, some research has been conducted on the political executive, the aim being to describe the way in which executive power is shared between the chancellor, the cabinet, and the ministries: the general conclusion is that power in the Federal Republic is dispersed rather than hierarchically structured. These studies have primarily an institutional character and are only partly concerned with behavioural patterns.[23]

The same conclusion can be drawn with respect to research on cabinets in the other Western European countries. In Austria, Italy, and the Netherlands, research on the structure and working of the cabinet basically focuses on the juridical aspects of the problem.[24] Only recently have empirical studies been published that devote some attention to questions of coalition formation, ministerial selection, governability, or the role of prime ministers, though even these studies do not systematically assess fully the process of cabinet decision-making.[25]

While this study has therefore largely benefited from the recent literature on Western European cabinets, a fully comparative dimension is added here as a result of two types of data sets. The first and more important data set is provided by the answers given by over 400 ministers and ex-ministers to interviews that were administered orally during 1989 and 1990 on the basis of a common questionnaire across the twelve countries.[26] This questionnaire was designed to elicit views about the practices of governments as well as impressions about the degree of satisfaction of respondents with respect to these practices. Meanwhile, a second data set was obtained by analysing newspaper reports on cabinet life and in particular on cabinet conflicts; these were examined over a substantial period for each of the countries covered in the study; the characteristics of the conflicts were then coded on the basis of a uniform scheme.[27] Cabinet behaviour can thus be compared across Western Europe in a way that had not previously been possible.

A comparative approach can therefore be adopted throughout the whole volume. Part I is concerned with the elaboration of a general framework of analysis. A model of cabinet decision-making processes is presented in Chapter 2 and the characteristics of the single-party/coalition distinction are examined in Chapter 3. Part II is devoted to structures. The role of cabinet rules and arrangements, of procedures in the cabinet meeting itself, of prime ministerial offices, and of parties is examined in order to assess how far they affect the extent to which cabinets members do govern together (Chapters 4 to 7). Part III considers the influence on decision-making processes of the members of the cabinets, from 'ordinary' ministers to the more powerful members, such as the ministers of finance and the prime ministers (Chapter 8 to 10). Part IV examines in conclusion the achievements and prospects of cabinets: it looks at the characteristics of both the agendas and the outcomes of cabinet deliberations and discusses proposals for reform as well as the fate of these proposals (Chapters 11 and 12). The aim of these chapters is to discover whether Western European cabinets have reached an equilibrium in which joint decision-making processes and more hierarchical arrangements are finely balanced: if such an equilibrium exists, the advantages that might be gained by changes in cabinet practices might be outweighed by the problems that might arise if these changes were brought about.

Cabinet government formally means to govern together; in practice, however, substantial limitations have to be introduced to this requirement. A satisfactory trade-off point has to be found so that the practical need for more streamlined decision-making is not forgotten. This is achieved in each country by means of rules and practices. These emerged gradually, sometimes even almost by accident; but the nature of the decision-making process is also markedly shaped by parties in the context of the major distinction between single-party governments and coalitions. The interplay between these factors is complex; it gives cabinet government different characteristics in different countries and leads to a great number of formulas. The task of disentangling the impact of these factors is difficult; it is also highly intriguing.

Notes

1. There has been an increase in the part played by the parliaments of Western European countries in the legislative scrutiny and even initiation, but the overall role of these parliaments in this context remains relatively small. See for example P. Norton (1990). On the other hand, the personal links between parliaments and governments are close in most Western European countries, although only in a few Western European countries, such as Britain, do ministers have to belong to parliament; in some countries, notably France, the Netherlands, and Norway, they have on the contrary to resign their seats on joining the government. The point is,

however, that, whatever the legal requirement, most ministers in cabinet-parliamentary systems proceed from the legislature and have links with the legislature. For a detailed examination of the situation in contemporary Western Europe, see L. de Winter (1991), pp. 44–69.

2. This was the view expressed by R. H. S. Crossman in the Preface which he wrote to the Fontana edition of Bagehot's *English Constitution* (1966). For a more balanced view, see J. P. Mackintosh (1977), pp. 75–84. The extent to which Western European cabinet systems can be regarded as 'prime ministerial' will be examined specifically in Chapter 10.

3. See for instance the first two volumes of the series entitled *The Future of Party Government* edited by R. Wildenmann, *Visions and Realities of Party Government* (F. G. Castles and R. Wildenmann, eds., 1986) and *Party Governments: European and American Experiences* (R. S. Katz, ed., 1987) published by De Gruyter (Berlin) as part of the European University Institute Series.

4. The concept of consociational democracy was originally developed by A. Lijphart (1968), in order to account for what had been a number of characteristics of Dutch politics. This concept remains of considerable importance even if there are some doubts as to whether Dutch politics continue to fit the model. The concept of 'adversary politics' was developed by S. E. Finer and a number of colleagues in S. E. Finer (1975), in order to make a case for proportional representation; but the idea can be regarded as applying as a matter of principle to single-party government, although not all single-party governments behave in an 'adversarial' manner with respect to the other parties.

5. See for instance A. Lijphart (1984), in which the average duration of single party and coalition cabinets is examined. See also W. Bakema (1988), pp. 79–83.

6. See K. Strom, (1984), pp. 199–228, and K. Strom, (1986), pp. 583–605.

7. See for instance V. Herman and J. Pope (1973), pp. 191–212. This has been the case of the French governments of M. Rocard, E. Cresson, and P. Beregovoy in the 1988–93 parliament as, after the 1988 General Election, the Socialist party did not have an overall majority in the National Assembly.

8. A good example of the nature and purpose of coalitions in the United States is given by W. H. Riker (1962). The type of 'coalition' that is being discussed in this connection (for the selection of a presidential candidate) is temporary and specific: this is very different from the concept of coalition developed in Western European parliamentary systems (see Riker, 1962, pp. 149–58). In Latin America, though, it seems that coalitions of a number of parties in the government occur relatively often in presidential systems. There are thus examples of the practice in Brazil, Chile, and Venezuela, and in other countries. However, the conditions under which these coalitions occur and are maintained have not as yet been systematically examined.

9. The part of the French president in the Fifth Republic has remained similar to that played originally by heads of State in parliamentary systems, however.

10. These agreements have begun to be studied in detail, especially as, since the 1970s, they have taken the form of lengthy written documents in some countries, such as Belgium and the Netherlands.
11. See note 4 above.
12. As was pointed out in note 9, there have however been coalitions in a number of Latin American presidential systems.
13. To borrow the expression of W. H. Riker (1962), *passim*; the approach that this expression characterises may be criticised as unrealistic and therefore clearly unsatisfactory: it none the less helped to launch the systematic analysis of coalition-building in parliamentary systems.
14. The role of governmental agreements in helping to reduce conflicts in coalition cabinets is still relatively understudied but is how beginning to attract attention.
15. The question of the role of factions and divisions within parties has begun to be studied in the context of coalition build-up. See M. Laver and K. A. Shepsle (1990), pp. 489–507.
16. See Chapter 4, p. 81, below. See also in J. Blondel and F. Müller-Rommel (1988), pp. 210 and 228–9.
17. See J.-L. Thiébault, 'The Social Background of Western European Ministers', in J. Blondel and J.-L. Thiebault (1988), pp. 19–30.
18. See J. Blondel and F. Müller-Rommel (1988) for a detailed bibliography on works on cabinets in the various Western European countries. See also the bibliography at the end of this volume.
19. J. P. Mackintosh (1977b).
20. On the British cabinet, see for instance, among the most recent works, S. James (1992). On the prime minister, see A. King (1985).
21. P. Avril (1987). J. Nousiainen (1990).
22. J. Fournier (1987). R.Py (1985).
23. N. Johnson (1983). R. Mayntz and F. Scharpf (1975).
24. M. Welan and H. Neisser (1971). A. Ruggeri (1981). E. Spagna Musso (1979).
25. See, for Ireland, B. Farrell (1987); for the Netherlands: R. Andeweg *et al.* (1980). W. E. Bakema and I. P. Secker (1988), pp. 153–70; for Belgium: A. Frognier (1988a), pp. 207–28; for France: M. Dogan (1989), pp. 19–44; for Italy: M. Dogan, 'How to become a minister in Italy', in M. Dogan (1989), pp. 99–140, S. Cassese (1981); for Austria: P. Gerlich, W. C. Müller and W. Philipp (1988), pp. 191–206; for Germany: F. Müller-Rommel (1988b), pp. 171–90; for Denmark: A. H. Thomas (1982).
26. See Appendix I for the description of the ministerial questionnaire.
27. See Appendix II for the description of the newspaper analysis.

Part I

General Framework of Analysis

2 A Model of the Cabinet System: the Dimensions of Cabinet Decision-Making Processes

Rudi Andeweg

The general category of cabinet government is heterogeneous. There are variations among the countries in which cabinet government exists; there are also variations from cabinet to cabinet within each of these countries. National variations are often described and are generally better documented than cross-national ones, since cross-national studies on the subject are rare, while national studies have become numerous.[1] Yet general remarks are not sufficient: we need to go further and attempt to assess *the extent* to which cabinets differ from one another. Such an endeavour is likely to be difficult and imprecise, however, for at least two reasons. First, it involves an assessment of the relative part played by the members of a cabinet: this amounts to a judgement on the relative *power or influence* of these cabinet members and precise judgements on power and influence have so far eluded political scientists despite the efforts undertaken in this field.[2] Second, the concept of 'cabinet government' is in common use, yet few attempts have been made to define it in such a way that it can be operationalised for further research. It is this second problem that this chapter seeks to remedy: its purpose is to determine the parameters of the general framework within which decision-making processes in cabinets take place and to undertake a preliminary categorisation of cabinets on this basis.

We can make at least some progress in the direction of such a measurement if we undertake three tasks. First, we must consider the part played by the cabinet in the national decision-making process: is the cabinet truly central or not? Second, we must describe the general framework within which decision-making processes in cabinets take place and, in particular, define the space in which all cabinets can be located irrespective of the extent to which their members truly govern together. Third, we must determine the 'temperature' of the process, so to speak; that is to say discover whether decisions are or not taken easily and without major disagreements. The purpose of this chapter is to examine these three aspects and to undertake a preliminary categorisation of cabinets in the context of the space within which decision-making processes take place.

EXTERNAL VARIATIONS AFFECTING CABINET DECISION-MAKING PROCESSES: THE EXTENT TO WHICH CABINETS ARE CENTRAL TO POLITICAL DECISION-MAKING

As was pointed out in the previous chapter, cabinets could not function at all if their members had to, or were able to, raise fundamental questions of both principle and implementation in the case of every issue that the government has to face. Restrictions of various kinds obtain: these make it possible for the cabinet to go about its business in an effective manner. Many of these restrictions are internal to the cabinet – and we shall examine these in the next section; but another type of restriction is external in that it ensures that some matters are not discussed at all because, if they are to be discussed, this tends to take place elsewhere. This point touches on the very important problem, which may seem at first sight peripheral to the subject of cabinet decision-making *per se*, of the extent to which the cabinet is central to national decision-making; to put it differently, this point raises the matter of the extent to which the cabinet is the most authoritative body in the nation or whether it is in some manner dependent on other bodies.

What is specifically at stake is the role of the political parties forming the government. This is a delicate matter in theory, as it touches on the relationship between 'representativeness' – which is held to be achieved by the parties – and governmental leadership. The question is also complex in practice, since it is concerned with the way in which governments and the 'supporting' parties of these governments organise their relations. Without going into detail here, it is clear that some parties are more anxious or able than others to supervise or even control the government: for instance, ruling communist parties did succeed in controlling entirely the apparatus of the State and party–

State relations in communist states were therefore hierarchical. This is not the case in either theory or practice in parliamentary cabinet systems, but some parties do wish and are able to exercise more influence than others on the government that they support. Yet neither the theory nor the practice of these relationships has been fully analysed so far and a full investigation of the problem would go markedly beyond the scope of this study.[3]

Yet the matter is too important not to be touched at all: the extent to which cabinets are 'dependent' or 'autonomous' and therefore less central or more central to the national decision-making process is manifestly critical to the overall purpose of life of governments and almost certainly to the behaviour of their members. The question must therefore be examined, would it only be by attempting to locate cabinets on a dimension ranging from full 'centrality' to total 'dependence', this last case being that of cabinets merely implementing decisions taken elsewhere and not concerned at all with, or at most very little concerned with, the crucial issues facing the polity.

INTERNAL VARIATIONS AFFECTING CABINET DECISION-MAKING PROCESSES: THE TWO DIMENSIONS OF THE GENERAL FRAMEWORK OF CABINET DECISION-MAKING

We can start from the proposition that 'ideal-type' cabinets in a parliamentary context are a form of collective decision-making. Sometimes the literature uses 'collegial' as a synonym of collective, but on closer inspection these two terms can be seen to denote distinct, but rarely distinguished dimensions of cabinet government.[4] Baylis, for example, defines what he calls 'collegial leadership' 'as the operation of continuing political leadership structures and practices through which significant *decisions are taken in common* by a small, face-to-face body *with no single member dominating* their initiation or determination'.[5]

The *collective* character of the government does not entail any specific distribution of power within the cabinet: it merely states that not one person (an individual minister or the prime minister) takes the decisions, but that all ministers are part of the process. Collective government is indeed the assumption that underlies the constitutional or customary rule of collective *responsibility*: it is largely concerned with the consequences of the involvement of ministers, whether such an involvement has been large or small, substantial or perfunctory.

The *collegial* character of the government is based on the principle that all ministers should have an *equal* say in the decision-making process. This corresponds to a different concept, that of collegial government, which is assumed by the principle of 'one man, one vote' within the cabinet. The idea is present, whether or not matters are decided by votes and notwithstanding the fact that in most countries where cabinet government exists the prime minister has the casting vote in the event of a tie.

Collegial and collective government are often confused, which is unfortunate. The failure to distinguish between the two dimensions led Max Weber, for example, to contrast monocratic and collegial government, and at the same time to see collective advisory bodies to a monocratic leader as one form of collegial government.[6] It also led one Dutch author to wonder about the paradox that in the Netherlands the cabinet has become more important while the prime minister has become more powerful.[7] It is essential to realise that all ministers may be involved in the decision-making process and yet the impact of their involvement may be different; conversely, even if all ministers have equal status, it does not follow that all decisions are taken by all ministers collectively.

The ideal-type cabinet can thus be defined as both collective and collegial, but such a 'golden age' of cabinet government probably never existed. Real-life cabinets stand at some distance from this ideal type on both dimensions, and the variations in cabinet government mentioned above lie in the fact that these distances are not the same for all cabinets. On the one hand, some will be more collective than others, the dimension of collective government ranging, at one extreme, from truly collective decision-making arrangements to, at the other, situations in which one person is involved in the decisions. On the other hand, some cabinets will be more collegial than others. Indeed, the deviation from the ideal of full equality is likely to be at least as large as the deviation from the ideal of a fully collective government; the ideal of perfect collegial government may even be regarded as less attainable than the ideal of collective government, if it can be attained at all: there will always be some ministers who are more 'senior' or more prestigious than others, even if one leaves aside for the moment the special role of the prime minister who is rarely the *primus inter pares* he is deemed to be according to the theory of cabinet government. We must therefore look at the characteristics of cabinets according to both dimensions if we are to give a comprehensive account of the nature of decision-making processes in these executives.

Deviations from collegial government

Let us examine first the extent to which cabinets are collegial. In some, a hierarchy is clearly visible, while in others members are more or less equal. In the literature, this distinction often takes the form of a contrast between 'prime ministerial' and 'cabinet' government, as if this was the main way, indeed perhaps the only way, in which the collegial character of cabinets could vary.[8] Perhaps because intermediate positions are less easy to define operationally, less attention has tended to be paid to the cases in which a small group of ministers, such as a formal or informal 'inner cabinet', dominates the life of the cabinet. Yet these cases do exist, both formally and informally, with cabinets ranging from those in which power is concentrated to those in which it is dispersed. It might therefore be more realistic to attempt to see whether cabinets are not merely monocratic or collegial, but occupy one of a number of intermediate 'oligarchical' positions.

It has sometimes been argued that there was a long-term trend towards 'monocratic' cabinets: this was indeed the contention of R. H. S. Crossman who claimed that the move towards 'prime-ministerial' government was the consequence of changes in the nature of modern political systems, arising for instance from the part played by the mass media.[9] Some evidence, superficial perhaps, but mentioned in a substantial number of countries, appears indeed to indicate the existence of a long-term trend towards a strengthening of the position of the prime minister, although the matter remains controversial, as others argue that, while electronic media do call for a symbolic personalisation of political leadership, the increasing complexity of modern government pulls towards a more collegial style of decision-making.[10] One potential indicator of such a 'monocratic' cabinet system can be the power that the prime minister may have to give instructions to individual ministers with respect to the scope of the activities of these ministers in their departments. The Irish Taoiseach and the German chancellor are among the government leaders who have such a power most overtly; their British and Belgian colleagues have it in certain cases; the French prime minister can also give instructions to ministers, but the matter has to be considered in the more general context of the position of the French president, especially when both presidential and parliamentary majorities are congruent. In other countries, on the other hand, as in Austria, the Netherlands, Finland, and Norway, the prime minister generally lacks such a power.

The indicator *par excellence* of an oligarchical cabinet system is constituted by the existence of an inner cabinet. The concept of inner cabinet is somewhat elusive, however, in part because such an arrangement may be wholly informal and in part because, in some cases, its very existence may be concealed and even denied. Thus, in Western Europe, only in Germany and Belgium does the arrangement seem to be a permanent feature of the cabinet's structure; an inner cabinet was also set up in Italy in the 1980s, but the mechanism does not appear to have become fully operative. Alongside the cases of formally constituted inner cabinets, however, one should also consider the 'coalition committees' that exist in some coalition governments: these typically include the prime minister and the deputy prime minister(s), all the coalition partners being represented in this way. Such a coalition committee can be found in Austria and in the Netherlands; in Belgium, the coalition committee consists of the party chairmen, although these are not necessarily members of the cabinet. While there are question marks about the presence or absence of 'inner cabinets' in many Western European governments, in two countries at least, Ireland and Finland, these institutional arrangements do not appear to exist at all.

It is difficult to draw a general conclusion about the *raison d'être* of these inner cabinets: their function seems to be diverse (and little is known about them in many countries). In some cases, they appear to reinforce the position of the prime minister: this seems to be the case in Germany and sometimes in Britain; in Italy, the inner cabinet has been set up for this reason, but the effect appears limited. In other cases, often in coalition cabinets, the effect of, and indeed the reason for setting up, an inner cabinet is the converse one, namely to reduce the potentially 'monocratic' ambitions of the prime minister. This is probably the case in Belgium. Only in the latter situation can the inner cabinet serve as an indicator of an oligarchical cabinet.

In the absence of an inner cabinet (formal or informal) and if the prime minister cannot be regarded as having powers (constitutionally or *de facto*) that strengthen him or her markedly in relation to the ministers, the cabinet should be regarded as collegial, on the understanding that such cabinets are collegial only in a relative sense and by comparison with monocratic and oligarchical cabinets. The Swiss Federal Council, with its rotating presidency and absence of an inner cabinet, is probably closest to the ideal collegial cabinet.

Little is known of the factors that determine the variation along this dimension of cabinet structure. Weller discusses a number of variables that may affect the power of the prime minister (and thus the degree of collegiality of the cabinet), such as the vulnerability of the prime minister from being removed from office, his or her control over patronage, cabinet committees, the hiring and firing of ministers, etc.[11] However, as Weller's analysis is restricted to Britain, Canada, New Zealand, and Australia, he largely measures variations within one category of monocratic government. In another attempt, Baylis lists nine determinants of collegial government: historical precedents, a cultural predilection towards consensus-seeking, a segmented society, coalition government, independent and pluriform mass media, neo-corporatism, a technocratic style of governing, a strong and specialised bureaucracy, and a weak prime minister.[12] As a weak prime minister is a defining element of collegial government, this last factor should be excluded, however. Baylis argues that the historical and cultural factors may explain the origins of collegiality, but that its persistence must be accounted for by neo-corporatism and bureaucratic specialisation. Our study suggests that coalition government may be at least as powerful in maintaining collegial, or at least oligarchical, government and inhibiting monocratic developments.

Deviations from collective government

It has become increasingly clear that cabinet government is not constituted merely by the weekly meeting of the fifteen to twenty plus ministers: to take account of the fact that it covers more than full meetings of the cabinet, concepts such as the *core executive* or the *cabinet system* have come to be used in the literature. In their work on *Unlocking the Cabinet*, Mackie and Hogwood introduced the term 'arenas' to refer to the different decision-making contexts that form part of the cabinet 'system'.[13]

In terms of 'arenas', a cabinet system may be collective where the plenary session of the cabinet is the most important place where decisions are taken; it may be fragmented where, in the most extreme case, each minister is individually responsible for the decisions to be taken in his or her department. If we wish to subdivide the continuum between collective and fragmented decision-making in order to allow for somewhat finer analyses, we need to introduce an intermediate category, that of segmented decision-making, between the two extremes; these segments are of two types, however: they can result from divisions based on policy areas, as is typically the case with cabinet committees, or from divisions based on party political cleavages, as tends to occur where there are coalitions or if there are factions within the cabinet; given differences in character between these two types of segmentation, it is best to keep them distinct in the elaboration of a typology of cabinet decision-making structures.

Cabinets typically meet at least once a week, but, as we shall see in greater detail in Chapter 4, the importance of these plenary sessions is subject to wide variations. In some countries, meetings of the full cabinet are a formality, a ritual that serves primarily to legitimise decisions taken elsewhere. Asked what purpose the plenary session serves in France, former prime minister Mauroy countered: 'A quoi ça sert la grand-messe du dimanche? C'est capital d'une certaine façon: ce n'est pas là où se fait la réalité de la religion, mais c'est la partie visible qui prouve qu'il y a une communauté qui fonctionne.'[14] In other countries the cabinet meeting is still the dominant arena within the government. Dutch ministers spend twenty to thirty hours per month in plenary cabinet sessions. If we add informal plenary sessions, such as the daily luncheon meeting of Swedish ministers or the weekly 'evening class' of their Finnish colleagues, Scandinavian ministers spend as much time in cabinet as their Dutch colleagues. French and British ministers, by contrast, spend little more than six to nine hours per month attending meetings of the full cabinet.

As we shall also see in Chapter 4, there are important variations across countries with respect to cabinet committees. They hardly exist in Sweden and Ireland. In Norway, the Netherlands, and Belgium, they do exist, but ministers spend more time in the full cabinet than in the committees and they can appeal against committee decisions to the full cabinet. In Britain, Austria, and France, on the contrary, ministers spend more time in committees than in the full cabinet; it seems that in Britain, but also in Belgium and Norway, committees can decide on some issues in lieu of the whole cabinet. An indicator of sectoral segmentation can thus be provided by the relative importance of committees, of the full cabinet, of the departments, and of factional meetings.

Segmentation based on party political characteristics occurs most in coalitions; factionalism does also exist in some single-party cabinets, however: this appears to be the case in Austria, Ireland, and occasionally in Britain. In coalitions, meetings of ministers belonging to the same party take place frequently: only in Ireland and in some French and Norwegian cabinets do such developments never take place. Furthermore, in most coalition cabinets, these meetings are also attended by the party chairman (although he or she may not be a member of the cabinet), as well as, at least in Belgium and in the Netherlands, by junior ministers, although these are not members of the cabinet either. It must be emphasised that political segmentation will normally be less complete than sectoral segmentation, as it is rare to find whole policy sectors more or less 'delegated' to one party. Such situations do occur, however, as is exemplified by the wartime British coalition in which the Conservatives concentrated on the war effort and seemed to have been happy to leave the domestic front to Labour.

Fragmented decision-making, finally, refers to the situation in which there are few interactions or common meetings of cabinet ministers and in which each minister, together with his or her department officials, in effect forms a self-contained decision-making system. The origins of most cabinets as collections of individual advisers to the king, without any collective responsibility, point to the historical relevance of this category. Today, the familiar complaints about 'sub-governments' and the lack of coordination of government policy indicate the continued existence of fragmented decision-making in cabinets.

Again, we can only speculate about the factors underlying the variations along the dimension of collectiveness of cabinets. Some of the factors that are said to explain the variations along the dimension of collegiality may play a part here. Traditions and cultural predilections emphasise the importance of the group in some countries and of the individual in others. Neo-corporatist networks and bureaucratic specialisation are likely to strengthen fragments or segments at the expense of collective action. Theoretically, it would seem that coalitions favour collective decision-making: in a coalition a party is by definition not in control of all departments; to influence policies in departments where it has no minister, the party will have to rely on some arrangement for collective decision-making. Empirically, however, the correlation appears not to be very strong: Belgian cabinets, for example, are coalitions of a large number of parties, but they are also characterised by strong cabinet committees.

In their attempt to explain the variations in 'arenas' and in the occurrence of cabinet committees in particular, Mackie and Hogwood argue that the size of the population is an important determinant, but they fail to explain how smallness would prevent the setting up of cabinet committees: they found only a weak correlation between the size of the cabinet and the occurrence of cabinet committees.[15] However, if we look not only at occurrence, but also at the importance of cabinet committees, large cabinets tend clearly to be more segmented than small ones (with Sweden as a notable exception). The literature on group dynamics and small group decision-making also indicates that the number of cabinet members is inversely related to collective decision-making. In addition to 'Parkinson's Law', Parkinson developed a similarly amusing theory about cabinet development based on a cross-country comparison of cabinet size. Beyond a certain number, he argues, no doubt tongue-in-cheek, the cabinet ceases to be efficient. 'A study of the British example would suggest that the point of ineffectiveness in a cabinet is reached when the total membership exceeds 20 or perhaps 21. The Council of the Crown, the Privy Council had each passed the 20 mark when their decline began.'[16]. In Parkinson's theory the cabinet is replaced by some smaller body when it has grown too large. Delegation of decision-making to cabinet committees or even to individual ministers seems to be a more likely response.

TYPES OF CABINET SYSTEMS AND THEIR CHARACTERISTICS

It is an empirical question as to whether the collective and the collegial character of cabinets happen to be correlated. Given the likelihood that some factors affect both the collegiality and the collectiveness of decision-making, such a correlation probably exists in some, perhaps many, cases. An example where the two dimensions are combined is provided by the fate of junior ministers who have not been considered so far as they are not formally members of the cabinet. Obviously, they are not of equal status and in most countries they are admitted to cabinet meetings only when their own department is affected: neither the principle of collegiality nor the principle of collectiveness applies to them. Despite such correlations, the distinction between the two dimensions is important in practice as well as analytically. For instance, while power may be concentrated in the hands of the prime minister in a particular cabinet (the case of the monocratic government), this power may be exercised in bilateral relations with individual ministers by way of presiding over cabinet committees or in the council of ministers itself. For instance, too, power may be dispersed and ministers may be equal but they may not be autonomous: the decision process may take place at the level of committees or in the cabinet meeting itself.

The two dimensions that have just been described make it possible to classify cabinets in terms of their internal decision-making processes. Within this two-dimensional framework, one can categorise in a broad manner the cabinets of some Western European countries. This categorisation is given here as illustrative, the classifications being based more

often on overall country characteristics than on individual cabinet idiosyncrasies, though the typology can help to describe individual cabinets;
indeed, some of the examples given here refer to specific cabinets.

(1) Globally dominated cabinets

These are cabinets in which the prime minister has all the power and
exercises this power by way of bilateral relations with individual
ministers. An extreme example would appear to be, outside parliamentary cabinet systems, that of the American executive: in this case, the
cabinet as such rarely meets (at least currently), there are few cabinet
committees, and individual ministers are dependent on the chief
executive who serves as his own prime minister. It is not surprising
that this type of arrangement should be characteristic of presidential
executives and in particular of the American executive.[17] However, in
parliamentary cabinet government, some examples approximate so
much to situations of this type that they should be included in this
group: these are, for instance, the cases of the Adenauer and Schmidt
cabinets in Germany and, in Austria, of the Kreisky cabinets, although
these last governments were probably not 'globally dominated'
throughout the whole of their existence, as will be pointed out shortly.

(2) Clientelist cabinets

These are cabinets in which a small group of ministers dominates the
decision-making process *and* where this group exercises its domination
by means of individual relations with the cabinet members who depend
upon them. Such cabinets are labelled 'clientelist' because the most
likely situations in which links of this type will be forged and remain in
being are where clientelism prevails, though strictly speaking bonds

Table 2.1   The two dimensions of the general framework of cabinet decision-
making

		Fragmented individual	Segmented Sectoral	Partisan	Centralised collective
Centralised	Prime-ministerial	(1)	(4)	(7)	(10)
	Oligarchical	(2)	(5)	(8)	(11)
Dispersed	Collegial	(3)	(6)	(9)	(12)

could be different; they could be, for instance, ideological, but each ideology would have then to correspond to a different 'dominant' cabinet member, a state of affairs that is likely to be rare and may be approximated only where coalitions include a large number of parties. The cases in which clientelist cabinets are most prominent are those of Mexico (where the dominant single-party system leads to a markedly different type of cabinet structure to that of the United States), and of Japan. In Western Europe, Irish coalition cabinets appear to come close to this type; in Germany, the Kiesinger and Brandt cabinets appear to have been of a rather similar character.

(3) 'Ressortprinzip' cabinets

These correspond to cases that are exemplified by a characteristic of the German constitutional doctrine, although this feature is not necessarily followed in practice, as is indicated by the examples of the Adenauer, Kiesinger, Brandt, and Schmidt cabinets that were mentioned earlier. In such an arrangement, ministers are equal and autonomous: they can and do take decisions within the jurisdiction of their department. The cabinet meeting thus loses much of its importance, most matters being settled by ministers individually. Such a situation has been found to exist in Germany in the Ehrard and Kohl cabinets; it also seems that, in Austria, Kreisky cabinets occasionally had such a characteristic, at least with respect to more routine decisions.

(4) Dominated cabinet committee arrangements

These are cabinets in which power is primarily exercised by the prime minister (the cabinet is 'monocratic'), but the prime minister tends to exercise this power through committees, while in globally dominated cabinets the prime minister exercises power by way of bilateral meetings with ministers; these committees are empowered to decide on many, and perhaps nearly all, matters in lieu of the full cabinet. The prime minister manipulates committees primarily by creating and disbanding them at will, by deciding on their composition, and/or by presiding over their deliberations and thus controlling the agenda.

Many British cabinets provide examples of this type of cabinet decision-making arrangements. French governments during the first phase of the Fifth Republic, from that of Debré to that of Barre (1959 to 1981), were dominated in this way by prime ministers: this occurred because these prime ministers had the crucially important backing of the president. They exercised their power in cabinet committees in a form that is described as 'arbitration' – that is to say, as a result of the prime minister's right to adjudicate in the last resort when there is conflict among two or more ministers. The only limit to this power of 'arbitration' of the prime minister was provided by the fact that during that period the president consistently retained his prerogative in foreign affairs and in defence matters. Interestingly, the president also exercises his power through committees: this gives the French cabinet two, largely overlapping, committee systems.

(5) 'Overlord'-based cabinets

These are cabinets in which there is an inner cabinet. The members of this inner cabinet oversee the work of clusters of departmental ministers. The cabinet is thus both oligarchical and segmented. There are no clear examples of such a type of cabinet in current European governments, but an (unsuccessful) approximation can be found in the Churchill experiment of 1951 where a number of 'overlords' were appointed in order to oversee the activities of a number of departments; the scheme was partial, as only a number of these superministers were appointed (three), covering a small number of aspects of governmental life.[18] Heath developed a somewhat analogous scheme when he came to power in 1970 and the results were not appreciably more encouraging; moreover, Heath's superministers were not 'overlords' in the strict sense of the word, as the ministers whom they supervised did not form part of the cabinet: as a result, it cannot strictly be claimed that the cabinet itself was segmented. As a matter of fact, the principle of appointing a superminister and of demoting subordinate ministers was adopted widely in one field, that of defence, after the Second World War; this was also to be the only field where the idea was successfully implemented.[19]

Although most of these experiments did not last long, the idea of a cabinet organised on the basis of a number of 'overlords' has been put forward repeatedly as a means of providing a solution to the difficulties of running collective and collegial cabinets, especially as these were becoming larger. Churchill's attempt was inspired in large part by the suggestion made in the 1930s by Amery, who had proposed the setting up of a much smaller cabinet whose members would be concerned primarily with broad policy development.[20] Similar ideas have surfaced in other countries from time to time, for instance in France and in the Netherlands.

(6) Autonomous cabinet committees

In such an arrangement, the cabinet is segmented into a number of elements, each of which is run by a cabinet committee. Decisions are collegial in that all members of the cabinet are equal, but they exercise this equality in the context of the committees to which they belong rather than in the context of the cabinet as a whole. Ministers have therefore to negotiate or coordinate with ministers from adjacent policy areas before decisions are taken. There are ostensibly few examples of such an arrangement, though some Norwegian cabinets seem to approximate a model in which cabinet committees are practically autonomous. Moreover, the formula can be regarded as an extreme case of committee dominance and therefore as an exaggeration of what takes place in cabinets in which committees are very influential, in Britain for instance; interestingly, English local government is run on the basis of such a decision-making structure, the decisions of the municipal and county councils being often largely formal ratifications of committee suggestions.

Types (7), (8) and (9) types apply only in cases of coalitions or where a single party in power is highly factionalised.

(7) Dominated consociational cabinets

These are cabinets in which the ministers of the governing parties meet separately, but the cabinet as a whole is dominated by the prime minister, either because of the strong personality of this prime minister or because the government is dominated by one party and the other coalition partner(s) are so small that they cannot claim for their leaders a position of equality with respect to the head of the government. The socialist–liberal coalition of 1983–6 in Austria is an example of such a situation; another example is that of the socialist–communist coalition of 1981–4 in France, though in this case the leadership of the prime minister (Mauroy) was perhaps not strong enough for the term 'dominant' to apply fully.

(8) Coalition committee-based cabinets

These are cabinets in which the ministers of the various parties of the coalition meet separately and in which the leading ministers of these parties, who often are deputy prime ministers, form an inner cabinet or a coalition committee; as we saw, party leaders who are outside the cabinet are sometimes included in these coalition committees. The general structure of such cabinets resembles that of those which are based on 'overlords', but the composition is different: the segments into which 'overlord'-based cabinets are divided have a technical character; the segments into which cabinets based on coalition committees are divided are party political. Belgian cabinets are those whose structure falls most closely in this category, though they are also divided to an extent according to technical segments; the Austrian 'grand' coalition of the second half of the 1980s as well as the Dutch christian–liberal coalition of the same period belong to this group.

(9) Consociational cabinets

In these cabinets, the ministers of the various parties of the coalition meet separately: the cabinet is thus segmented according to political cleavages. On the other hand, such cabinets are collegial as all the ministers of each party have an equal amount of influence at party meetings: no coalition committee or dominating prime minister attempts to influence, let alone succeeds in influencing, the decisions of the cabinet. This type of arrangement characterised Dutch cabinets before the 1980s; Finnish cabinets are also normally organised on this basis.

(10) Cabinets with a dominating chairman

In this case, the cabinet remains collective, but the influence of the prime minister on decision-making processes is fundamental. This means in practice that decisions have to be taken by the cabinet as a body and that there is no or very little formal or even effective delegation either to individual ministers (including the prime minister) or to committees; at the same time, the decisions are markedly influenced by the prime minister, for instance because of his or her personal power or position in the party. The prime minister will often make his or her mark on cabinet policy by formulating the conclusions of the deliberations: Steiner and Dorff have labelled this process 'decision by interpretation'.[21] Although operating in a different type of cabinet system, former British prime minister Wilson once called 'summing up' the 'fine art of cabinet government'. This kind of situation seems to have occurred in a number of cases in the past, at a time when cabinets were smaller and had less business to transact.

Matters were then decided in the full cabinet meeting, which was therefore the place where prime ministers used their influence to obtain what they wished. In the contemporary world, Norwegian cabinets sometimes seem to have this character.

(11) Cabinets with an 'inner circle'

These are cabinets where the decision-making process is also based on the involvement of all the ministers, but where considerable influence is exercised, not by the prime minister alone, but by two or more senior ministers. This type of arrangement also probably characterised many parliamentary cabinets in the past, for instance in Britain, in the cases in which the prime minister did not have a towering personality: a number of key ministers, such as the chancellor of the exchequer, the home secretary, the foreign secretary, as well as probably one or two senior ministers without portfolio, could exercise true dominance over the decisions of the cabinet. Swedish contemporary cabinets often appear to have this character, primarily because of the critical part played by the minister of finance alongside the prime minister; some Norwegian governments are also examples of 'tandem' cabinets, at least those in which the prime minister is not dominant.

(12) Truly collective and collegial cabinets

These are the 'ideal' textbook cases of cabinets in which ministers are all equal and are involved directly in the affairs of all the departments. This type of arrangement may have existed in the past in some countries, though its occurrence was probably less frequent than may have been suggested: it does not seem to be the case, for instance, that British governments ever had such a character, given the large part played traditionally by senior ministers and by the prime minister in the cabinets of that country. Such cabinets are probably relatively weak: their decision-making capabilities are likely to be somewhat limited and very often slow; French governments in the Third and Fourth Republics may have sometimes had this character. In the contemporary world, some Norwegian cabinets may approximate this model, though seemingly infrequently. It is highly improbable that this type will be found frequently in large and complex modern societies.

THE 'TEMPERATURE' OF THE DECISION-MAKING PROCESS: THE DIMENSION OF CONFLICTUALITY IN CABINETS

The decision-making process may vary because it is internally more or less collective or collegial as well as externally because it is more or less central; it can also vary because the 'temperature' may differ widely. Some cabinets may take decisions without any real difficulty and on the basis of a wide extent of consensus; others may arrive at the solution of the problems that they face only after bitter conflicts: at the limit, if these conflicts are too harsh and the 'temperature' is therefore too high, the cabinet may 'explode', so to speak, and disintegrate. Even if the 'temperature' does not reach such extremes, there are many levels, and indeed a whole dimension of intensity of conflicts: this dimension is of considerable importance for the understanding of the nature of cabinet decision-making.

The extent and the degree of cabinet conflicts need therefore to be examined if one is to have a comprehensive picture of the way in which ministers do govern together. The measurement of conflict does remain rather imprecise, however, although in theory one could at least know the incidence of conflicts that occur in cabinet; but there are difficulties if one wishes to compare the levels of these conflicts. As a matter of fact, neither levels nor incidence can be adequately discovered, in large part because ministers are typically not prone to divulge the extent of the disagreements in cabinet and in part also because, on the contrary, some disagreements may deliberately be exaggerated. Yet it is at least possible to obtain a broad composite image of the amount of conflict in given cabinets and participants are likely to be as reliable when they provide such a broad impression as when they provide an impression of the extent to which cabinets are central to national decision-making, are collective, or are collegial.

COUNTRY CHARACTERISTICS, INDIVIDUAL CABINET CHARACTERISTICS, OVER TIME CHANGES AND POLICY AREA VARIATIONS

The type of cabinet structures that were described earlier constitute a marked simplification of the reality, since that reality is characterised by continuous dimensions and not by a number of discrete categories.

Naturally enough, real-world cases are somewhat difficult to locate within these categories, as they may be at the borderline between two positions. This is inevitable and will be remedied only when the instruments of measurement at our disposal become less imprecise.

Yet beyond the fact that dimensions rather than discrete points should form the basis of the analysis, four further types of variations affect the characterisation of cabinet decision-making processes. The first has already been mentioned and concerns the distinction to be made between various cabinets in the same country: the existence of a common political culture no doubt results in all the cabinets of a country having many similarities; but they are also likely to differ appreciably from one another. To begin with, some cabinets may be based on coalitions, others may be single party: as was noted in Chapter 1, this has been the case in particular in Ireland, Norway, Denmark, and Sweden; changes in composition, especially changes of prime ministers, are also likely to affect the nature of the cabinet decision-making processes within the same country.

Second, the characteristics of decision-making of a cabinet may vary over time: the part played by the prime minister may change as he or she acquires more influence, for instance as a result of a major electoral victory; the influence of ministers may also increase, for instance if they become regarded as irreplaceable because they are vote-winners or excellent managers; conversely, ministers may lose some of their influence for opposite reasons. These variations may not be measured precisely nor even always traced, given the instruments of analysis at our disposal, but, at least in some particular cases, they might well be important.

Third, variations from cabinet to cabinet in a given country as well as within a single cabinet raise the general question of the dynamics of decision-making characteristics of cabinets. It was suggested earlier that, according to some observers, cabinets are now more 'monocratic' than previously, as there are reasons to believe that the power of prime ministers may be on the increase. This means that there may be a long-term evolution of cabinet decision-making structures, an evolution that may also be fostered by practices of other countries: Western European integration may have the effect of strengthening such cross-national influences. Meanwhile, the dynamics of cabinet decision-making structures are also likely to have short-term characteristics and these may also develop according to a particular path: the influence of prime ministers may at first increase, for instance, and later decrease.

Finally, the location of a cabinet along the dimensions that have been described here may vary according to the different policy areas in which the government is involved. The prime minister may thus be dominant in one field, for instance in foreign affairs (as is manifestly the case of the French head of State); in aspects of social or economic policy, committees may be dominant; in yet other aspects, the cabinet may operate on a collegial basis.

The large number of variations that may affect cabinet decision-making structures suggest that the present study is likely to be in the nature of an exploration of the forms that these may take and of the factors that account for these forms. By and large, such an exploration will have to concentrate on the most obvious aspects of these cabinet decision-making structures – that is to say, on country differences rather than on individual cabinet differences; on overall differences between cabinets rather than on those within cabinet dynamics; and on overall cabinet decision-making characteristics rather than on decision-making features relating to particular policy areas. The general picture that will emerge in this way will help to provide a framework within which more detailed analyses can more easily have their place. We can now turn to the specific examination of the most important factors likely to affect cabinet decision-making patterns and in particular to the exploration of the extent to which the distinction between coalition and single-party governments constitutes a major discriminating element in this context.

Notes

1. See the bibliography at the end of this volume.
2. The measurement of power exercised political scientists to a considerable extent in the 1960s, in particular under the influence of R.A. Dahl. The outcome was rather disappointing, however.
3. This question is the object of a current study undertaken by a number of members of the team involved in the cabinet decision-making study. For a preliminary examination of the concept of 'partyness' of government, see R.S. Katz (1986), *passim*.
4. A well-known example is Max Weber's use of the concept of 'Kollegialität' in *Wirtschaft und Gesellschaft* (1921) (1972 ed.), pp. 158–65.
5. T.A. Baylis (1989), p. 7.
6. See Weber's typology of 'collegial' decision-making in Weber, *op.cit.*, pp. 158–63.
7. J.P. Rehwinkel (1991), p. 233.

8.   See Chapters 1 and 10.
9.   See R. H. S. Crossman (1963), *passim*.
10. See J. Mackintosh (1977b), *passim*.
11. P. Weller (1985), ch. 9.
12. T. Baylis (1989), pp. 147–54.
13. T. T. Mackie and B. W. Hogwood (1985), especially chapter 1.
14. P. Mauroy, interviewed by members of this research team at Lille, on 12 December 1987.
15. T. T. Mackie and B. W. Hogwood (1985), pp. 16–17.
16. C. N. Parkinson, 'Directors and Councils or Coefficient of Inefficiency', in Parkinson (1971).
17. We noted already in Chapter 1, however, that this situation did not obtain to the same extent in Latin American presidential governments. As a matter of fact, the US cabinet itself was more collective in the nineteenth century.
18. The 'overlord' idea was adopted by Churchill in part following suggestions made by L. S. Amery (1936) before the Second World War. See also Chapter 4.
19. After the Second World War, most Western countries adopted gradually the idea of a single minister of defence and the process of unification of the armed services departments was relatively painless. See Chapter 4.
20. As pointed out in Note 18, L. S. Amery was the politician who exercised most influence in pressing for a smaller cabinet.
21. J. Steiner and R. H. Dorff (1980).

3 The Single-Party/ Coalition Distinction and Cabinet Decision-Making

André-Paul Frognier

Of the general variables that might help to account for differences in cabinet decision-making processes, the single-party/coalition distinction is the one that appears intuitively to be the most important. The impact of the single-party/coalition distinction in accounting for differences among types of cabinets has long been singled out, indeed somewhat exaggeratedly, as it appears to relate closely to the effect on governments, and in particular to the stability of these governments; to the distinction between two-party systems and systems of more than one party; as well as to the effect on governments of the distinction between majority electoral laws and proportional representation. The stability aspect of the problem has now been systematically examined and the (somewhat limited) relationship with the party composition of the government is well documented.[1] These matters do not need further analysis.

What has not been analysed so far, however, is the effect of the distinction between single-party and coalition governments on the characteristics of the life of cabinets: admittedly, the possible impact of the distinction needs to be examined together with other elements, and in particular with individual country characteristics and with the nature of the party or parties included in the government, as one has to determine which of these factors appears to play the major part in both general and specific cases. The purpose of this volume is to fill this gap, at least in part, by looking at what ministers think about cabinet decision-making processes. Of course, a variable such as duration does provide an indirect measurement of the quality of decision-making; but a more direct measurement is needed, which only a survey of ministers such as the one that was undertaken for this study can give. The aim of this Chapter is to assess on this basis the specific effect on decision-making of the single-party or coalition composition of the government.

After an examination of the types of single-party and coalition governments that exist in Western Europe and a summary of the findings on the relationship between these types and governmental stability, this chapter will consider possible hypotheses relating to the relationship between the single-party/coalition distinction and the four aspects of the characteristics of cabinets that were identified in the previous chapter – these being the centrality of decisions, the collective character of the process, the collegiality of the body, and the conflictuality of the relationships. The chapter will then examine to what extent these hypotheses can be said to be supported by the evidence from the ministerial survey; it will then assess generally the impact of the single-party/coalition distinction on the characteristics of Western European cabinets in relation to the part played by the nature of parties and by country characteristics.

TYPES OF CABINETS AND CABINET SYSTEMS

The measurement of the impact of the single-party/coalition distinction raises difficulties, however. First, cabinet governments, whether of the single party or of the coalition variety, may or may not have majority support in parliament: this is likely to affect their behaviour. Second, there are many types of coalitions. These differ among themselves, not only as a result of the number of parties involved, but also as a result of the relative weight of these parties: a coalition comprising a large party and one or more smaller ones is not likely to function in the same way as one in which the parties are equal. Yet even the number or posts may not reveal the whole story: one can use relative parliamentary strength as an indicator, since there is often some correspondence between the number of seats in parliament and the number of ministerial portfolios; but a 'pivot' party may exercise an influence disproportionate to its parliamentary strength.[2] Moreover, the importance of the different posts is not the same: in some countries such as Belgium, points are even given to each ministerial position when parties negotiate to form a coalition.

If we take these different aspects into consideration, we come to the following classification:

(1) *Single-party cabinets*: (a) single party minority; (b) single-party near-majority; (c) single-party majority.

(2) *Coalition cabinets (majority or minority)*: (a) two parties with or without a dominant party; (b) three parties with or without a dominant party; (c) four parties with or without a dominant party; (d) more than four parties with or without a dominant party; (e) grand coalitions.

Single-party near-majority cabinets are found in a number of countries (Sweden, Ireland, occasionally Britain); they have to be distinguished from true minority cabinets.[3] Grand coalitions are a category apart because of their ideological scope, although they can be composed of only a few parties, as in Austria where they have included two parties only. The distinction between coalitions with or without a dominant party is somewhat imprecise, for this dominance can be more or less marked; moreover, more than one party can dominate the others.

As was noted earlier, there is a relationship between party systems and cabinet party structure: single-party cabinets are more often to be found in countries with two-party systems than in countries with multi-party systems, whereas coalition cabinets are most often found in multi-party systems. Yet this is only a tendency: some multi-party countries – the Nordic countries for instance – alternate between single-party and coalition cabinets: this illustrates the point that, in cabinet-building, there is both a mathematical logic (the search for a majority in parliament) and a political logic (the choice between several possible majority combinations). Consequently, the party system in the cabinet does not necessarily mirror the party system in the country and in parliament.

One must therefore distinguish between single party cabinet countries, coalition cabinet countries, and mixed cases. Some coalition systems can be ranked according to the dominance criterion: Germany and France have experienced coalitions in which the dominance of one party was clear, while the Netherlands and Belgium (mainly after the parties split along the language divide), and to some extent Italy (except in the immediate post-war period) are countries in which there is not such a marked one-party dominance in the cabinet. Meanwhile, these countries have 'pivot' parties, the christian democrats in Belgium and Italy, or the christian parties in the Netherlands: although these may not have a disproportionate share of the cabinet portfolios, they exercise considerable influence as a result of their permanence in government (an influence that in some cases is buttressed by a politicised public administration).

Mixed systems are even more varied and the historical evolution of each country accounts for each situation. Thus Ireland, Austria, Denmark, Sweden, and Norway oscillate between single-party and coalition government, an oscillation that is due in large part to the nature of the social cleavages on which the parties are based. In Austria and Ireland, there has traditionally been near-two-party dominance. Austria is closer to Britain in that the two parties have historically been almost equal in strength; in Ireland, one party (Fianna Fail) is near-majority, while the second (Fine Gael) is appreciably smaller. In Denmark, Norway, and Sweden, there is a dominant party, but this party is in decline; alongside that party, there are a number of smaller parties that are typically more distant ideologically from the dominant party than the two major Austrian parties have been since 1945.

Majorities are easier to achieve in the first two cases: the political market is clearer and more open. In Ireland, cabinets are based either on one party (often enjoying an absolute majority) or one large party and a small party;[4] in Austria, cabinets are based on one party only, on one large party and a small party, or on both dominant parties. In Denmark, Norway and Sweden, the choice is restricted to the dominant party alone (which is then often in a minority situation), to a coalition between the dominant party and a rather difficult partner (the Communist Party in Sweden), or to an alliance comprising several parties, sometimes with very dissimilar programmes.

Western European party systems in cabinets can therefore be classified from the point of view of their party composition into: (a) pure single party; (b) mixed with 'shared' dominance (such as Ireland and Austria); (c) mixed with incomplete dominance (such as the Nordic countries); (d) coalitions with a dominant party; and (e) coalitions without a dominant party or pure coalitions. In theory, all types include both majority and minority situations, but in practice the distinction arises more often in mixed cabinets with incomplete dominance, because of the marked Left–Right division that characterises these cases.

However, on the basis of this typology, it is difficult to place the twelve countries analysed here on a continuum. The cases at both ends are clear, but intermediate positions are not: with mixed systems with incomplete dominance, in particular, the question arises as to whether greater emphasis should be given to the number of parties in the coalition or to the fact that there is a dominant party. If the mean and the modal number of parties is taken into account for the period 1965–85, the classification seen in Table 3.1 is obtained.

Table 3.1 Country classification according to the number of parties in cabinet

Mean		*Mode*	
Britain	1	Britain	8/8 cabinets
Austria, Ireland	1.3	Austria	5/7
		Ireland	7/10
Sweden	1.5	Sweden	8/11
Denmark	1.7	Denmark	9/13
France	1.9	France	6/11
Norway, Germany	2.0	Norway	7/12
		Germany	10/10
Italy	2.9	Italy	6/20
Netherlands	3.3	Netherlands	4/11
Finland	3.4	Finland	8/18
Belgium	4.0	Belgium	8/18

Note: Column 2 gives the number of cases in the mode over the total number of cabinets in the country concerned during the period.

France is difficult to locate in terms of the mean number of parties in cabinet: as a matter of fact, the positions of France and Norway should be inverted. The classification based on the modal distribution corrects this point, but it has the defect of not helping to distinguish between the first three categories; moreover, the similar values of the mode for Italian and Dutch cabinets tend to give an unrealistic and rather unclear picture. It is thus difficult, if not impossible, to rank countries according to a quantitative criterion alone. Such a criterion is valid for Britain, on the one hand, and for the four countries at the other extreme, on the other (Netherlands, Italy, Finland and Belgium). The seven remaining cases have to be located in the middle, but their relative position is somewhat arbitrary. Consequently we have to adopt an ordinal scale of the following type:

Britain < Austria = Ireland < Sweden = Denmark = Norway
< Germany = France < Italy = Netherlands = Finland = Belgium.

THE INDIRECT MEASUREMENT OF DECISION-MAKING BY MEANS OF OBJECTIVE DATA

So far, little has been discovered about the effect on the internal workings of cabinets of the distinction that we just elaborated between single-party and coalition governments. In order to examine this effect, both 'objective' data and the opinions of the actors can be considered. The 'objective' data can provide some clues if we consider duration as an indicator, on the assumption that more stable cabinets are more efficient (as well as probably being less conflictual). Duration has now come to be explored in some detail. First, as a class, minority cabinets last less well than majority cabinets. Second, with respect to coalitions, Blondel states that, for the period 1945–71 in the Atlantic area,

> the average duration of single party governments was 4.6 years, while the average duration of coalition governments was little under 3.0 years . . . two-party governments lasted on average 3.3 years, three-party governments 3.0 years, four-party governments 2.4 years and governments of five parties less than one year. The unstable governments are therefore the governments of five parties . . . [5]

Thus, on the whole, little difference is observed between two-party, three-party, and four-party cabinets, as the big difference concerns five-party cabinets; but these are relatively rare. It should be noted that the duration of ministerial life tends to compensate somewhat for the relatively shorter life of coalition cabinets: this is particularly so in Italy, Belgium, and Finland; moreover, a subsequent cabinet may have the same party composition or the same prime minister.[6]

There are some differences between the findings for the 1965–85 period and the findings for the earlier period. Single party cabinets are still more durable (almost 24 months) than all other cabinets, as compared with little more than twenty-one months for coalition cabinets, although the difference is again quite small. Yet there is a substantial gap between single-party *majority* cabinets and coalitions, single-party minority cabinets being less durable than five-party coalition cabinets; strangely, three-party cabinets are less stable than four- and five-party cabinets, as Table 3.2 shows.[7]

While the single-party/coalition distinction does affect duration, the existence of a dominant party does not appear to have any significant effect. The correlation with duration is almost non-existent (.08), and the discrepancies are very small. Cabinets with strong dominance last one month more than cabinets without strong dominance (21.09 months *v.* 19.56); the middle category is the one in which cabinets last longest (22.64 months).[8]

Finally, the number of ministers in cabinet appears to have a substantial impact: while cabinets with less than 20 ministers last on

Table 3.2   Duration and number of ministers in cabinets

	Duration (months) (1965–85)	Number of ministers
Single party	23.9	18
Single-party minority	14.4	
Single-party near-majority	24.9	
Single-party majority	32.9	
Coalition	21.2	
2 parties	25.8	18.7
3 parties	17.2	19.5
4 parties	20.6	19.9
5 parties	20.4	20.4
6 parties and more	9.0	24.0

average 23.8 months, those with between 21 and 30 ministers last 18.1 months only. As the number of ministers is related to the number of parties in the cabinet (from 18 in single-party cabinets to 24 in cabinets of six parties or more), the chain seems to be the following: the more parties, the more ministers; and the more ministers, the less durable the cabinets.

THE MEASUREMENT OF CABINET DECISION-MAKING: THE POSSIBLE EFFECT ON DIMENSIONS OF CABINET DECISION-MAKING OF TYPES OF PARTY ARRANGEMENTS IN CABINET

In chapter 2, we identified two descriptive dimensions of cabinets as well as a dimension of centrality and a dimension of intensity of conflicts. The two descriptive dimensions, as we saw, relate respectively to the extent of collegiality and to the collective character of the cabinet. Collegiality means equal participation: it is concerned with the presence or absence of a hierarchy; collective government relates to the fact that decisions are taken jointly by the group rather than by a section of it, such as, for instance, committees. The dimension of centrality raises the question of the extent to which the decisions taken by the cabinet are the major decisions taken by the nation. We will therefore examine here four broad characteristics of cabinets to see to what extent these are central, collective, collegial, and free of conflicts. The aim is to see how far the single-party/coalition dimension is likely to affect the position of cabinets with respect to the four dimensions that we have just listed. In order to undertake this task, let us first hypothesise what these relationships can be expected to be and then turn to the empirical evidence to see how far these hypotheses are validated.

The single-party/coalition distinction and the extent to which the cabinet is central to decision-making

The first question relates to the extent to which the cabinet is central in the political decision-making process. To be central, the cabinet must be able to debate and to settle 'major issues'. If this does not occur, the cabinet must be regarded as peripheral or as dependent on other bodies.

A priori at least, the effect of the single-party/coalition distinction is not immediately apparent. Two alternative hypotheses can be advanced. On the one hand, coalitions, whose essential feature is diversity, are situations in which discussion and negotiation take place, while single-party cabinets would appear merely to have to put a party programme into practice. On the other hand, as parties exercise some control on coalitions, by means of governmental pacts, party summits, and other arrangements, major issues may well be more often discussed outside than inside the cabinet: coalition cabinets may therefore be regarded as not being central. Conversely, single-party cabinets seem to have more freedom to modify their party's initial programmes, especially if the party leaders belong to the cabinet, and provided the party is united. If, though, the party is sharply divided, the situation would seem to resemble that of a coalition. Finally, single-party *minority* cabinets also resemble coalitions, since, being minority, these governments may well depend markedly on other parties.

Party composition and the extent of cabinet collective decision-making

The second question relates to the extent to which ministers are able to take part collectively in discussions or whether they tend to confine their interventions to their departmental field. The first type can be expected to lead to longer, more lively, and more conflictual debates than the second type. Presented in another way, the point could be that a more departmentalised cabinet is also more technical and is characterised by a higher level of agreement than a more collective cabinet.

Here also, it is difficult to advance one single hypothesis. Ostensibly, it might seem reasonable to hypothesise that global agreements are more difficult to achieve in coalitions than in single-party cabinets. Yet if parties strongly control coalition governments, agreement is also likely to be high in those cases, especially if socio-political cleavages are not too sharp; conversely, as we already noted, if there are marked divisions in a party that alone forms the cabinet, that cabinet may have many of the characteristics of a coalition.

Party composition and the extent to which the cabinet is collegial

Some cabinets are more hierarchical, others are more collegial: not just the prime minister, but deputy prime ministers and generally senior cabinet members (such as ministers of finance) may have leading positions. There may thus be a hierarchy or in some cases a kind of oligarchy, with the top ministers being fairly equal (as in Belgium), while other cabinet members are in a subordinate position.

It seems reasonable to hypothesise that fully hierarchical arrangements are less likely to prevail in coalition cabinets; indeed the more numerous the coalition parties, the less likely there is to be a hierarchy. On the other hand, as was pointed out, single-party cabinets may well develop factions, corresponding to those existing in the party at large: this is likely to have an effect on the extent to which the cabinet is hierarchical.

Party composition and the extent of conflict in the cabinet

The fourth question relates to the incidence of conflict. This may be thought to be linked to the extent to which the cabinet is central, as conflict may be expected to be higher when major issues are debated. However, major conflicts may arise on minor issues as well, as on the distribution of patronage, the quest for electoral advantages, etc. On major issues, no clear general hypothesis can be advanced, since, on the one hand, the more ideologically close to each other cabinet members are, the less conflict there will tend to be, but, on the other hand, conflicts are reduced in coalitions by the fact that the party leaders outside the cabinet may exercise a moderating influence. Moreover, the extent of conflict also depends on the type of conflict-solving arrangements that exist in each case. These can be internal (search for a consensus, prime ministerial action, referral to committees, referral to individual departments) or external to the cabinet (national party executives can play a part, for instance): which of these forms are the most efficient ones is not immediately clear.

It might seem permissible to hypothesise that the search for consensus is probably more characteristic of coalition cabinets than of single-party cabinets, unless the single-party governing party is seriously split. Second, prime ministers in coalition cabinets are likely to be less able to impose their views than their single-party cabinet counterparts (in single-party cabinets, the personality of the head of the government may be a more important differentiating factor). Third, the presence or absence of specific interparty mechanisms is likely to affect the level of conflict, especially if these mechanisms are fully institutionalised (party summits, for instance). Finally, the more conflictual cabinets are also likely to last for a shorter time than the others.

THE OPERATIONALISATION OF THE FOUR DIMENSIONS AND THE RELATIONSHIP BETWEEN THESE DIMENSIONS

The analysis of the effect of party composition on the four dimensions that have just been examined can be undertaken on the basis of answers to the survey of cabinet ministers on which this study is based. First, in relation to the extent of *centrality* of cabinets, ministers were asked whether the cabinet was a place where major issues were thoroughly discussed. Second, in relation to the *collective or departmentalised* structure of the cabinet, ministers were asked whether it was common for cabinet members to participate in discussions that did not relate to their departmental matters. Third, in relation to the extent to which the cabinet structure was *hierarchical or collegial*, a number of questions were asked about prime ministerial influence on the structure and the processes of cabinets, in particular whether this influence was exercised on overall governmental organisation or on departments only, and whether it aimed at consensus-building or at forcing a decision. Finally, in relation to the extent to which there was *conflict*, ministers were asked to state how frequently there were instances of substantial disagreement among cabinet members.

One can expect these variables to be interrelated to an extent. For instance, it would seem that the more a cabinet is able to debate (central), the more it is collective and the more it is conflictual.

Empirically, it appears that the more the cabinet is autonomous, the more it is conflictual (there is a significant correlation of 0.19), and the more it is collective, the more it is also conflictual (there is a significant correlation of 0.34). The relationship between the autonomous and the collective character of cabinets is positive and almost significant (0.16). We have therefore good reasons to conclude that there is a positive relationship between the autonomous, collective, and conflictual character of cabinets. With respect to the relationship between the collegial dimension and the other dimensions, one observes only that there are negative correlations between the collective character of cabinets and the hierarchical power of the prime minister: this is so with respect to the structure of the governments, the correlation being −0.39 on the question of overall governmental organisation; this is so also with respect to the manner in which the prime minister acts on the decision-making process in cabinet: the correlation is −0.54 on the question of the prime minister acting in a consensual manner and −0.30 on the question of the prime minister forcing issues in cabinet.

The nature of interparty arrangements in coalitions

By and large, the smooth working of a coalition can be expected to depend on the existence of arrangements designed to solve difficulties that might arise between the parties belonging to the coalition. These arrangements are more or less formal and can be based, for instance, on party summits. Admittedly, a substantial minority of coalition cabinets do not seem to have any such arrangements: over a fifth of the ministerial respondents stated that there were either no contacts between the coalition partners or that there was competition between

Table 3.3   Frequency of types of relationships among parties in coalitions

	Party summits and formal	Informal collaboration	Informal competition	No contact	N
All coalitions	37.7	40.1	16.5	5.7	212
2-party	22.1	51.6	17.9	8.4	95
3-party	34.8	43.5	17.4	4.3	46
4-party	65.1	30.2	23.0	2.3	43
5-party and more	53.6	10.7	32.1	5.6	28

them. This situation affects a minority of cases only, however significant these may be: the large majority of respondents do mention some contacts between the parties, these being apparently more formal as the number of these partners increases: half the respondents who had experienced two-party coalitions stated that the collaboration was informal while this was only the case with 10 per cent in coalitions of five parties or more.

On a country basis, the cabinets in which arrangements are most institutionalised are those of Germany, Belgium, Italy, and Finland: at least the last three cases correspond to countries in which there is no truly dominant coalition partner. In the Netherlands, there is a high level of informal collaboration, but also a relatively high level of informal competition. It is in Ireland and Norway that there appears to be least contact between the partners in cabinet.

The single-party/coalition distinction and the dimension of centrality of the cabinet

There is a manifest relationship between the single-party/coalition distinction and the centrality of cabinets. First, on the whole, at the level of each cabinet, coalitions appear to be somewhat more central to

Table 3.4   Frequency of types of interparty relationships in coalitions, per country

	Party summits and formal collaboration	Informal collaboration	Informal competition	No contact	N
Finland	100				31
Sweden			100		1
Norway		75			12
Denmark	45.5	54.6			11
Ireland		56.3	18.8	25	16
Belgium	45	30	15	10	41
Netherlands	11.8	47.1	35.3	5.9	17
Germany	60.9	39.1			23
Austria		100			10
France		56.3	43.8		32
Italy	52.6	21.1	26.3		19

Note: The highest figure for each country is underlined.

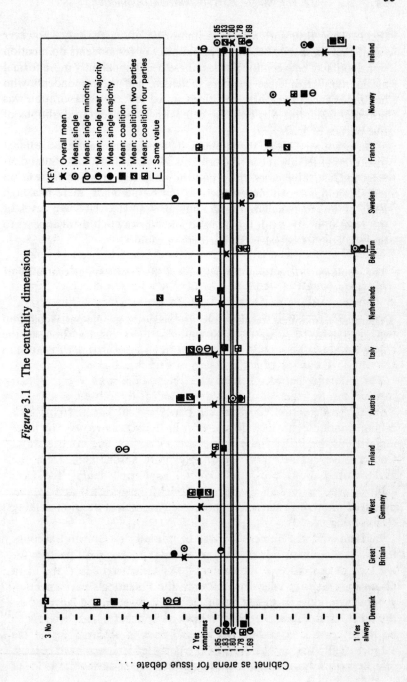

Figure 3.1 The centrality dimension

decision-making than single party governments in general and single-party majority governments in particular (single party: 1.83; single party majority: 1.85; coalitions: 1.78). However, single-party minority cabinets are more dependent and single-party *near-majority* cabinets are not only more central than other single-party cabinets, they are even more central than coalition cabinets (1.69). There is, moreover, a relationship, albeit rather weak, between the number of parties in a coalition and the extent to which major issues are debated: the larger the number of parties, the more open the debate is, as can be seen from the cases of Belgium, the Netherlands, Denmark, and Italy. Finally, country variations are substantial: for instance, while in Denmark, Austria, and Sweden, single-party cabinets appear to be more central than coalitions (in conformity with the the initial hypothesis), the situation is the reverse in Ireland, Norway, and Italy.

Indeed, at the national level, no clear relationship can be found. There is apparently less discussion in British cabinets than in the cabinets of countries where coalitions have a large number of parties; in between, variations from country to country are rather erratic: specifically, there is less discussion in British than in Irish cabinets; there is a marked difference between Danish cabinets and those of other Scandinavian countries; and there appears to be a substantial amount of discussion of major issues in French cabinets.

The difference between Britain and Ireland does seem to correspond to what can be regarded as the 'demotion' of the cabinet meeting in Britain, this demotion being in turn partly a result of the strength of cabinet committees, which do not exist in Ireland; moreover, the large majority of the British interviewees were Conservative ministers and Conservative cabinets are appreciably more autonomous from the party than Labour cabinets.[9] Overall, as Farrell states, 'the Irish cabinet, even more than the British model from which it derives, has managed to preserve the secret garden of government decision-making from prying eyes'.[10]

In Denmark, the numerous cases of minority government account for the predominant role of the parliamentary party and therefore for the lack of centrality of the cabinet.[11] As a matter of fact, the main discussions seem to take place more in the Folketing's parliamentary groups than in the parties as organisations. In Sweden and Norway, on the other hand, cabinets appear to have more debates and therefore to be more central: co-ordination in coalitions is achieved inside the cabinet itself either by the aides of the party leaders who have become ministers (this was the case in particular in Sweden during the 1976–82 coalition) or by 'undersecretaries' (as in Norway).[12] Inter-party co-ordination thus tends to be performed outside the cabinet in Denmark, and inside the cabinet in Sweden and Norway; this could explain the Swedish and Norwegian cabinets' greater centrality.

The apparent ability of French ministers to discuss important matters frequently is surprising, given the powers of the president and those of the prime minister. Moreover, committees play a crucial role in French cabinets and these are likely to reduce discussions in the cabinet itself, as seems logical; this will be examined in greater detail in the coming chapter. Perhaps the explanation comes in part from the fact that many interviewees were drawn from the 1981 government of the Left, a government in which ministers had more freedom of speech than previously and where the leadership style was more flexible.

Overall, therefore, it does not seem to be the case that coalitions impede discussion more than single-party governments. This is indeed reinforced by the answers given by the small number of ministers who belonged to more than one government and experienced both single-party and coalition cabinets. Despite the fact that the number of cases is very small, it appears that more debate on major issues takes place in coalition cabinets than in single-party cabinets. Specifically, Austrian and Danish respondents from single party cabinets give answers that differ from the rest of the respondents in these countries. Considering the fact that the opinion of those who have actually experienced both types of cabinets must surely be regarded as more valid than the opinion of those who did not, it seems clear that there is more debate in coalitions, that this trend is definite in a number of countries, and that there is therefore probably more cabinet centrality in coalitions than in single-party governments.[13]

This conclusion seems to suggest that the control mechanisms in coalitions, and especially party summits and other forms of formal collaboration between parties, have little effect, either because these mechanisms are not often used or because they are not strong enough to achieve dependence. The point can be tested by considering the extent to which these institutionalised mechanisms are used: on this basis, as was indicated in Table 3.4, the cabinets of Finland, Germany, Italy, Denmark, Belgium, and the Netherlands (in that order) would be expected to have coalitions that are less central than their counterparts: this is indeed the case for Denmark, Germany, and Finland, which score rather high on the scale, while the French, Irish, and Norwegian cabinets – three countries where the institutionalisation of cooperation mechanisms is seldom mentioned by the ministers – obtain a very low score: they are indeed the most central cabinets. Italy, the Netherlands, and Belgium occupy a middle position, as they indeed do in Table 3.4.

It seems therefore that the arrangements that reduce discussion in coalitions are not adopted sufficiently generally to affect the majority of coalition cabinets. Meanwhile, the use of these mechanisms does have the effect of reducing debate and of decreasing cabinet centrality, as Table 3.5 shows. If one calculates the mean scores of those who quote these mechanisms, *vis-à-vis* those who participate in single-party cabinets or in coalitions in which the collaboration mechanisms are not used, one finds that the practice of party summits and of formal collaboration leads – on the aggregate – to less debate and less cabinet centrality, compared with coalition cabinets in general but also with single-party majority cabinets (but not with single-party minority cabinets): party summits are thus effective.

The respective positions of the different countries on the centrality scale shows that national situations are contrasted and diverse, however. One must therefore investigate further the extent to which institutional mechanisms have the effect of reducing debate, especially in the countries that experienced both single-party and coalition cabinets. If cabinets in which party summits or other formal arrangements have existed have less debate than other single-party and other coalition cabinets in these countries, these mechanisms can be regarded as indeed very likely to be at the origin of the reduction of debate in cabinets: as Table 3.6 shows, this is the case in the Netherlands, Belgium, and Italy, but not in Denmark. Meanwhile, informal collaboration mechanisms have a similar effect in Denmark,

Table 3.5   Effect of cabinet type and of type of relationships on cabinet centrality

	Mean	*N*
Single-party minority	2.0	33
Coalitions with party summits and formal collaboration	1.94	77
Single-party majority	1.85	107
Coalitions with informal collaboration	1.80	77
All coalitions	1.78	267
Coalitions with no interparty contacts	1.42	12
Coalitions with informal competition	1.44	32

Note: Only the first experience of respondents is considered.

Table 3.6   Effect of cabinet type and of types of relationships on cabinets centrality, per country

	Single-party minority	Single-party majority	All coalitions	Coalitions with summits and formal collaboration	Coalitions with informal collaboration
Finland	2.5		1.85	1.84	
Norway	1.25		1.23		1.2
Denmark	2.23		2.54	2.4	2.67
Ireland		1.29	1.05		1.11
Belgium			1.83	1.94	1.58
Netherlands			1.85	2.0	1.86
Germany			2.0	2.0	2.0
Austria		1.8	2.1		2.1
France			1.62		2.07
Italy	2.0		1.87	2.0	2.0

France (strongly), and Ireland. In Belgium, on the other hand, informal collaboration does not lead to less debate (while party summits do), but, on the contrary, results in more debate; finally, there does not seem to be any apparent effect in Germany, Finland, Austria, and Norway. In Finland, Germany, and Denmark, there is indeed little debate in cabinet, as can be seen in Figure 3.1: in these countries, the lack of centrality of the cabinet may be a result of other factors. Formal and informal mechanisms aimed at reducing discussion are thus not universally effective.

The situation can thus be summarised in the following way:

(1) In Denmark and Austria, coalition cabinets are in all cases less central than single-party cabinets and institutional mechanisms maintain this lack of centrality.

(2) In Italy, institutional mechanisms decrease cabinet centrality on parties somewhat, but the level of centrality is the same in single-party cabinets.

(3) In Finland, institutional mechanisms have little effect on the extent of centrality.

(4) In Norway, there is also little difference in the extent of centrality between single-party and coalition cabinets.

(5) In Ireland, institutional mechanisms tend to reduce somewhat the amount of debate in coalition cabinets, but single-party cabinets are even less central.

One can therefore conclude that, in general, there is somewhat more debate in coalition cabinets than in single-party cabinets, but the difference is small; and that institutional mechanisms that reduce debate in coalition cabinets are effective in a number of countries (the Netherlands, Belgium, Italy), but not in all; moreover, these mechanisms do not succeed in making coalition cabinets as a whole less central. This is probably because some mechanisms, highly institutionalised in some countries, are less practised elsewhere (for instance in France, Austria, Norway, and Ireland), and/or are not always effective enough (as in Denmark, Germany, Finland, Austria, and Norway). If these mechanisms do not function adequately in coalitions, major debates do take place in these cabinets.

The single-party/coalition distinction and the collective dimension of the cabinet

At the cabinet level and in general, the extent to which cabinets are collective is exactly the same in coalitions and single-party majority cabinets (1.69) and is slightly greater than in single-party cabinets in general (1.60), while single-party near-majority cabinets are more collective (1.41); at the country level, coalition cabinets are less collective in Denmark, Italy, and Norway, while they are more collective in Finland and Ireland; Austrian and Swedish cabinets are intermediate cases. Cabinets comprising socialists are somewhat more collective, especially in France, Britain, Norway, and Ireland. This is perhaps because there are more ideological divisions among coalition partners and major issues are therefore more likely to lead to debate.

At the national level, there is no apparent relationship between the single-party/coalition distinction and the extent to which cabinets are collective. In some cases at least, the distinction seems primarily based on cultural differences. Thus Dutch and French cabinets, in particular cabinets of the Right in France, tend to be highly departmentalised.[14] Conversely, in Sweden and Ireland, cabinets are markedly collective, independently from the fact that they may or may not be based on coalitions.[15] Only in Norway does it seem that the 'potential for collective decision is higher in coalition cabinets than in single party cabinets'.[16] This dimension is thus scarcely affected by the single-party

or coalition character of the cabinet. Moreover, there is no clear effect
of the conflict-reducing mechanisms on the degree of 'departmentalisation'.

The single-party/coalition distinction and the collegial-hierarchical dimension

One of the ways in which the collegial character of the cabinet can be
assessed is by examining how respondents assess prime ministerial
action, both with respect to the structure of the cabinet and the process
of decision-making. Table 3.7 shows that the effect of the prime
minister on the structural aspects of the cabinet is more limited in
coalitions, which are thus, to this extent at least, more collegial than
single-party majority cabinets, while single-party near-majority
cabinets are close to coalitions.

There are some peculiarities, however: the action of the prime
minister appears to increase when there are four parties or more in the
coalition, perhaps because, in these cases, cabinet organisation tends to

Table 3.7   Cabinet hierarchy: prime ministerial involvement

| | Influence of prime minster | | Style of prime minister | |
	On overall cabinet organisation	On departments	Consensual	Forceful
Single party	1.12	1.61	1.07	1.39
Single-party minority	1.2	1.7	1.03	1.47
Single-party near-majority	1.3	1.71	1.03	1.09
Single-party majority	1.0	1.5	1.14	1.22
Coalitions	1.33	1.74	1.25	1.75
2-party	1.37	1.57	1.31	1.76
3-party	1.39	1.71	1.27	1.77
4-party	1.24	1.95	1.13	1.8
5-party or more	1.19	1.82	1.13	1.62

become more complex. Meanwhile, the influence of the prime minister on ministerial departments diminishes as the coalition grows from two to four parties, but increases again with five or more parties, although this increase remains limited. The specific way in which prime ministers act does not seem clearly related to the party structure of cabinets, however. There is a tendency for prime ministers to be more prepared to seek consensus as the number of partners in the coalition increases, but only in coalitions of four parties or more do prime ministers seek consensus as much as they do in single-party majority governments and, in all types of coalitions, prime ministers seek consensus less than in single-party minority or single party near-majority cabinets.

Detailed country variations broadly follow the overall pattern. The only exceptions concern the power of the prime minister on individual departments in Swedish, Italian, Austrian, and Finnish cabinets (though with limited effectiveness) and the extent to which consensus is sought in the Austrian cabinets. In the Belgian and Finnish cabinets – the two countries with the largest coalitions – prime ministers are said consistently to avoid forcing a decision; indeed, the larger the coalition, the more they avoid doing so. Moreover, single-party majority cabinets are always less collegial in countries where both single-party majority and coalition cabinets have been in office.

Furthermore, an analysis of the extent to which prime ministers are said to force issues shows that, in single-party cabinets, and in particular in single-party majority cabinets, prime ministers tend to force issues more often than their counterparts in coalition cabinets, while the situation of single-party near-majority cabinets resembles here again that of coalition cabinets. This type of action of prime ministers emerges none the less more clearly in coalitions of five parties than in the other coalitions.

There are some surprising country idiosyncrasies, however. French and German cabinets are judged by the ministers of these countries to be those in which prime ministers are least likely to force a decision: in the French case, this may be because, in the ministers' opinion, the president of the Republic plays a major part; the German case is difficult to account for. According to Müller-Rommel, while the chancellor has substantial influence, the leadership style varies from one head of government to the other;[17] yet a close scrutiny does not reveal any significant differences in this respect. The Dutch findings are also rather unexpected: the Netherlands appears to have a more authoritarian prime minister than other multi-party coalition countries. This runs counter to what might be expected in a nation

63

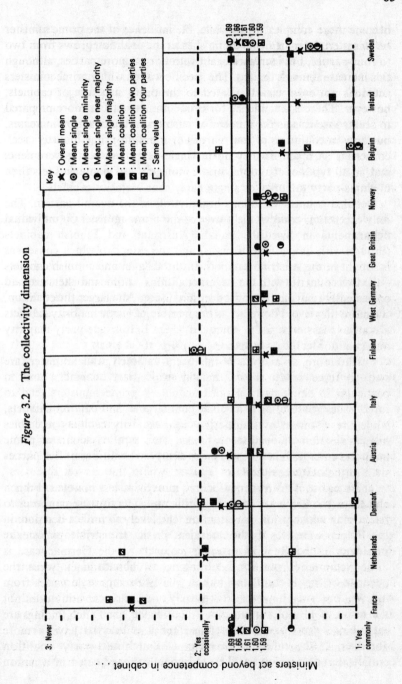

Figure 3.2 The collectivity dimension

with a *primus inter pares* tradition; R. Andeweg does state that the Dutch prime minister's powers have gradually increased, however.[18]

A close look at the answers to the questions regarding collegiality in the cabinet (though limited to those concerned with the prime minister's action) suggests that the hypothesis according to which coalition cabinets are more collegial can be sustained. However, coalitions are less subjected both to prime ministerial authoritarianism *and* to attempts at consensus-building, especially in two-party and three-party coalition cabinets. Furthermore, as with the centrality dimension, single-party near-majority cabinets are nearer to coalition cabinets in terms of relative collegiality.

The single-party/coalition distinction and the management of conflict in cabinet

On the aggregate, ministers judge coalition cabinets to be more conflictual than single-party cabinets (2.33 *v.* 2.06) and the trend is confirmed for all the countries studied here. Moreover, there is an increase in the level of conflict as the number of parties in the coalition increases (two-party: 2.16; three-party: 2.13; four-party: 1.98; five-party: 1.76). The different types of single-party cabinets do not exhibit here substantial differences: single-party majority and single party near-majority cabinets score 2.36 and single-party minority cabinets score 2.24.

At the national level, British cabinets appear less conflictual than those of countries with multi-party coalitions. This result is congruent with the above-mentioned trend, i.e. the more conflictual character of coalition cabinets. When Figure 3.3 is compared with Figure 3.1, there is a sharp contrast, except for France, where the cabinet discusses major issues but is not very conflictual; moreover, as was noted earlier, cabinets of the Right are the least conflictual. The French presidential system may account for this situation: the level of conflict is reduced globally as a result of the president's and the prime minister's dominance, especially in non-socialist cabinets.

The Netherlands' position is surprising, as cabinets in that country appear to be highly conflictual although they are reputed not to be so. Andeweg observes, however, that as only one Dutch cabinet has fallen as a result of loss of parliamentary confidence since 1965, it follows that cabinets must have collapsed as a result of interparty conflicts.[19] Moreover, as the collective character of Dutch cabinets is low, the conflicts that do develop are likely to remain confined to a narrow zone

65

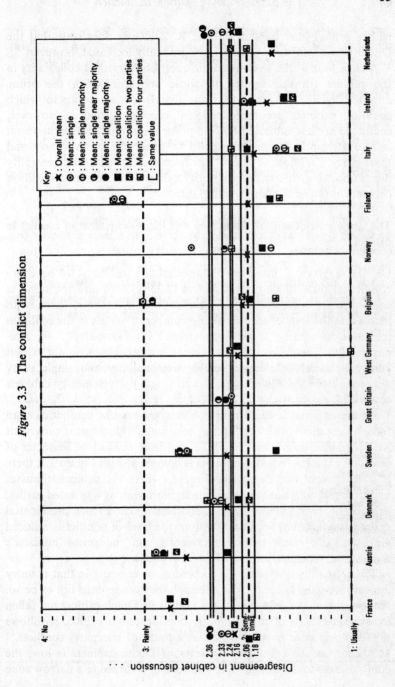

Figure 3.3   The conflict dimension

and be therefore less spectacular. An analysis of the answers of the ministers who have experienced both single-party and coalition cabinets confirms the more conflictual character of coalition cabinets.[20]

The management of conflict

We noticed earlier that coalition cabinets were on the whole somewhat more central than single-party cabinets, despite some tendency for this centrality to be reduced as a result of arrangements between the parties; the effect of institutional arrangements on conflict levels in coalition cabinets needs to be examined in order to see whether these arrangements lead to a reduction in the incidence of conflict.

Conflicts can be settled internally or externally. Internally, they can be solved by means of consensus, by referral to a department or to a cabinet committee, by discussions among ministers, or by prime ministerial action. Table 3.8 lists the frequency of use of these conflict-management mechanisms as well as their relative effectiveness.

Consensus is frequently used everywhere; committees are used more often by coalition and single-party minority cabinets than by single-

Table 3.8　Use and efficiency of conflict management procedures in cabinet (rank ordering)

Procedures	Single-party minority	Single-party majority	Coalitions
Consensus	1	1	1
Committees	3	7	2
Prime minister and minister	4	3	3
Discussion among ministers	4	2	4
Prime minister imposes	2	4	5
Prime minister and one minister impose	7	6	5
Departmental decision	6	5	7
Votes	8	8	8

party majority cabinets; prime ministers tend to act unilaterally more often in single party minority cabinets than in single-party majority and coalition cabinets where the extent of their involvement is about the same; voting is the mechanism of decision-making that is the least used of all.

Frequency of use and effectiveness are not as closely linked as might have been expected. Discussions among ministers appear to be the most effective mechanism in single-party minority cabinets, referral to individual departments in single-party majority cabinets, and the power of the prime minister in coalition cabinets.

Coalition cabinets thus do not appear to resort more to consensus-building than single-party cabinets (and it will be recalled that prime ministers were found to be stronger in coalition governments than might have been expected); meanwhile, the role of the prime minister is particularly manifest in single-party minority cabinets, while it is not as strong in single-party majority cabinets or in coalitions; yet, in coalitions, the best conflict-reducing mechanism is provided by prime ministerial unilateral action: thus, although the prime minister does not often try to force issues in coalitions, as Table 3.9 shows, the mechanism is effective when it is used.

At the national level, too, consensus stands out as the procedure that is most often used. In Britain, however, there is also often referral to the department concerned; the extent to which matters are referred to committees varies from country to country: it is used frequently in Danish-single party minority cabinets (but not in coalition cabinets) in Germany, Belgium, France, Italy, Finland, and Norway (single-party minority and coalition cabinets); the procedure is more rarely adopted in the single-party cabinets of Austria, Ireland and Britain (the British result being rather surprising, given the importance of cabinet committees in that country).

Of the external mechanisms aimed at reducing conflict, the one that appears to be the most effective in coalitions is informal collaboration; the other arrangements, namely party summits and formal collaboration, do not contribute to the reduction of conflicts in coalitions. Meanwhile, single-party majority and single-party minority cabinets are less conflictual than coalitions with formal mechanisms of conflict reduction. Thus formal and institutionalised arrangements are not able to reduce conflict in coalition cabinets, but they succeed in decreasing the centrality of these cabinets.

At the national level, the picture is rather unclear. Party summits diminish conflict in Denmark, the Netherlands, and Finland, but in

Table 3.9   Use and efficiency of conflict-management procedures per country

	Party structure	First	Second	Third
Finland	Single min.	Consensus	PM decides	PM + 1 min.
"	Coalition	Consensus	Committees	Disc. among mins.
Sweden	Coalition	Consensus	Disc. among mins	PM + 1 min.
Norway	Single min.	Consensus	Committees	Disc. between mins.
"	Coalition	Consensus	Committees	Department
Denmark	Single min.	Department	Consensus	Committee
"	Coalition	Department	PM decides	Consensus
Ireland	Single maj.	PM + mins	Consensus	Disc. among mins
"				
Belgium	Coalition	Consensus	PM + mins	Department
Netherlands	Coalition	Committees	PM + mins	
Germany	Coalition	Consensus	Committees	PM decides
Austria	Single maj.	Consensus	Department	PM decides
"	Coalition	Consensus	Disc. among mins	PM decides
France	Coalition	Consensus	PM and mins	Department
Italy	Coalition	Consensus	Department	PM decides

Germany (admittedly only to an extent) and in Belgium they seem to have the opposite effect and increase conflict. Informal collaboration reduces conflict everywhere, except in Denmark, Ireland, and Norway; this mechanism even compensates for the deficiencies of party summits in Germany and even more in Belgium. Moreover, even if use is made of conflict-reduction mechanisms in a country, the level of conflict seems higher in coalition cabinets than in the single-party cabinets of that country. Overall, external and internal conflict-reducing mechanisms have combined effects: for instance, there is an interesting compensating effect between external mechanisms and the role of the prime minister in coalition cabinets. The more competition predominates over collaboration and the more informal collaboration predominates over formal relations, the more the prime minister tends to play an important role.

The hypothesis of the less conflictual character of coalition cabinets is not validated. On the contrary, coalition cabinets are globally more

Table 3.10   Effect of the cabinet type and of type of relationship among
parties on conflict levels

	Mean	*N*
Coalitions with no interparty contacts	1.83	12
Coalitions with informal competition	1.97	35
Coalitions with party summits and formal collaboration	2.01	80
All coalitions	2.06	267
Single-party minority	2.24	33
Coalitions with informal collaboration	2.29	85
Single-party majority	2.36	107

conflictual: this trend is general and is independent of the different
political cultures. Three more specific points can be made, however.
First, the recourse to consensus-building is not more frequent in
coalition cabinets than in single-party cabinets nor is consensus-
building the most effective conflict-reducing procedure; second, the
more parties in coalition cabinets relate to one another in an informal
manner, the more conflict is reduced; yet, third, even when these
mechanisms of conflict-reduction are effective, they do not succeed, on
the aggregate, in ensuring that coalition cabinets become less
conflictual than single-party cabinets.

The single-party/coalition distinction, conflictuality and the duration of cabinets

We noted earlier that coalition cabinets lasted less time than single-
party cabinets, but that the difference was not very large, except for
coalitions that include five parties or more. We suggested that this
might be because of a link between conflictuality and duration, as well
as because coalition cabinets are more conflictual than single-party
cabinets, an assumption that the data analysed here shows to be
correct.

If we consider the two longest-lasting cabinets in each country, the
majority of these (15 out of 24) display a low level of conflict; this does
indirectly confirm the scale's validity as well. However, the link

between conflict and coalition is not marked since, out of 14 low-conflict cabinets, 8 are coalitions and 6 single party, while out of the cabinets that are longer-lasting and conflictual, 5 are coalitions and 3 single party (Britain being excluded since there was not a coalition in that country during the period).

However, in France, Germany, Belgium, and the Netherlands, highly conflictual coalition cabinets are – on average – the least durable cabinets, while in Sweden the one coalition cabinet studied was more conflictual and less durable than the two single-party cabinets. The hypothesis according to which coalitions are less durable is thus confirmed in five countries out of eleven studied (Britain being excluded) and, on the aggregate, highly conflictual coalition cabinets are also the least durable.

The single-party or coalition composition of governments does therefore affect, but only to a limited extent, the characteristics of decision-making in Western European cabinets. This relatively small effect is in part a result of the fact that there are both many types of single-party governments (minority, near-majority, majority) and many types of coalitions (from two to five or more parties, with or without a dominant party, ideologically close or very broad). In many ways, for instance, single-party minority governments resemble coalitions rather than other single-party governments from the point of view of the characteristics of decision-making.

Thus factors other than the single-party/coalition distinction manifestly play a substantial part in shaping the style of cabinet decision-making processes. Specifically, country idiosyncrasies are important: indeed, in many cases, country idiosyncrasies are inextricably intertwined with the single-party/coalition divide: Britain has always had single-party governments since the Second World War and almost always single-party majority governments; single-party minority governments are a feature of Denmark, while the two-party coalition with a dominant party is a feature of Germany. In many cases at least, it is therefore difficult to distinguish between the effect of idiosyncratic country characteristics and that of the single-party/coalition dimension.

This distinction does none the less have an impact and it is also valuable to discover where this impact is small or negligible: this is what the cross-national survey undertaken for this study enables us to do. It is thus clear that there are greater opportunities for debate in coalitions than in single-party governments; it is also clear that coalitions are more egalitarian and conflictual, this last effect being the most prominent in the survey analysed here. Moreover, both these characteristics become increasingly marked as the number of partners in the government grows, a finding that accounts for the fact that coalitions that include many parties result, by and large, in less stable governments. Meanwhile, the limitation of debate and the taming of conflict are often, but not always, achieved better by arrangements within the cabinet, informal discussions being more successful in general than formal meetings, although these can be used and be effective, especially when the number of parties in the coalition is large.

The role of the prime minister can be substantial in both single-party and coalition governments, a point to which we shall return in Chapter 10. In coalitions, prime ministers do not merely make their presence felt by endeavouring to create a consensus: they do try to force issues in these types of cabinets as well as in single-party cabinets. Indeed, it is typically the same prime ministers who both use consensual means and strong forms of unilateral power.

Coalition government is, by and large, a feature of Continental Europe and single-party government is characteristically a feature of Commonwealth countries, although there are substantial exceptions to this generalisation. It is not possible to say whether it is because these exceptions exist that the distinction between the effects of single-party and of coalition governments on the characteristics of cabinet decision-making is not as great as might have been expected; but all types of party structure of cabinets, whether of the single party or coalition types, achieve manifestly a balance between consensus and conflict and between the centrality of debate and streamlined decision-making. That this should be the case is a tribute to the realism of Western European ministers when confronted with the tasks they have to fulfil, a realism that might in turn explain why both single-party and coalition forms of parliamentary government have been, in their different ways, broadly successful, when compared to other forms of government in other polities.

Notes

1. See A. Lijphart (1984), pp. 124–6.
2. In Belgium, the Netherlands, and Italy, for instance, the christian democrat parties have been in power always, or nearly always despite

the fact that, especially since the 1970s, these parties have often obtained only about a third of the votes.

3. Near-majority cabinets (with the support of 45 per cent of the parliamentarians at least) can usually count on the votes of members of small parties and some independents. To this extent, their strength is greater than that of 'true' minority cabinets. Swedish social democratic governments, for instance, have needed and typically obtained the consistent support of the small Communist party.

4. Fianna Fail cabinets have typically been able to govern alone and indeed to dismiss the very idea of coalition as characteristic of weak and divided government. With the emergence of the Progressive Democrats, however, even Fianna Fail had to accept leading a coalition.

5. J. Blondel (1982), p. 115. A government is defined in this case by the same leader and the same party or parties in power, but not by a new parliament, let alone by a change in the composition of the cabinet.

6. A.-P. Frognier (1991), p. 121.

7. Ibid.

8. For these correlation levels the level of significance is .01 and $N = 185$. In order to measure dominance, we have used an indicator inspired from the notion of 'entropy' in information theory: on the basis of the repartition of portfolios among coalition parties, entropy is maximal if all the parties possess the same number of portfolios and minimal if one party holds all the portfolios.

Entropy is measured in the following way. First, absolute entropy is computed by using the following formula:

$$E = \frac{(\ln 1/Pi) \times Pi}{i}$$

where $Pi = NMi/NM$, and where NMi = the number of ministers in the party, i and NM = the total number of ministers. E varies between 0 and $\ln NP$.

Second, relative entropy is

$$rE = E/(\ln NP)$$

E varies now between 0 and 1.

There are three categories: coalitions with strong dominance of a party ($rE < .84$: 32 cases); coalitions with medium dominance (rE from .84 to .94: 28 cases); and coalitions with weak dominance (rE from .95 to 1: 32 cases).

9. M. Burch (1988b), p. 24.

10. B. Farrell (1988), p.41.

11. T. L. Schou (1988), p. 179.

12. S. Eriksen (1988b), p. 207.

13. Among ministers having participated in two cabinets in five countries (Finland, Norway, Denmark, Austria, and Italy), the trend was the following. Of those who went from a single-party to a coalition cabinet, 7 respondents stated that there was more debate in the first

than in the second cabinet and only one stated that there was less; of those who went from a coalition to a single-party cabinet, 5 respondents stated that there was less debate in the second than in the first cabinet and only one stated that there was more.

14. J.-L. Thiébault, (1988), pp. 100–1. R. B. Andeweg (1988), p. 63.
15. T. Larsson (1988b), p. 198. B. Farrell (1988), p. 43.
16. S. Eriksen (1988b), p. 194.
17. F. Müller-Rommel (1988a), p. 166.
18. R. Andeweg (1988a), p. 55.
19. In the Dutch case, however, only two respondents were found to pronounce in the opposite direction.
20. Among ministers having participated in two cabinets in six countries (Finland, Sweden, Norway, Denmark, Austria, and Italy), the trend was the following. Of those who went from a single party to a coalition cabinet, 8 respondents stated that there was more conflict in the first than in the second cabinet and only two stated that there was less; of those who went from a coalition to a single-party cabinet, 6 respondents stated that there was less conflict in the second than in the first cabinet and only one stated that there was more.

Part II

The Role of Structures in Cabinet Decision-Making

4 The Organisational Structure of Western European Cabinets and its Impact on Decision-Making

Jean-Louis Thiébault

In the previous chapter, we outlined in broad terms the effect of the distinction between single-party and coalition governments on the characteristics of cabinets and in particular on the extent to which these are central, collective, collegial, or conflictual. At this point, however, we need to pause somewhat and examine the part that legal arrangements, as well as traditions and customs, may play on cabinet decision-making processes. For it is widely believed that certain types of rules, for instance about the frequency of meetings or about the procedures adopted at these meetings, have an impact on the extent to which decision-making is collective or not; it is also widely believed that the development of committees markedly contributes to a segmentation of cabinets and therefore to a decrease in their collective character. These matters need to be explored in some detail, although information is not always as readily available as one might have hoped and expected: it is to these questions that we turn in this and the following chapters with a view to assessing how much impact rules, procedures, and other arrangements may have on the way in which decisions are taken.

Such an analysis will naturally be based partly on 'received opinion' as it emerges in the published literature; but it will also be based on the views expressed by cabinet members in the responses that they gave to the ministerial questionnaire. Throughout the chapter, the emphasis will be on distinctions between groups of countries: legal arrangements and traditions tend to emerge on a country, not on a cabinet basis. Yet we will also examine whether the single-party/coalition distinction and the party composition of governments have a noticeable effect on the cabinet organisational structure.

A tripartite distinction between collective, segmented, and fragmented cabinets was outlined in Chapter 2 in order to identify the different arenas in which cabinet decisions tend to be taken. In practice, these arenas correspond to the full cabinet meeting, to committees (which can be, as we also saw, interdepartmental or party political), and to ministerial departments, this last category being the arena where decisions are taken by cabinet members individually. This chapter will explore further the relationship between these structures and the nature of the decision-making processes. To do so, we shall first elaborate somewhat on the points made in Chapter 2 and examine how far decision-making structures in the cabinets of the various countries tend to be primarily based on cabinet meetings, on committees, or on individual departmental autonomy. We shall then endeavour to assess the impact that these structural arrangements have on the characteristics of decision-making processes.

THE THREE MAIN ARENAS OF GOVERNMENT DECISION-MAKING AND THEIR RELATIVE IMPORTANCE IN WESTERN EUROPEAN CABINETS

The cabinet meeting

Since many cabinets are not, or have ceased to be, collective or collegial, the full meeting has also ceased to be regarded as crucial for decision-making, at least in a large number of cases and in most countries. Co-ordinating committees, party committees, as well as the ministers individually or in bilateral discussions are probably felt to be the real sources of decisions in the majority of cases. While there are differences from country to country and perhaps from cabinet to cabinet, as was pointed out in Chapter 2 and as we shall see in more detail in the course of this chapter, the ideal of a cabinet meeting truly taking the most important decisions does not correspond to the reality, although there are naturally variations from case to case.

Even if the role of the cabinet meeting has been reduced, however, it does still remain important, both substantively and symbolically. In the majority of countries, the cabinet meeting is often the constitutionally (or at least customarily) compulsory channel through which governmental proposals have to pass; this is true even where the decisions of the cabinet do not have a truly legally binding character, as in Britain. Moreover, the cabinet meeting has a crucial part to play in preventing the government from being wholly divided into a number of independent segments, if only because it is the one place where all the members of the cabinet are together and can therefore exchange ideas, often in private, before or after the meeting proper. Finally, the cabinet meeting provides an occasion for the government to announce its decisions: in many countries, a press statement is made at the end of the deliberations. The cabinet meeting can thus be regarded as having an overall, if somewhat ill-defined, impact on decision-making patterns: this broader general impact is difficult to determine, however, and we need to look at other more specific indicators if we are to assess how the full meeting of the cabinet can affect decision-making processes.

Four such indicators can be identified. First, the composition of the cabinet might affect decision-making because of differences in size and possible fluctuations in this size over time. Second, variations in the frequency and duration of meetings can be expected to have an effect on the extent to which individual cabinet members are involved in discussions. Third, who determines what the cabinet discusses at each meeting seems highly critical to the general decisional environment. Finally, the rules of procedure for the conduct of the meeting are likely to influence modes of decision-making.

Composition

By and large, Western European cabinets are composed in a broadly similar manner. They all include the top ministers, most of whom are heads of departments, but some of whom are without portfolio. There has been some increase in the size of cabinets in the post Second World War period, but this increase has remained modest, at least in Western Europe:[1] thus most cabinets have between fifteen and twenty members, except in Iceland and Luxembourg, where they are much smaller (but these two countries are outside the scope of the present study), and in Italy, Belgium, and Britain, where they typically have somewhat over twenty members.

One major difference in composition could have come from the presence or absence of the head of State (monarch or president) at the meetings; but, except for the Finnish and French presidents, heads of State have now ceased to attend cabinet meetings. The customary rule adopted in Britain in the eighteenth century gradually became the norm elsewhere, though of course much later: it was adopted in

Belgium for instance between the two world wars.[2] By the 1980s only
the Norwegian King, among the monarchs, attended cabinet meetings,
but he attended only the formal Friday sessions.[3] Nor do the German
or Italian presidents attend cabinet meetings. In fact, even in France,
the practice of holding many meetings of the cabinet without the
president had also developed under the Third and Fourth Republics;
but this custom was stopped with the advent of the Fifth Republic,
when, as the Finnish president, the French president asserted his right
to chair meetings. In the French case at least, the presence of the head
of State at cabinet meetings does by itself have an effect on decision-
making, as the president appears to the ministers to be the final
decision-maker.

While full ministers thus belong to the cabinet, junior ministers
(often called ambiguously 'secretaries of State' in Continental Europe)
are not part of it; they are typically invited to attend when issues that
concern them directly are discussed, though. This is the case in Ireland,
the Netherlands, Belgium, Germany, Austria, France, Italy, and
Norway; in Germany, junior ministers may even replace cabinet
ministers when they are absent. This practice obviously contributes to
some variations in the composition of cabinets over time, but probably
not to such an extent as to affect the structure of decision-making.

Finally, some advisers of the head of the government or of ministers
also regularly attend meetings, but they do not technically 'belong' to
the cabinet: they do not have the right to intervene in debates and their
influence is therefore covert; it takes place in particular through the
part that they may play in helping to shape the agenda or in drafting
the minutes of meetings. A cabinet secretary is typically present, this
secretary being normally, but not always, a civil servant: in Belgium,
for instance, the secretary is one of the collaborators of the prime
minister. In some countries, more than one adviser attends the
meetings. Thus, in Norway, the prime minister's press officer and the
permanent secretary to the prime minister's office are both present.[4] In
France, the general secretary of the presidency of the Republic and the
general secretary of the government attend the cabinet meetings every
week. In Germany, since 1974, a few ministers of State and the heads of
the chancellor's office and press office also attend cabinet meetings.[5]
Finally, in Italy, the under secretary to the prime minister acts,
according to an old practice, as secretary to the cabinet.[6] It is doubtful
whether the presence of these officials affects markedly the way the
meetings proceed, however. Overall, therefore, it seems permissible to
suggest that variations in composition are not sufficiently large across

Western Europe to have a significantly different impact on decision-making patterns in cabinets.

Frequency and duration of meetings

On the contrary, the frequency and duration of meetings vary appreciably across Western Europe. One can divide countries into three groups in this respect. First, in four countries, Sweden, Norway, the Netherlands, and Ireland, meetings of the cabinet are frequent and/or long. In Sweden, formal cabinet meetings take place once a week to approve decisions already taken elsewhere, but these formal meetings are normally followed by a more informal meeting, known as the 'general cabinet meeting', in which more important matters are discussed. There are also other occasions, both regular and frequent, that provide opportunities for discussions and include all the ministers: this is especially the case of the daily lunches, at which the level of attendance is high and during which important policy matters are discussed informally.[7] In Norway, the cabinet meets three times a week, although one of these meetings, the one that is presided over by the King, is formal: the other two meetings last about three hours each.[8] The Dutch cabinet meets only once a week, but the sessions are long: they lasted in the past until the small hours; more recently, they typically end in the late afternoon, Dutch ministers thus spending about thirty hours a month in cabinet meetings.[9] In Ireland, the cabinet meets twice a week, the duration of the meetings being markedly affected by the personality of the prime ministers, some of whom appear to favour long discussions.[10]

In two other countries, Finland and Austria, the relatively shorter frequency and overall duration of cabinet meetings is compensated by the existence of preliminary gatherings of all the ministers in a more informal setting. In Finland, the equivalent of the Swedish lunches is provided by an evening session which takes place the day before the official cabinet meeting and is known as the 'evening school'.[11] In Austria, official cabinet meetings are preceded by unofficial preparatory sessions. Originally, these were meetings of the individual parties represented in the grand coalition, but they continued to take place during the seventeen years of single-party government. Since the return to a coalition government in 1983, both intra- and interparty preparatory meetings are held, the composition of the two bodies being approximately the same.[12]

In the other countries that are studied here – that is to say, the four larger countries (Britain, France, Germany, and Italy) as well as in

Belgium and Denmark – cabinet meetings are typically less frequent and last for a shorter time. In Britain, the cabinet meets weekly for between one and a half and three hours (on Thursdays): in the early postwar period, under Attlee and Churchill, it met twice a week; more recently, the once-a-week meeting became the rule.[13] In France, the cabinet meets also once a week for about two hours (on Wednesdays), while in Italy meetings were irregular during the Rumor and Moro governments, but came to be held weekly afterwards, each session being relatively short.[14]

The cabinet agenda

The influence of the cabinet meeting on decision-making is likely to be affected also by the extent to which members are free to raise issues for discussion. As a matter of fact, the head of the government now has marked powers in this context, he or she being helped by the secretariat of the cabinet. Admittedly, many topics placed on the agenda are the result of lengthy discussions that have taken place previously in arenas other than the cabinet itself; yet there is always room for flexibility and this flexibility is what may give the prime minister, on the one hand, or individual ministers, on the other, greater or lesser influence. By and large, the balance is tilted in favour of the prime minister in most countries and, correspondingly, of the president of the Republic in the French case since the establishment of the Fifth Republic, except when the president and the government are of different parties: thus, during the 'cohabitation' period of 1986–8, the president did not refuse to have political matters discussed on the grounds that he disagreed with them.[15]

There seem to be two countries only, Austria and Finland, where ministers have the right to demand that a question be discussed at the meeting.[16] One might therefore hypothesise that ministerial influence on decision-making is substantially larger as a result in these two countries.

Management of the cabinet meeting

Finally, the role of the cabinet meeting can be enhanced or reduced as a result of management rules, some of which are formal, while others are customary. Formal rules prevail in Germany, France, Finland, the Netherlands; customary rules prevail in Britain. In Germany, there are 'government rules' (*Regierungsverordnungen*) which state, among other things, that meetings must allow for statements to be made on certain matters, even though they do not entail decisions: this is the case with statements on foreign affairs or the economic situation.[17] In France, guidelines were adopted in 1947 and amended a number of times; they stipulate that the meeting is to be divided into three parts: one dealing with draft bills, ordnances, and decrees; the second dealing with top appointments that have to be made in cabinet; and the third devoted to ministerial statements, particularly on foreign affairs and, increasingly, on European developments.[18] In Finland, the cabinet must effectively adopt almost every governmental decision: thousands of items thus go through the cabinet every year.[19] In the Netherlands, rules state all the items that need to be approved in cabinet: these are, on the one hand, draft bills, decrees, treaties and international agreements, white papers, policy plans that have financial implications, including plans on which the ministers concerned have failed to agree, and all other matters affecting overall government policy; on the other hand, the meeting must ratify the appointment of senior civil servants, judges, and mayors of large local authorities.[20] This very long list contrasts with the British situation, where the cabinet has essentially a general policy-making function but does not have the legal powers that Continental cabinets possess.[21]

The fact that large numbers of matters have to pass through the cabinet for decision-making does not mean that the meeting is more influential as a result: on the contrary, the more the decisions that they have to take are formal, the less members have time to scrutinise the main points in detail. One indicator seems to be of value, though, namely whether or not issues are settled by a vote. There are major variations in the way in which conflicts are handled in the various countries, indeed in the various cabinets. In some (France and Britain, for instance), there is considerable reluctance to settle issues by votes; this is true in other countries as well, as the ministerial survey indicates. Indeed, Finland and to a lesser extent the Netherlands and Norway are the only countries where votes are routinely taken at cabinet meetings; in the four larger countries of Western Europe, on the contrary, as well as in Denmark and in Belgium, votes take place rarely or almost never. While this does not mean that the cabinet meeting is necessarily weak in this second group of countries, vote-taking does suggest that the cabinet meeting is indeed influential in the first group, even if voting is sometimes a prelude to a crisis among the coalition partners.[22]

We have thus identified a number of ways in which the cabinet meeting can be expected to exercise influence as a result of structural or procedural arrangements. While composition is not likely to vary enough to have an effect, except perhaps marginally in Britain, Italy,

Table 4.1 Votes in the cabinet; disagreements solved by votes

	Yes	No
	(absolute figures)	
France	0	37
Britain	0	31
Germany	0	24
Denmark	0	28
Belgium	1	8
Austria	1	26
Italy	3	22
Norway	9	27
Netherlands	11	5
Ireland	15	14
Finland	26	19

Note: Sweden gave almost no responses to this question.

and Belgium, where the cabinet is larger than in the other countries, the duration of meetings, agenda-setting, and the use of votes at meetings vary enough to suggest that decision-making processes may be affected. Taking all three indicators together, one might hypothesise that the countries where the full cabinet meeting is most likely to have an impact are Scandinavia, except Denmark, as well as the Netherlands, Ireland and, perhaps surprisingly, Austria. We will see in the final section of this chapter whether there is evidence to support this hypothesis.

The cabinet committees

Meanwhile, the widespread use of committees constitutes perhaps the most important change affecting governments since the 1950s, this development being largely a result of the increased complexity of governmental affairs and the consequential overload on ministers and the cabinet. Sometimes, the committee structure remains rather informal; in most cases, it is formal and it can indeed be very elaborate in some countries.[23] The mushrooming of committees is usually regarded as having been directly instrumental in reducing the collective character of cabinets and in increasing the segmentation of these bodies.

Cabinets can be divided into three groups according to their committee structure. In three countries, Britain, France, and Italy, they are very numerous; it is difficult to provide truly reliable data for the number of committees in these countries because of the existence of temporary as well as permanent committees, because of rules of secrecy, and because of variations over time, although it seems that numbers have become more stable in the 1980s than in previous decades. According to Mackie and Hogwood, there were 38 committees in Britain in the early 1980s; but, according to the *Financial Times* and the *Economist*, there were only 26 committees in 1992.[24] Numbers are similar in France and Italy.

In the majority of other Western European countries, the number of committees is about half the number found earlier in Britain: according to Mackie and Hogwood, there were about 14 committees in the Netherlands, 17 in Germany, and 21 in Denmark. Committees do not appear to play a major part in Germany, however, and they meet only occasionally.[25]

Finally, in two countries, cabinet committees have not developed at all. In Ireland, the only committees that exist are *ad hoc* or are entirely informal, the prime minister being in charge of the coordination of day-to-day work and of the preparation of long-term policies. In Sweden, they do not exist. According to Mackie and Hogwood, the reason might be the stability of party control (from 1932 to 1976 and from 1982 to 1991) and the long duration of many cabinet ministers in office: ministers are therefore able to decide informally on many matters without having to rely on a committee structure.[26] Thus, if one takes the number of committees as an indicator of segmentation, one might expect that the impact will be most marked in the first group of countries and least in the third.

Composition

The size and composition of committees seem likely to have an impact on the part played by these bodies in decision-making. By and large, small committees are more powerful as they tend to take decisions on behalf of the cabinet. Some of the large committees are those set up by statute or regulation; they include a substantial number of ministers, in order to obtain a representative cross section of the cabinet: examples are provided by the committees for economic and social coordination in Belgium and the Netherlands; but large committees can also be set up more informally, whether they are constituted by a cabinet decision, as in the Netherlands, or by a decision of the prime minister, as in

Britain. Permanent committees are naturally more formal than temporary committees: these are likely to be set up when two or more ministers have to settle an issue.

An important and growing component of the membership of committees is constituted by civil service members; indeed, this practice is now widespread. In France and in the Netherlands, senior civil servants participate actively in committees. Dutch officials are members of twelve of the fourteen cabinet committees; they are mostly directors-general of ministerial departments, but other civil servants, such as the director of the central bank, are also included in the committees.[27] Britain adopted a similar practice in the 1970s, ostensibly in order to improve the efficiency of the cabinet system, but the experiment was a failure and the only important mixed committee to survive is the one dealing with national security. Senior civil servants attend ministerial committee meetings, but they do not take part in the discussion.[28] When civil servants are present in committees, the sectional or segmented character of the cabinet is likely to be increased.

It is indeed further increased when, below these 'mixed' committees, there are also bodies exclusively composed of civil servants. Although these are outside the cabinet *stricto sensu*, they have to be considered here as they prepare the work for the regular cabinet committees, in particular if these do not include civil servants. Committees of civil servants may thus be asked to handle a specific problem, as in Britain.[29] In Austria, Denmark, Norway, and Germany, committees of senior civil servants have been set up to deal with technical aspects of issues and therefore to prepare the political decisions to be taken subsequently by cabinet committees – or even sometimes directly by the full cabinet. There are indeed cases in which these committees of civil servants are given formal decision-making powers: cabinet committees or the cabinet itself will intervene only if the civil servants' committees have been unable to resolve their disagreements. Such committees are thus truly part of the broader 'cabinet system'.

The trend is even more marked in France, where numerous meetings of senior civil servants take place in the prime minister's office and cover entire areas of government. The number of such meetings doubled during the early period of the socialist government of the 1980s: 592 took place in 1971 and 607 in 1975; there were 1300 or more in the first half of the 1980s; with the return to power of the Centre-right in 1986 their number fell to 845.[30] By and large, therefore, at least in France and in the Netherlands, and perhaps in Britain, outsiders are sufficiently numemous and sufficiently influential in committees to be able to erode substantially the role of the cabinet meeting.

Powers

One must be careful about drawing conclusions too quickly about the impact of committees on the basis of the formal powers of these bodies. These formal powers differ widely, some committees having a broad remit, others being more specialised.[31] Those that have a broad remit are more likely to have a substantial impact than those that are specialised, but such an impact consists more in reducing the collegial nature of the cabinet than its collective character. At the limit, if the policy scope is as large as that of the cabinet itself, committees may be embryonic inner cabinets; this is rare, however, and in most cases committees are concerned with only some aspects of governmental policy, even if these are the most important aspects.[32]

In the Netherlands, for instance, in the early 1970s, a committee was set up, interestingly rather informally, in order to discuss social and economic questions. It started as a 'triangle' comprising the ministers of finance, of economic affairs, and of social affairs. These were subsequently joined by the prime minister and the minister for internal affairs and thus constituted a 'pentagon'. For a period, this committee tended to dominate social and economic policy-making: as these problems typically form the bulk of the cabinet agenda, the 'pentagon' has sometimes been considered as an inner committee.[33] The influence of the committee did decline in the late 1980s, however. Similarly, in Belgium, the committee for economic and social coordination did have considerable influence: as it has been composed of twenty members since the middle of the 1970s, however, it is no longer a committee, but the cabinet itself insofar as it deals with economic and social matters.[34] In Finland, the two main permanent committees, the finance committee and the economic policy committees, exercise a power of political and administrative coordination: they are filters for matters to be subsequently decided in cabinet. Thus, in many cases, ministers are required to secure formal authorisation from the finance committee before embarking on expensive projects. Moreover, the economic policy committee meets twice a week and acts as a policy-drafting body: it thus often acquires the character of an inner cabinet.[35]

Segmentation is more likely to result from the activities of the more 'normal' committees dealing with different aspects of governmental policy and aiming at achieving coordination in a particular sector. They may thus be concerned with agriculture, industry, transport, public works, housing, health and social security, science and technology. They are set up to ensure that due regard is paid to the interests of the various departments that may be involved; they are therefore likely to reduce significantly the part played by the whole cabinet.[36]

This conclusion can also be drawn with respect to the committees set up to coordinate government policy in fields that are politically 'hot' at a given moment in time. This was the case in the 1970s with committees dealing with energy and the environment, and, in the 1980s, with urban affairs and problems of drug addiction. Depending on the circumstances, their policy scope may be broad or narrow.[37] Meanwhile, however, the potential impact of some committees dealing with one-off issues that are regarded as politically sensitive is not entirely clear. These committees are often rather large because of the need to involve a cross-section of the cabinet in the preparation of the decisions, probably politically painful, that will have to be taken.[38]

Overall, on the basis of the number and composition of these bodies, committees seem strongest in Britain, France, Italy, as well as perhaps in the Netherlands, and weakest in Ireland and Sweden. The first group is composed mainly of those countries that are not expected to give a high premium to decisions taken by the full cabinet; it also includes the Netherlands, though, which seems to be a somewhat special case.

Individual ministerial decisions and the level of departmental autonomy

Some Western European cabinets are characterised by a high degree of individual ministerial autonomy. This may result from administrative traditions, as is the case in Sweden, Finland, Norway, Denmark, Austria, and Germany; ministerial autonomy may also develop on political grounds, often in order not to upset a fragile equilibrium between the parties, as in Italy, Belgium, and the Netherlands.

There may be substantial ministerial autonomy when the cabinet resembles a body of top civil servants meeting from time to time, on an egalitarian basis, to thrash out common problems and to take important decisions. This description fits principally the Finnish situation, as the cabinet emerged there when the country was still an autonomous grand duchy within the Tsarist empire. The ministers were civil servants and formed a board, similar to other boards in Russia at the time; the notion survived as did another element, namely the fact that ministers are expected to be able to act freely within their own sphere.[39] A similar situation exists in Austria and in Germany where departments are largely immune from cabinet interference and individual ministers maintain this independence. Thus, in Germany, every minister is personally and fully responsible for the activities of his or her department, as the tradition of ministerial autonomy coexists with the view that the whole cabinet is held to be collective: within the sphere of responsibility of each department, a minister cannot be given orders, in theory at least, even by the chancellor.[40]

In other countries, the autonomy of departments stems from the need to maintain a given political equilibrium. In the Netherlands, the tradition of departmental autonomy is strong and the Dutch cabinet can be regarded as a group of heads of administrative departments. Yet the autonomy of the ministers is assured, not for administrative reasons, but because of the large part played by interest groups in policy-making in the Dutch system: many decisions are taken in the departments after consultation with the relevant groups; this type of arrangement does naturally assume that ministers are broadly autonomous within their own sphere. It should also be noted, moreover, that in the Netherlands each department has its own criteria for civil service recruitment.[41] In Italy, too, the cabinet can be regarded as a collection of ministries, on the understanding, however, that the autonomy that ministers enjoy stems as much from the fact that they represent their party or a faction of their party as from the fact that they are heads of their departments.[42]

Ministerial autonomy thus prevails in some countries, whether for administrative or for political reasons. On the other hand, there are countries where the autonomy of ministers is played down and collective responsibility emphasised: this is in particular the case in Britain and Ireland. In France, since the Fifth Republic, ministerial autonomy is also limited, but primarily because of the somewhat hierarchical character of the cabinet: ministers relate to the president and to the prime minister in a manner somewhat akin to that of senior civil servants to their superiors.[43]

There are as yet no truly reliable indicators of the extent of autonomy of ministers in the various Western European countries: one has to use impressions and descriptions given in the literature. In many cases, therefore, the real extent of autonomy is difficult to ascertain. There are clear differences, however, between countries where ministers do not have an autonomous sphere of action (Britain, Ireland, France) and countries that are manifestly autonomous, for administrative reasons (Finland, Austria, and Germany) or for political reasons (the Netherlands, Belgium, and Italy). It can be seen from this list that, with the exception of the Netherlands, the group of countries in which ministerial autonomy is large coincides with the group of countries where the cabinet as a whole does not appear to have (or have any longer) the opportunity to be truly collective.

CABINET STRUCTURES AND CABINET DECISION-MAKING PROCESSES

Structural arrangements thus differ appreciably among Western European cabinets, with more or less emphasis being placed on full meetings, on committees, or on individual departments. As we examined the structural differences, we suggested some hypotheses about the impact that these structures could have on decision-making processes: the expectation is that cabinets will be more collective where the meeting of all the ministers has a substantial scope of activity, that they will be more segmented where committees are highly developed, and more fragmented where individual ministers have a large amount of autonomy. In the course of the analysis, we identified a number of indicators of these structural arrangements; we need now to relate these to indicators of decision-making processes to see whether structural arrangements appear to affect these processes. We need also to consider other factors, and especially the single-party/coalition dimension and the party composition of cabinets and examine the part these factors play in this configuration.

The impact of structural arrangements on decision-making processes: the evidence from the ministerial survey

Two types of evidence can be used to ascertain the extent of the relationship between decision-making processes and cabinet structures. These two types supplement each other. One is richer and more colourful: this is the evidence provided by the literature that describes the broad characteristics of decision-making on a country-by-country basis. More systematic comparative evidence is found in the answers to the ministerial survey undertaken for the present study.

To take the ministerial survey first, the characteristics of decision-making processes can be derived from answers to a number of questions which indicate the part played by the full cabinet, by committees, and by individual ministers. Thus respondents were asked to state how far they were able to take decisions individually without referring to the cabinet; they were asked to say how they brought issues to the attention of their colleagues and, in particular, whether they used the channel of cabinet committees or went directly to the full meeting; they were asked to give their opinion as to whether the cabinet was a place where major issues were debated or whether, among other arenas, cabinet committees were a place where they were typically debated; finally, they were asked to say whether, in cases of disagreements, issues were settled by means of referring these back to a committee and whether, when decided on in full cabinet, they were settled by a vote.

Thus cabinets of countries whose ministers scored high on the first set of questions could be regarded as cabinets of countries where considerable autonomy was given to ministers and where the cabinet could be regarded as fragmented, at least relative to the cabinets of other countries; cabinets of countries where committees were mentioned as essential channels could be regarded as having a segmented pattern of decision-making; cabinets of countries where the full meeting was most mentioned as a decision-making arena could be regarded as characterised by centralised or collective decision-making patterns.

Answers to the questionnaire provide strong evidence for the view that structural arrangements have an impact on patterns of decision-making. On the basis of the indicators mentioned earlier, the cabinet

Table 4.2   Going directly to cabinet to raise an issue; number of ministers answering

	Yes	No
	(absolute figures)	
Netherlands	14	0
Austria	27	2
Norway	31	5
Sweden	20	3
Britain	17	11
Ireland	16	16
Belgium	9	9
Finland	13	21
Germany	6	17
Italy	3	16
Denmark	5	22
France	0	37

meeting appears strongest in Finland, Sweden, Norway, Ireland, Austria, and the Netherlands: in four of these six cases, a large majority of ministers stated that, if they wanted to raise an issue, they would bring it directly to cabinet, while in the other two countries of the group, between a third and half the respondents replied in the same way. On the other hand, of the other six countries, only in two, Britain and Belgium, was half or a majority of the respondents of the opinion that they would go directly to the cabinet; in the other four, Germany, France, Italy, and Denmark, the overwhelming majority stated that they would not go directly to the cabinet.

We noted earlier that Britain, France, Italy, and the Netherlands were the countries where committees were most developed, while, at the other extreme, Sweden and Ireland had few or no cabinet committees. Cabinet life could therefore be expected to be more segmented in the first group of countries, and more collective in the second. The answers given by ministers confirm this hypothesis. In France, Britain, and Italy, as well as in Belgium, all or nearly all the respondents stated that they would send to committees matters that they wanted to see discussed. In Germany, Ireland, and, surprisingly, the Netherlands (but, in this last case, the number of answers to the question was very small), the majority of the respondents stated that they would not use the committee channel, while in Norway, Finland, Denmark, and Austria, the response was more mixed (the question was

Table 4.3 Matters referred to cabinet committee in case of disagreement

	Yes	No
	(absolute figures)	
France	37	0
Britain	23	2
Belgium	38	0
Italy	11	2
Finland	24	21
Norway	18	18
Denmark	11	16
Austria	11	17
Ireland	9	23
Germany	6	18
Netherlands	0	7

Note: Sweden gave only one response to the question.

not asked of Swedish ministers). Thus, with the exception of the Netherlands, the expected pattern of segmented decision-making was found to exist in the countries where the structure of cabinet committees was known to be most developed.

Finally, some indication can be obtained from the examination of answers to the scope of action of ministers. The replies do not provide a very clear picture of the extent of ministerial autonomy as they tap more directly the degree of activism of ministers, a point that will be examined in Chapter 8. They show, however, that the freedom of cabinet members is more restricted in Belgium, Britain, and particularly Ireland, as well as, more surprisingly, in Austria, while it is greater in Germany and Finland. By and large, these findings correspond to the patterns that were anticipated and confirm the broader hypothesis.

Overall, therefore, there seems to be an impact of cabinet structures on decision-making. Full cabinets are more collective and therefore central to decision-making in the Scandinavian countries, in Ireland, and in the Netherlands. They are more segmented, with a considerable dose of committee decision-making, in Britain, Belgium, and France, as well as, in a somewhat ambiguous manner, in the Netherlands. Finally, cabinet decision-making is more fragmented in Germany, while the other examples of ministerial autonomy are less clear-cut.

The impact of structural arrangements on decision-making processes is further reinforced by the fact that, on the other hand, neither the

Table 4.4 Ministers can act individually even if a matter is politically 'hot'; number of minister answering

	Yes	No
	(absolute figures)	
Germany	13	8
Finland	23	16
France	18	19
Austria	8	21
Britain	9	25
Italy	5	17
Norway	13	21
Denmark	4	23
Ireland	4	25
Sweden	0	21
Netherlands	0	4

distinction between single-party and coalition government that exists among parliamentary cabinets nor indeed the party distinction between cabinets of the Right and cabinets of the Left appear to have any impact on these processes. Single-party cabinets are just as likely either to be structured collectively or to have segmented patterns of decision-making as coalition cabinets; cabinets of conservatives or christian democrats are just as likely as socialist cabinets to be structured collectively or to have segmented patterns of decision-making. In almost no case can one detect any apparent relationship and in no case is there a statistically significant association between either factor and the indicators of decision-making patterns. The single-party coalition distinction does not even seem to have an effect on the size of cabinets: Italian and Belgian coalition cabinets are larger than average, but so are British single-party cabinets, while other coalition cabinets are not particularly large. Indeed, the large size of Belgian cabinets is probably more a result the difficulties resulting from the cultural and linguistic conflict than of the existence of coalitions.

The evidence from the literature

The broad conclusions of the ministerial survey go in the same direction as the evidence drawn from the examination of the country cases described in the literature, but these more detailed and more

Table 4.5   Association between the single-party/coalition distinction and the party composition of cabinets and decision-making patterns

	Single-party/coalition distinction	Party composition of cabinets
Politically 'hot'	0.0002	0.28
Referring to cabinet committees	0	0.03
Sending direct to cabinet	0	0.03
Cabinet the main arena of decision-making	0.02	0.17
Votes	0.0008	0.006
Prime ministerial staff draws agenda	0	0

specific analyses also provide nuances that are of some importance. Thus, while the distinctions that have been made between collective, segmented, and fragmented cabinets are broadly supported by country descriptions, there are some reservations. First, it is typically noted that, in the Scandinavian countries and in the Netherlands, matters tend to be debated thoroughly in the full cabinet: ministers report on the issues that concern them and these are then discussed. Yet, even in these cases, the collective aspect of the cabinet is limited. Exchanges between ministers are often limited by informal rules: for instance, conventions prevent ministers from criticising proposals from their colleagues if their department is not at stake.[44] Moreover, the collective aspect of cabinets is also limited when the prime minister plays an important part and conducts the general policy of the government. In the Netherlands, the position of the prime minister has been strengthened over time because of his increasing role in foreign affairs. Prime ministerial influence seems to be a major factor in accounting for the reduction of the power of the cabinet.[45]

Second, the role of cabinet committees in segmenting policy-making is stressed in the descriptive evidence relating to a number of countries; but it is also pointed out that the consequences of the development of committees are not the same everywhere. In France, cabinet committees meet at irregular intervals and the number of meetings varies each year according to the successive presidents: De Gaulle and Pompidou convened few such meetings. These multiplied under Giscard d'Estaing and took place then almost as frequently as cabinet meetings (between 30 and 50 a year between 1974 and 1981). They met to the same extent during the first Mitterand presidency (34 meetings in 1982), but since 1986 they have occurred less often. Coordinating committees initiated and chaired by the prime minister on a specific matter were summoned fairly frequently in the early period of the Fifth Republic and after 1981: these committees are powerful instruments in the hands of the prime minister, who can control ministers better in this way.[46]

In Britain, too, the prime minister tends to set up committees to deal with specific issues: this has become an easy way of handling governmental problems and this procedure has made it possible to summon only one weekly meeting of the cabinet. The participation of the prime minister at these meetings has reinforced the position of the head of the government at the expense of collegiality. To this extent, British and French governments can be regarded as segmented.

Elsewhere, cabinet committees are more likely to be set up at the request of ministers, for instance to achieve coordination. Such committees sometimes boost the autonomy of individual departments. The role of the cabinet as such is weakened, but the intended coordination is not always achieved: individual departments may simply use the committees to increase their veto power. This may be because some of the committees function as 'inner cabinets', as we noted earlier has been the case in Belgium and the Netherlands, at least for a period; this is often because committees can be instruments legitimising the autonomy of individual ministerial departments:[47] every minister chairs his or her cabinet committee. Committees do not then merely segment the government: they fragment it. In Italy, committees are instuments designed to legitimate the autonomy of some ministerial departments rather than to achieve coordination; coordination has been replaced by institutionalised political bargaining. Committees thus become instruments designed to promote the particular interests of departments. Every minister chairs departmental committees: this emphasises a form of governmental polycentrism which in practice escapes from the control of the prime minister and of the cabinet.

Third, although, as we noted earlier, the historical origins of individual ministerial autonomy could be administrative or political, there are variations. In Germany and Austria, where departmental autonomy is regarded as large, it is compensated to a substantial extent by the influence of the chancellor, who conducts the general policy of the government and whose strength stems from his constitutional authority, from the dominant position that he holds within his party, and from the support that he receives from this party.[48] To this extent, ministerial autonomy in Germany and Austria is less marked than in those Scandinavian countries where an administrative tradition also leads to ministerial autonomy but where the role of the prime minister is less pronounced.[49] Finally, in the two countries where ministerial autonomy is large for political rather than administrative reasons, Belgium and the Netherlands, the existence of inner cabinets and of other committees appears to counterbalance to an extent the influence of the individual ministers.[50]

Fourth, the analysis of the structures of cabinets and of their impact tends to leave aside the question of the extent of centrality of the cabinet, that is to say the part played by external bodies in cabinet decision-making. As was noted in the previous chapter, in a number of countries, and in particular in a number of coalition governments, cabinet decisions are prepared or markedly helped by 'party summits' which may include a smaller or larger number of non-cabinet members

– for instance, party secretaries. This has been particularly the case in Austria, Italy, or Belgium, while in other cases (in Norway and the Netherlands, for instance) these party summits have existed but have included cabinet members only.[51] We shall return to this question in Chapter 7, in the context of the role of parties in the general development of cabinet decision-making, as both cabinet structures and the impact of these structures on decision-making processes are markedly affected as a result.

Western European cabinets are thus organised more specifically around the full meeting, around committees, or around individual departments, but the distinction is far from watertight: especially the part played by committees can and does vary, since these can help the prime minister, achieve coordination, or even protect individual ministerial autonomy. There are therefore committees in countries in which the full meeting is given prominence as well as in countries where individual ministers have considerable autonomy.

Yet, although we are confronted with a continuous dimension and intermediate cases can be closer to one or the other of the extreme positions, the relationship between cabinet structural arrangements and cabinet decision-making processes is strong. In Western European cabinets, decision-making processes developed on the basis of the different country 'cultures' that produced different structural arrangements. These 'cultures' appear to be truly alive; in particular they cut across both the distinction between parties of Right and Left and the distinction between single-party governments and coalitions. We now need to turn to cabinet working procedures to see whether these amplify or limit the impact of structural arrangements.

Notes

1. The proportional increase in the number of ministers was larger taking the world as a whole than in the Atlantic countries in the post Second World War period. See J. Blondel (1982), p. 180.
2. A. P. Frognier (1988b), p. 74.
3. J. P. Olsen (1980), p. 211.
4. J. P. Olsen (1980), p. 210. S. Eriksen (1988b), p. 189.
5. F. Müller-Rommel (1988a), p. 154.
6. M. Cotta (1988), p. 129.
7. T. Larsson (1988b), pp. 202 and 209–10.
8. S. Eriksen (1988b), p. 188.

9. R. B. Andeweg (1988a), p. 56.
10. B. Farrell (1988), p. 40.
11. J. Nousiainen (1988a), p. 221.
12. P. Gerlich and W. C. Müller (1988), pp. 149–50.
13. M. Burch (1988b), p. 21.
14. S. Cassese (1980), p. 175.
15. J.-L. Thiébault (1988), p. 92.
16. P. Gerlich and W. C. Müller (1988), p. 143. J. Nousiainen (1988), p. 213.
17. R. Mayntz (1980), p. 154.
18. J. Fournier (1987), pp. 227–8. J.-L. Thiébault (1988), p. 92.
19. J. Nousiainen (1988a), p. 220.
20. R. B. Andeweg (1988a), p. 56.
21. M. Burch (1988b), *passim.*
22. R. B. Andeweg (1988a), p. 57.
23. T. T. Mackie and B. W. Hogwood (1985), pp. 1–15.
24. Ibid., p. 19. *Financial Times,* 20 May 1992. *The Economist,* 23 May 1992.
25. Ibid., p. 19. Also F. Müller-Rommel (1988a), p. 159.
26. Ibid., p. 17.
27. R. B. Andeweg (1985), p. 141.
28. P. Hennessy (1986), pp. 30–1.
29. M. Burch (1988b), p. 27.
30. J. L. Quermonne (1987), p. 506.
31. J. G. Christensen (1985), pp. 120–4.
32. Ibid., p. 120.
33. R. B. Andeweg (1988a), p. 65.
34. A.-P. Frognier (1988b), pp. 79–80.
35. J. Nousiainen (1988a), p. 225.
36. J. G. Christensen (1985), pp. 129–30.
37. Ibid., pp. 120–1.
38. Ibid., pp. 132–3.
39. J. Nousiainen (1988a), p. 218.
40. P. Gerlich and W. C. Müller (1988), p. 139. F. Müller-Rommel (1988a), p. 152. R. Mayntz (1980), p. 143.
41. R. B. Andeweg (1988a), pp. 63–4.
42. S. Cassese (1980), p. 175.
43. J.-L. Thiébault (1988), p. 90.
44. H. Heclo and A. Wildavsky (1974), p. 141.
45. R. B. Andeweg (1988a), p. 55.
46. J. L. Quermonne (1987), pp. 203–6.
47. R. B. Andeweg (1988a), p. 65. A.-P. Frognier (1988b), pp. 79–80.
48. P. Gerlich and W. C. Müller (1988), p. 139. F. Müller-Rommel (1988a), pp. 161–5. R. Mayntz (1980), pp. 144–50.
49. J. G. Christensen (1985), p. 133.
50. R. B. Andeweg (1988a), p. 65. A.-P. Frognier (1988b), pp. 79–80.
51. R. B. Andeweg (1988a), p. 62. A.-P. Frognier (1988b), pp. 83–4. S. Eriksen (1988b), p. 189. P. Gerlich and W. C. Müller (1988), pp. 149–50. M. Cotta (1988), p. 130.

5 Organising the Flow of Business in Western European Cabinets

Martin Burch

To understand the operation of cabinets, it is essential to extend the scope of analysis beyond formal ministerial meetings to cover the wider set of organisations that make up what has been termed the 'cabinet system'.[1] This consists of the organisations whose members are involved in handling issues once they move beyond the jurisdiction of individual government departments. Characteristically the issues that these personnel deal with are those which, in order to be settled, need to be handled by an authority above the department. As the matters that are referred upwards have become both more numerous and more complex, the 'cabinet system' has, as a consequence, expanded beyond the confines of the cabinet itself. It includes advisers, typically organised in offices and secretariats, whose function it is to smooth and coordinate the ways in which issues are brought forward and determined.

The way in which business is handled is important. In cabinet systems, as in all organisations, certain formal boundaries help to shape behaviour: members of cabinets cannot raise matters as they wish, or discuss these at any time they choose, or take them out of the agenda at will. There are thus limits to the way in which members can participate; these reduce the degree of flexibility and the scope for individual discretion and tend to channel decisions along established pathways.[2] These boundaries are partly a consequence of the structures that were examined in the previous chapter, but they are also the product of rules and operating procedures and, in particular, the manner in which these are customarily applied.

Rules and procedures serve to shape behavioural patterns either directly, by prescribing and determining an activity, or indirectly when they are attended to but with the aim of avoiding them: in such instances the rule is being addressed, but it is not being followed.[3]

Nevertheless, in both instances, behaviour has been shaped by the existence of a rule or established procedure. Moreover, the framework of rules and operating principles can either be tightly drawn and thus operate in a highly restrictive way or it can be loose and fragile and thus allow wide discretion. The degrees of restriction and flexibility are obviously relative; one result is that marked differences exist from country to country.

Rules and operating principles establish only a part of the framework through which decision materials pass and are shaped and altered. In addition, a consideration of the process whereby decision materials originate, are developed, and resolved is essential to understanding the general operation of cabinet systems. Of course patterns of behaviour will show particular and varied manifestations according to the issue being handled, the exact circumstances pertaining at the time, and the personalities and the skills of the individuals holding this or that position. In all instances, however, general patterns underlie and shape everyday behaviour. They are the framework within which the everyday and incidental have to find accommodation.

The previous chapter was essentially devoted to the examination of the *structures* that help cabinet decision-making to take place, often at the expense of its collective character. In this chapter, the stress is on the *procedures and practices* that are used to handle, and in some cases expedite, business. These procedures and practices also have an impact on the collective character of decision-making. As we shall see, the operating principles and the processes whereby decisions are prepared significantly affect the extent to which a government can operate collectively, both by limiting the actions of cabinet members and by providing some of the ministers (and some senior civil servants) with particular opportunities to exploit the arrangements that are in being.

Attention is also given in this chapter to ascertaining the ways in which the rules, operating procedures, and processes of cabinet systems are applied in practice. The powers granted to particular incumbents holding certain positions are explored as well as the general characteristics of the rules and procedures involved, and how and by whom these rules and procedures are established and adapted. The chapter falls into three parts: the first considers the rules; the second, the main processes or tasks involved in the handling of business; and the third examines which key actors have the best opportunities to manage the flow of business.

As in other parts of this study, the analysis is based on the ministerial interviews as well as on published secondary sources. In addition, a 'checklist' was completed by members of the research group. This was an attempt to collect information on the procedures governing the conduct and handling of business that have become established since the 1960s. The answers that were provided were based on the personal knowledge of these scholars or were compiled with the help of other experts such as ministers and top civil servants both in office and retired. The data fully covers ten of the twelve countries surveyed plus some material on Italy. Information relating to Denmark was not available.

RULES

How precise are the rules and operating procedures of Western European cabinets and who has the power to change these rules and procedures?

The part played by rules in cabinet decision-making raises three sets of general questions. First, what is the status of the rules and what is their legal character? Are they to be found in the constitution, in statutes, in standing orders, or merely in codes of procedure? Second, how precise, extensive,and binding are these rules and, in particular, how wide a range of activities of the cabinet do they cover and with what degree of authority? Do they substantially constrain procedure or do they leave many 'loose ends' and much room for manoeuvre? Finally, who advises on the rules and who has the power to change them? From answers to these three questions one can distinguish between types of cabinet systems. The extent to which there are precise and written rules gives a measure of the institutionalisation, and even formalisation, of the system; variations in the procedures from one cabinet to another in a given country also provide some indication of the stability of the operations in the cabinet system of that country. The extent to which rules are precise and cover a wide range of activities provides some indication of the degree of discretion within the cabinet system, while the existence and nature of rules provides an indication of the potential for holding personnel accountable or for encouraging them to act collectively.

Table 5.1 rank orders Western European cabinets according to the extent to which they are subject to rules of procedure and to the extent to which these rules are binding. This latter point is based on the

Table 5.1   Institutionalisation and stability

Countries		A	B	GB	SF	F	D	IRL	NL	N	S
1. Are there any cabinet rules and operating procedures mentioned in:											
a) written constitution	a)	2	2	3	2	2	3	1	2	2	2
b) legislative statute	b)	3	3	3	1	3	1	2	2	2	2
c) standing orders	c)	2	2	3	1	3	1	3	1	1.5	2
d) written code of practice?	d)	3	2	2	1	2	1	1	1	1.5	2
Score: 1 = extensively, 2 = marginally, 3 = no											
TOTAL a)–d)		10	9	11	6	10	6	7	6	7	8
2. Do the above sources of written rules cover most or few of the actual procedures of the cabinet?		2	2	2	1	1	1	1	1	1	1
Score: 1 = most, 2 = few											
Total scores for 1 and 2		12	11	13	7	11	7	8	7	8	9
First ranking: 1 = most instiutionalised		9	7	10	1	7	1	4	1	4	6
3. On the whole, do the procedures of cabinet: 1 = remain relatively unchanged across cabinets 2 = vary in some respects, but most procedures remain stable 3 = vary considerably?		3	2	2	1	1	2	1	1	2	2
Total scores questions 1–3		15	13	15	8	12	9	9	8	10	11
Second ranking: 1 = most stable and institutionalised		9	8	9	1	7	3	3	1	5	6

A = Austria, B = Belgium, GB = Britain, SF = Finland, F = France, D = Germany, IRL = Ireland, NL = Netherlands, N = Norway, S = Sweden.

proposition that rules contained in a national constitution, in a legislative statute, or at least a publicised set of standing orders, are likely to be more binding than rules solely laid down in an informal code of practice, even if it is written. On the basis of the scores presented in Table 5.1, Britain is the only country in which there is not only no written constitutional basis for cabinet government, but also where the written code of practice covers only limited parts of the actual procedures of cabinet. In the British case, the cabinet is mentioned only in two pieces of legislation and then only in passing, though there are a number of confidential notes of guidance to officials working in the cabinet system.[4] At the other extreme are to be found Finland, Germany and, to a lesser extent, the Netherlands, where binding bases for rules, such as legislation and standing orders, cover a significant number of the procedures involved in handling business in the cabinet system.[5]

There are two sets of implications stemming from these variations in the extent to which rules are binding. On the one hand, ministers and others involved in the cabinet system have more discretion to act as they please in the less institutionalised systems. On the other, where rules of procedure are laid out in a written document which is publicised, the members of the cabinet system are more capable of being controlled by outside bodies such as a constitutional court or a parliament. For, where there are no clear rules, it is manifestly impossible to assess whether given forms of behaviour are acceptable or not. Admittedly, effective accountability to outside bodies with respect to rules of procedure depends on the nature and the operation of the machinery available for scrutiny and enforcement of these rules; but it is also clear that, when rules and operating procedures are scarcely formalised, as in Austria, Britain, France, and Belgium, the potential for surveillance and control through judicial or parliamentary mechanisms is minimal. It should be noted, however, that over and above such forms of control, cabinet systems are also supervised indirectly and more informally in other ways and in particular by parties and, ultimately, the electorate.

The fact that rules are spelt out in detail also has a consequence for the continuity of procedures across cabinets in each country. It is a reasonable assumption that the more rules are embodied in formal documents, the less they are likely to be altered over time: the procedure for changing them is likely to be more lengthy and more onerous. Material relevant to this point is also presented in Table 5.1, which provides some indication of the extent to which procedures remain relatively unchanged across cabinets and the extent to which they vary. Overall, all Western European cabinet systems can be described as stable as there is a great deal of continuity in terms of procedures from cabinet to cabinet; there are degrees in this stability, however. Among the cabinets that are the most stable in this sense are those of the Netherlands, Finland, France, and Ireland: this is a mix of cabinet systems that do not otherwise have much in common, since some have strong committees while others do not, some have collective structures while others do not. At the other extreme, there are appreciable variations from cabinet to cabinet in Austria. Finally, those changes that do take place across cabinets are partly explained in Austria, Germany, and, to a lesser extent, Britain as a consequence of the discretion granted to the prime ministers and the style of managing the cabinet that he or she adopts.

Not only do cabinet systems vary in terms of the extent to which they are rule governed and there is continuity in the procedures, but also in terms of how and by whom these procedures are established and altered. Clearly in any circumstances where rules apply and serve to shape behaviour, the power to create or alter rules is vital. In relation to those matters of procedure that are not covered by comprehensive sets of written rules our range of cabinet systems reveals some variation when it comes to distinguishing who is primarily responsible for advising an incoming cabinet (that is, a wholly new set of incumbents) on the nature of its operations. It is in relation to this task that those who belong to the bodies that help to streamline cabinet business can be markedly influential. In Belgium, France, and Britain members of the cabinet secretariat advise cabinet ministers (in the case of Britain, the secretary of the cabinet with one or two other top officials); in Sweden, individual cabinet ministers are advised on cabinet procedure by their departmental civil servants, while in the Netherlands, Ireland, Austria, and Norway both sets of personnel are involved. This is a task that is always fulfilled by civil servants, which may in part help to explain the continuity of cabinet procedures between administrations. The potential for civil servants to influence procedures at this point is clearly substantial, though it is bound to be constrained by the need to maintain accepted and established ways of working. Ministers with previous cabinet experience may also occasionally make a contribution and cabinets may come into office with proposals for procedural reform, but this is likely to be rare: generally most procedures remain in currency. It is civil servants who act as guardians of these procedures and it is their task to socialise new arrivals into the accepted way of doing things. Where our systems differ is in the degree to which this is handled by civil servants at the cabinet system level, at departmental level, or at both levels.

Being influential in the initiation of rules is important. The establishment of rules helps to set the operating conditions for the organisation and the framework within which it works. Generally speaking, changes to these rules are, once they have been accepted, marginal. Yet changes do take place, and the ability to change rules and thereby seek to alter practice is obviously an important power.

Who, then, in general, changes the written rules governing the operation of cabinet and, where relevant, its committees? There are appreciable differences in this respect among the countries studied here. First, as was pointed out earlier, parliament may be involved: this is the case in Germany, Finland, Italy, Ireland, the Netherlands, Norway, and Sweden, at least for some of the rules. For the other rules in these countries and for all the rules in the others, there is a sharp distinction between the more collective and the more 'prime ministerial' cabinets. In Germany, France, and the Netherlands, the cabinet as a whole is responsible for the rules: the system is (in theory at least) 'collective' in this respect. The system also contains significant collective elements in Finland and Norway, since the cabinet is drawn into the process along with the prime minister, who may take the lead but does not always do so. At the other extreme, in Italy, the rules that are not determined by parliament are issued by the prime minister, while in Belgium and Sweden rule changes appear to be almost entirely the responsibility of the prime minister. In between are a number of systems in which both the cabinet and the prime minister are involved. In Ireland, changes arise usually as a result of discussions between the cabinet secretary and the prime minister but they may on occasion be ratified by the cabinet; a similar situation pertains in Britain, although ratification by the cabinet is unusual while the prime minister may, 'very occasionally', act alone without the guidance of the cabinet secretary. In practice, however, one must not exaggerate the real power entailed by this authority to change the rules. While altering the rules may give ministers, prime ministers, and their advisers an opportunity to innovate in the area of procedures, the extent to which they are able to do so is partly shaped by the amount and pressure of business that they have to handle and by the extent to which existing procedures are accepted and embedded in the organisation. Few cabinets have time to review the rules and operating procedures to which they are subjected: this may not necessarily be an advantage as, perhaps, if cabinets were truly able to change the rules, cabinet government might be the better for it.

The process for handling decision materials

The making of decisions involves two activities that are closely interlinked but are analytically distinct. On the one hand, there are activities concerned with the *content* or the policy substance of the decisions reached; on the other, there are activities concerned with the *handling* of decision materials such as cabinet and committee papers and memoranda. As we are concerned in this volume with decision-making processes, we are not primarily examining here the content of the decisions, though to the extent that content does affect processes, we shall look at the matter in Chapter 11. In this chapter, we are concerned with the way materials are handled from the point at which they are initiated into the cabinet system to the point at which they emanate from it as decisions to be implemented.

The established ways in which decision materials are handled form another part of the framework within which members of cabinet systems are obliged to act. These, like the rules examined in the previous section, serve to constrain and shape behaviour. They also provide opportunities for influencing the flow and content of materials and thus help to form what is decided. The handling of cabinet materials involves a number of tasks. First, access has to be gained into the system and decision materials have to be initiated; second, these materials have to be circulated, distributed, and in some cases reformulated; third, items have to be timetabled and prioritised; they have then, fourth, to be placed in a particular arena where decisions are formally taken; fifth, decisions and proposed actions need to be recorded and disseminated; and finally the implementation of the decisions has to be monitored. For each of these tasks, one needs to consider how and by whom they are usually carried out and who is formally placed in the best position to influence the process. It is worth distinguishing among these tasks between those that are largely concerned with the initiation of the flow through of materials, those largely concerned with their determination, and those largely concerned with their application.

INITIATING BUSINESS

Gaining access to the system

In all the countries points of access to the cabinet system are restricted to certain individuals who are subject to certain procedures. Those in key positions to control access have considerable potential to influence what enters the system, how it is to be interpreted and to whom it is to be made known.[6] There is the important matter of access by outside interests. In all countries a considerable process of consulting outside interests takes place before matters are initiated into the cabinet system: what matters is whether this is done directly from within the cabinet system or indirectly from the departments and whether it is ministers or civil servants who are largely involved. A contrast can be drawn between *centralised* and integrated approaches, where external interests have direct access to cabinet institutions, and *decentralised* and diffused approaches, where these external interests have contacts mainly with the departments. Most Western European countries can be described as decentralised in this respect, as the main contact points with outside interests are the departments. Yet there are variations: in Belgium, Ireland, Germany, and Austria, the cabinet secretariat and/or prime minister's office is also involved in these links. In Britain and Germany relations with interest groups are usually handled by civil servants, in France and Sweden by ministers, while in other countries both groups are involved. Some cabinet systems are more open than others to external influences: respondents to the ministerial questionnaire were asked to state where discussions over major issues tended mainly to take place: over 40 per cent of the Italian and over 30 per cent of the Austrian and Norwegian interviewees mentioned interest groups, while no mention was spontaneously made of these by their British, Finnish, and French counterparts.

Providing information and advice and originating proposals

Those within government who originate a decision proposal and who provide the information and advice attached to it are in a strong position to influence the final outcome since it is they who establish the framework of ideas and assumptions within which discussions take place; originators can therefore have a critical role. In general, this initiative is with the departments and not at the level of the cabinet system: this is especially the case so far as the provision of detailed information and advice is concerned. In the matter of actually originating a proposal there are certain exceptions to this rule; this is especially so for the broadest policy proposals, such as the governmental programme or the electoral platform, which tend to emerge at a level above departments, though the latter may be drawn in as contributors within their areas of responsibility. Beyond these cases, there are four types of exceptions to the principle that initiatives are departmental. One concerns Sweden, where commissions often provide the original inputs.[7] Another concerns the two semi-presidential systems that exist in Western Europe, France, and

Table 5.2 Involvement of external interests

Countries	A	B	GB	SF	F	D	IRL	I	NL	N	S
Through whom are external interests mainly brought in to the government? D=Department; S=Cabinet Secretariat; M=Individual ministers; PM=PM's office	PM	M/PM	D/M	D	D	D/S /PM	D/S	*	D/M	D/M	D/M
Who mainly handles relations with outside interests? M=Ministers; C=Departmental civil Servants; S=Secretariat	M/C/S	M/C /S	C	M/C	M	C	M/C	M/C	M/C	M/C	M
Percentage of ministers in each country mentioning relations with interest groups as the place where discussions on policy outside cabinet mainly take place (percentage rounded to nearest full point)	35	10	0	0	0	12	18	42	8	31	3

Note: * = not available. A = Austria, B = Belgium, GB = Britain, SF = Finland, F = France, D = Germany, IRL = Ireland, I = Italy, NL = Netherlands, N = Norway, S = Sweden.

Finland, where, in particular in some policy fields (notably foreign affairs and defence), the initiative sometimes lies with the president or the president's office.[8] Third, in coalitions, the initiative is often at cabinet level, as can be seen in particular in Belgium and the Netherlands where meetings of the coalition partners often have some part to play in this respect. Finally, in Ireland, Italy, Belgium, Germany, and, to a lesser extent, France and Britain (particularly under Thatcher), the prime minister's office plays a significant part in originating policy proposals, as respondents to the ministerial questionnaire pointed out.[9] Even in these cases and therefore in general, the key agents for the preparation and development of policies coming to the cabinet are in the departments, though some systems are more decentralised than others.

Table 5.3 The extent to which cabinet systems are centralised/decentralised (sources within government from which (1) external interests and (2) cabinet agenda items are drawn into the cabinet system)

	(1) External interests		*(2)* Agenda items
	(a)	*(b)*	
Austria	C	O/M	D
Belgium	C	O/M	C/D
Britain	D	O	C
Finland	D	O/M	D
France	D	M	C
Germany	C	O	C
Ireland	C	O/M	C/D
Netherlands	C	O/M	C/D
Norway	D	O/M	D
Sweden	D	M	C/D

Key: (a) = structure
(b) = personnel
C = centralised – i.e. those systems in which, in addition to individual ministers and departments, cabinet system institutions (such as the cabinet secretariat and/or prime minister's office, or cabinet committees) have an important part to play.
D = Decentralised – i.e. those systems in which the departments are predominant
M = Ministerial (politician)
O = Official (civil servant)

Collecting and reformulating materials

Drawing together and disseminating the various materials required for decision-making provides an obvious opportunity for the exercise of at least negative influence in that the flow of materials can be slowed down, blocked, altered, or directed towards particular participants to the exclusion of others. There may even be an opportunity for exercising a positive influence on the content of policy if some measure of reformation of the materials is undertaken. In Western European cabinet systems, these tasks are, in nearly all cases, handled by civil servants.

Again a distinction can be drawn here, between systems that are departmentally based and those that primarily use central and coordinating institutions. With respect to bringing together materials for cabinet committees, France, Britain, and Norway have the most centralised arrangements – that is to say, the 'cabinet system' handles these matters. Yet the task of formulating papers for cabinet committees is usually undertaken by the departments, except in Norway and in the less committee-based system of Germany where the prime minister's office or secretariat is substantially involved in drafting the content. When it comes to the cabinet itself, the bringing together of materials to be placed before it is undertaken by 'cabinet system' institutions; the only decentralised cabinets in this respect are those of the Netherlands, Sweden and, surprisingly, Norway, where individual ministers and departments handle these matters. In France the prime minister's office is also substantially responsible for formulating cabinet papers. The key role of this office in France is indicated in the responses of ministers interviewed: 89 per cent felt that the prime minister's staff acted to control their policy proposals; similar comments were made, though not as overwhelmingly, by German (62 per cent) and Italian (57 per cent) respondents.[10] Thus the prime minister's office/cabinet secretariat has an opportunity to exercise a measure of control over the flow of materials in the majority of countries and to influence substantially their content in France and, at the committee level, in Germany and Norway.

Circulating and distributing materials

Once materials are drawn together and formulated or reformulated, they have to be distributed. The manner in which and the extent to which they are made available can clearly affect collective discussion within the cabinet in a major way. If a cabinet member does not receive full information (and at the right time), he or she cannot participate in the making of the decision to the same extent as those who are more fully informed. Moreover, if ministers are not fully informed about the overall activities of government, they are less likely to be able to influence the general strategy of the administration and are more likely to be confined to their departmental responsibilities. One can thus distinguish between *exclusive* cabinet systems in which information is limited only to members of the cabinet or its committees, and *inclusive* cabinet systems where all ministers (including junior ministers) and even top civil servants receive all the information.

In Western Europe, cabinet agendas and papers always go to all cabinet members, but they are not automatically circulated more widely to *all* members of the government. One possible consequence of this limited circulation is that cabinet members may not be fully alerted to the implications of some technical questions outside their departmental responsibilities by non-cabinet members who may be more aware of them. This restriction of papers to cabinet members takes place in half the countries: in Norway and Sweden, in three of the largest countries (France, Britain, and Germany), and in Ireland. Moreover, while cabinet papers and agendas are in every instance circulated to all cabinet members, this is not the case when it comes to cabinet *committee* agendas and papers. They are distributed only to members of the committee in Britain, France, and Belgium. Indeed, no cabinet system is fully inclusive, for none allows the circulation of committee materials throughout the government. Those systems in which the committee agendas and papers are not circulated can be characterised as being segmented and compartmentalised in that information is likely to be kept within sub-areas of the cabinet system. This is particularly the case in Britain, France, and Belgium, which are three of the four countries in which, as noted in the previous chapter, committee systems are most developed. Finally, if there is any ambiguity about whom to distribute papers to, the matter is settled in Britain, France, Germany, and Ireland by *officials* of the secretariat of the cabinet; in Belgium, the prime minister decides.

Timetabling and agenda setting

Determining the sequence and pace at which materials are handled and the moment at which meetings are held is often regarded as one of the more covert ways in which influence can be exercised. In some Western European cabinet systems there are rules about how these matters should be handled; in others, practices are fairly well established, but there is always some leeway. Moreover, because of the pressure of business, the planning of timetabling has to be worked out over a fairly long period. In Britain, for instance, the business of cabinet and its committees is planned in outline three months ahead and in detail over the next two weeks.[11] Indeed, even the timing of the meetings is not based everywhere on a rule: such a rule exists only in France and Norway. Austria is the one case in which a potentially collective solution exists in this respect: the cabinet itself decides. In all the other countries, it is the prime minister who has the discretion to determine or alter the timing of meetings, though usually subject to the advice of officials. In the case of cabinet committees timing is usually determined by the chair of the committee, who is often the prime minister; Britain is an exception in that, because of the complexity of its committee system, timetables tend to be organised by the secretariat and in the less committee-based systems of Austria, Germany, and Norway usually the committee members collectively determine schedules.

The opportunity to submit items, to prioritise them and to ensure that they are discussed at one of the formalised points of decision-making (cabinet or committee) lies at the heart of the effective management of decision-making. Though most systems are decentralised in that the departments are the main sources from which items placed on the cabinet agenda are drawn, committees are clearly an important source in Britain, France, Italy, and Belgium, and, except in Britain, Norway, and Finland, the prime minister's office has an important part to play; the chancellor's office is especially critical in Germany as are the offices of prime minister and president in France. The sources from which items placed on ministerial cabinet committee agendas are drawn hardly vary from this pattern, except that in Britain and France, which have the most extensive committee systems, an additional important source of items for discussion are submissions from other committees, often at an official level. The requirements for getting a matter to cabinet or, where appropriate, to committee for decision, often serve to filter out or to delay proposals substantially at a lower level. This point will be considered later in this chapter.

The final drawing up of cabinet and committee agendas are centralised operations in all cabinet systems. The prime minister's office or the cabinet secretariat are in charge (a point to which we shall return in Chapter 6), but the prime minister also has a part to play in what can of course be a crucial element in the control of the flow of business. The influence of the prime minister is important at least in Britain, Ireland, Germany, Sweden, and Finland, while in France, the president is in charge of drawing up the cabinet agendas. In the case of cabinet committees, the chairman of the committee, who may be the prime minister, is usually involved in setting the agenda.

DETERMINING BUSINESS

In Western European cabinet systems business is either formally determined in cabinet or cabinet committee. The distinction between countries in which cabinet committees play a large part and those in which they do not was examined in the previous chapter. Notably the most committee-based systems in terms of the number of committees are Britain, France, Belgium, and Italy, though committees are also important in Norway and the Netherlands and they play some part in all other countries with the exception of Ireland and Sweden, and indeed in the latter case until 1990 only, since a committee system was then established for the first time.[12]

The creation and management of committees offers some important opportunities for affecting the handling, and therefore the content, of business. Attention is therefore given to the powers to establish and determine the remit and composition of committees, before considering factors that help to shape the process of determining business within the cabinet itself. Four factors are particularly important, namely the amount of major policy business that can be handled in cabinet given constraints of time and routine matters, the shape in which matters reach the cabinet and the extent to which these matters are predetermined by the departments and the committees, the structure of the cabinet meeting, and the nature of the cabinet group.

Shaping the decision arena: controlling cabinet committees

In those systems where committees are used extensively, members of these bodies are at least shaping, if not fully determining, policy decisions. It is therefore important to discover who is responsible for

Organising the Flow of Business

Table 5.4   Managing ministerial cabinet committees

Countries	A	B	GB	SF	F	D	I	NL	N
Who chooses the chair?									
1 = PM, 2 = cabinet,	3	1	1	1	1	1	1,2	1	1
3 = committee members	(a)	(b)		(c)	(d)			(f)	(g)
Who decides the membership?	2	2	1	2	1	1	1,2	(j)	1
1 = PM, 2 = cabinet				(h)	(i)		(e)	(g)	
Who determines the terms of reference (i.e., responsibilities and remit)?									
1 = PM, 2 = cabinet,	2	1	1	1,2	1	n.a.	1,2	2	1,2
3 = committee chair		(b)	(k)		(l)		(m)	(n)	3
Are committees able to decide issues or do they only prepare them for the full cabinet to decide?	2	2	1	2	2	2	1	2	2
1 = decide, 2 = prepare		(o)							(p)

Notes: For country codes see notes to Tables 5.1 and 5.2.
Sweden and Ireland are excluded because they do not operate committee systems.
n.a. = not available.
(a)   Austria: if the Chancellor is a member he usually is in the chair.
(b)   Belgium: the Prime Minister is chairman of most of the committees. Committees are created by a decree of the Prime Minister at the beginning of a new government. The decree lays down the number of cabinet committees, their composition, and chairmanship, and it also covers the organisation of the cabinet operation of the committee system across cabinets.
(c)   Finland: for *ad hoc* committees only; chair of others laid down in statutes.
(d)   France: the Prime Minister is chairman of all committees, but he can and does delegate this power to others.
(e)   Italy varies in that the chair for formal committees it is either the Prime Ministers or cabinet who chooses the chair.
(f)   Netherlands: Prime Ministers, 'ex-officio'.
(g)   Norway: to some extent institutionalised as chair is laid down in regulations.
(h)   Finland: *ad hoc* committees; composition of others laid down in statute.
(i)   France: Prime Minister decides the composition of interministerial committees.
(j)   Netherlands: composition of committees is decided though negotiations on cabinet formation.
(k)   Britain: advised by, and sometimes at the suggestion of the Secretary of the cabinet.

(l)   France: in the case of *ad hoc* committees it can either be the Prime
      Minister or the President, though the terms of reference of permanent
      committees are laid down in decrees.
(m)   Italy: in some cases it is laid down in statute that certain decisions should
      go to a cabinet committee.
(n)   Netherlands: formally speaking the cabinet decides terms of reference,
      but in practice this is sometimes settled during negotiations for the new
      cabinet coalition.
(o)   Belgium: only certain matters handled by the Social and Economic
      Committee.
(p)   Norway: the Security and Defence Committee decides top secret matters
      on its own.

———————

determining the operation of the committee system especially when it
comes to choosing the chair and establishing the composition an terms
of reference of committees. The clearest distinction is between, on the
one hand, those systems in which the prime minister, advised by officials
in the secretariat or prime minister's office, has the main say on these
matters and, on the other hand, those in which the cabinet is also
involved. A further distinction can be drawn about the amount of
discretion that can be exercised in terms of the extent to which they are
partially determined by an established rule laid down in a regulation or
statute.

In three of the four major committee-based systems, Belgium,
Britain, and France, the choice of committee chair and the composition
and terms of reference are matters for the prime minister. In the fourth,
Italy, these tasks also involve decisions by the cabinet. As far as the less
committee-based countries are concerned, in Norway the prime
minister is most influential when it comes to determining chair and
composition, but the establishment of the terms of reference for a
committee involves the cabinet; in Austria, Finland, and the
Netherlands the cabinet is more involved in all these choices.
However, everywhere except Britain, the extent of choice is restricted
by the existence of regulations that affect the choice of committee chair
as well as the composition or the terms of reference of the committee.
In all cases these points apply only to some of the major committees
but they suggest that the powers and freedom of manoeuvre of the
British prime minister are the most extensive in Western Europe. Given
the committee-based nature of the British system, the management of
committees provides the prime minister with one of his or her most
significant opportunities to influence the flow and content of business.

SHAPING THE DECISION ARENA: THE PHYSICAL CAPACITY OF THE CABINET

As far as the factors that affect the taking of decisions within cabinet itself, an important constraint is the sheer capacity of the cabinet to handle business. This capacity is partly a function of the number, duration, and frequency of meetings, and the extent to which there are formal, routine items that crowd out the discussion of other issues. Broadly speaking the more often a cabinet meets, the longer its sessions, and the more it deals with non-routine items, the more central the cabinet is likely to be and the more it will be able to discuss matters thoroughly and determine the shaping of decisions.

Material relevant to the duration and frequency of cabinet meetings, both formal and informal, was examined in Chapter 4.[13] A clear distinction was made, on the one hand, between a majority of countries that are most cabinet-centred in terms of the time spent in cabinet, notably Norway, the Netherlands, Ireland, Finland, Sweden and, to a lesser extent, Austria and Germany, and those countries that are least cabinet-centred, namely, Britain, France, Italy and, to a lesser extent, Belgium. Not surprisingly, these are all systems in which committees are used extensively. The difference between the extremes is substantial: ministers in Sweden usually spend more than forty hours a month on cabinet meetings, both formal and informal, and in the Netherlands often more than thirty, while in Britain, since 1974, only between six and ten hours are spent in cabinet, and in France, between six and twelve. The frequency and duration of meetings is thus a clear indication of the importance of the cabinet meeting in relation to the overall cabinet system.

Although the opportunity for collective discussion and decision-making seems likely to be far greater in cabinets that meet frequently and at length, it does not follow that the time spent in cabinet in some countries is necessarily well spent in terms of the classical model of cabinet government. The need for cabinets to handle routine issues can have a substantial effect on the level and extent of participation in cabinet meetings, as there will be less time to devote to major policy questions. Moreover, the need to consider routine and formal items often gives a less spontaneous character to the whole meeting. As a matter of fact, routine matters make up a significant proportion of the business in cabinet meetings in several countries. In France, Norway, and Austria, the cabinet has to ratify formally many of the actions and orders of the government. Indeed, only the Irish cabinet has no regular set items that are always placed on the agenda, though the situation in Belgium, Italy, and Germany is unknown. Furthermore, reports on foreign policy, as in France, Britain, and the Netherlands, on European affairs, as in France and Britain, on the general state of government expenditure, as again in France, on civil service appointments and reimbursements, as in Austria and France, and on the parliamentary situation, as in Britain, can take a substantial part of the time of the cabinet meeting. In the British case, for example, the outline and discussion of this type of 'regular' business usually takes about thirty minutes and can often span out to a full hour, while, as was already noted, the overall duration of the meeting is often only about two hours.[14] The capacity of the cabinet to fulfil its tasks of deciding major policy questions is clearly substantially impaired as a result. Of those countries whose cabinets meet least frequently, France appears to be the country where formal matters and regular statements appear to loom largest: this may well explain in part the disaffection that French cabinet members feel and to which we shall return in Chapter 8.

Types of major policy business coming to cabinet

The space that is left in the cabinet meeting after time constraints and routine business are taken into account is available for the discussion of policy matters. The kinds of non-routine items that reach cabinet vary substantially across Western Europe. In some cases, there are rules or traditions that ensure that some matters are presented, though there are also rules that prevent certain questions from being raised. In Finland, for instance, only since 1985 has it been possible to require a minister to bring a matter to the cabinet meeting.[15] Starting at the lowest level, there are, generally speaking, substantial variations in the extent to which issues need to be brought outside departments, as the answers to the ministerial questionnaire show: while in Sweden and Finland less than 20 per cent of the respondents felt obliged to bring 'innovative' matters outside their departments, the proportion is much higher in other countries.

A matter drawn into the cabinet *system* from a department may of course never actually reach the cabinet *meeting* itself because of the arrangements that stipulate where items are decided on. It is therefore important to distinguish between those cabinet systems where business is expected to be settled at the lowest possible level regardless of the intrinsic importance of the issue and those in which an attempt is made to select out major or significant items. We examined committee

Table 5.5   Matters brought outside departments

Ministers were asked, 'In matters relating to your department, what kinds of
decisions did you not feel able to take on your own?' (variables 3, 4, 5 and 6 of
the ministerial questionnaire)

Countries	A	B	GB	SF	F	D	IRL	I	NL	N	S
% of ministers in each country specifically mentioning decisions on:											
Innovation matters (27.1)	40	14	35	19	51	n.a.	76	12	n.a.	36	n.a.
Politically hot issues (57.8)	70	76	63	34	51	33	76	65	n.a.	58	60
High expenditure (39.9)	20	41	33	17	30	42	100	15	n.a.	61	50
Coordination reasons (53.2)	78	16	100	6	95	25	56	35	n.a.	81	77

Notes:
For country codes see notes to Tables 5.1 and 5.2.
n.a. = not available.
Percentages in brackets are the overall proportions of ministers in the cross-
national sample specifically mentioning these four types of matters.
Percentages for responses in each country have been rounded to the nearest
full point.

systems in the previous chapter and the extent to which issues are either
determined at that level or first discussed in committee before coming
to cabinet; in addition, however, over and above the existence of
structures such as committees, which tend to shape the way matters are
handled, there is what can be described as a 'philosophy' of the role of
the cabinet meeting.

Thus, in Norway, the cabinet is obliged under constitutional rule to
give priority to major matters:[16] there are naturally problems in such
instances in determining what is 'major', but the fact that the cabinet is
asked to consider matters in this fashion is clearly significant.
Meanwhile, some cabinets, and the British cabinet in particular, can
be regarded as having basically what amounts to a residual function as
they deal mainly with matters that cannot be settled elsewhere.[17] This is
a reflection of the extent to which cabinets, if they are involved at all,
are very often at the end of a long process involving the formulation
and pre-determination of decision materials. If and when issues get to
the cabinet they are often substantially pre-shaped and pre-formed
before they arrive: sometimes what is left to cabinet is simply, as it

were, to dot the 'i's' and cross the 't's. On many issues it is the function of cabinet to tidy up what has gone on elsewhere, perhaps to arbitrate, or act as a court of appeal, or be a place where issues are settled that cannot be settled at committee or departmental level.

Among the issues that do reach the cabinet, fairly stringent procedural requirements have to be met before an item is sent to the cabinet for deliberation, though there are variations in the number and extent of these requirements. This affects the degree to which matters are refined and pre-determined before being considered at the highest level. The likelihood of conflict and disagreement within cabinet is also reduced. The approval of the finance ministry for any proposed extra expenditure has to be obtained and ministries must show that there has been full consultation with all the departments concerned. In Germany, discussions must also take place with the chancellor's office and a number of conditions have to be fulfilled, including, where relevant, consultation with the Laender and communal authorities. In Britain and the Netherlands, the ministers responsible for legal matters must be consulted: indeed, in Britain, since the late 1980s, a statement must be made about any potential legal liability that might result from the proposal. In Britain, too, as well as in Germany and in Norway, the administrative consequences and costs of any initiative have to be contained in the proposals. Thus in those systems where such pre-requirements for the consideration of business at the cabinet meeting are both more numerous and more onerous and where time constraints are strong, the role of the meeting in the effective decision-making process is liable to be downgraded considerably.

The nature of the cabinet group

Cabinets always tend to break into sub-groups. In the previous chapter, we examined not merely committees, but 'inner cabinets'; there are also ideological factions as well as very informal discussions taking place around key senior ministers. The result may be a clear hierarchy which can even be reflected in the seating arrangements: this is the case in France, Britain, Belgium, Ireland, and Norway. The 'top ministers' can thus constitute an informal inner circle who discuss matters beforehand: having these ministers in agreement over an issue can greatly bolster the position of whoever presents this issue; the result will also be that the extent of cabinet debate will be reduced. By contrast, ideological factions tend to heighten conflict in cabinet.

This aspect of the handling of business is one of the few in which the distinction between single-party and coalition government does have some importance: yet the contrast is not altogether clear-cut as there are also distinctions to be made within each of these two categories of cabinets. Thus, in single-party governments, ideological divisions can be sharp. Cohesive factions have been prevalent in Austrian cabinets; in Britain, there have been loose alliances between Left-inclined ministers during the 1974–9 Labour governments of Wilson and Callaghan.[18] On the other hand, not all coalition cabinets have been markedly divided, in part because organisational arrangements for dealing with such problems may have become institutionalised. However, in coalition governments, as was indicated in the previous chapter, the most important cabinet decisions are typically first discussed in separate meetings from each coalition party: this is the case in Germany, Austria, Belgium, the Netherlands, and Finland, while in the Netherlands and Austria it is usually the practice for important cabinet decisions to be first discussed in a committee of coalition party leaders. Such practices add a further source of refinement and pre-determination to the issues that are later brought before cabinet.

DISCUSSION IN CABINET

All the factors that have been explored so far – extent of pre-determination of matters, refinement of issues, time and capacity constraints, formal and informal pre-cabinet meetings, as well as the structure and importance of committees – affect the extent to which there is conflict within the cabinet. Not surprisingly, therefore, there are substantial differences across Western Europe in the extent to which disagreements occur. These seem most frequent in Finland, where 34 per cent of the ministerial respondents claimed that arguments were frequent; disputation in Irish cabinets also appears to be high. Though most ministers also recalled conflicts in Belgium and to a lesser extent in France, Germany, and Austria, the level of these disagreements appears connected in these countries with particular cabinets rather than being endemic to the system.

The manner of solving disagreements in cabinet is partly a product of tradition and practices and partly related to the specific complex of personalities making up individual cabinets. There are, at one extreme, the consensus cabinets, that is to say those where issues are expected to

Table 5.6 The extent and resolution of conflict in cabinet ministerial questionnaire: percentages of ministers in each country

Countries	A	B	GB	SF	F	D	IRL	I	NL	N	S
Do you recall discussions in cabinet involving substantial disagreement amongst cabinet members? (V. 25)											
usually	10	10	0	34	0	13	22	23	20	14	11
sometimes	20	70	80	34	51	63	69	58	72	69	52
rarely of never	70	14	20	30	49	25	9	19	4	17	32
How were these disagreements usually solved? (note: the categories are not mutually exclusive)											
By consensus in cabinet (V. 28)	93	74	85	72	0	88	78	77	n.a.	94	77
By prime minister's decision (V. 29)	61	6	75	9	100	21	27	42	n.a.	25	14
By cabinet committee (V. 30)	39	78	58	53	100	25	n.r.	42	n.a.	50	n.r.
By prime minister and ministers (V. 32)	46	n.a.	45	7	97	n.a.	91	77	n.a.	44	63

Notes:
For country codes see notes to Tables 5.1 and 5.2.
n.a. = not available
n.r. = no reply

be solved on the basis of general agreements. Austria is prominent among these: the principle of unanimity has been enshrined in the working practices of its cabinet systems since the Second World War.[19] Not surprisingly, Sweden is also in this group, its cabinet being expected to solve matters through cooperation.[20] Elsewhere, the *idea* of consensus is widely supported as a way of solving disagreements and it is emphasised by a clear majority of respondents in all countries except France. Indeed, in Britain, Belgium, Finland, and especially France, a majority of respondents also stated that cabinet committees were used as means of solving disagreements in cabinet, as did half the ministers in Norway, which suggests that consensus may in the end be achieved, but outside the forum of the cabinet itself. The central role of the prime minister acting alone in solving conflicts is also emphasised in Britain, France, and Austria and, along with ministers, in Sweden, Ireland, and Italy. This suggests that the prime minister may also have an important arbitrating function. Certainly, in these instances, consensus is found, though in a rather 'hierarchical' and contrived manner. In the Netherlands, the prime minister also arbitrates, but apparently only when called to do so by the ministers concerned.[21] One mechanism for solving disagreements that can often prove divisive is the vote. It is hardly ever used in cabinet in Germany, Britain, France, Italy, and Austria, while its use is more common in the Netherlands, Ireland, Finland, and, to a lesser extent, Norway. The usual practice is for the prime minister to sum up the spirit of the meeting, weighing perhaps some of the voices more heavily than others because of their seniority or reponsibility for the policy. This is another way of stressing the value of consensus, even if it is contrived. The overall picture that emerges is thus one in which cabinets, with the exception of France, actively strive to reach agreement, but do not always succeed, Austria and Sweden providing the clearest examples of 'real' consensus. The idea of a divided cabinet seems to be regarded as repugnant in most countries, possibly because it is assumed that party, parliament, and public opinion view such a division as a sign of ineffectiveness; the exceptions to this type of behaviour appear to be only Ireland and Finland. Thus some form of unanimity tends to be aimed at, even if it is often achieved in a rather contrived manner, at the prime ministerial or at the sub-cabinet level. It is therefore true to say that, generally speaking, the cabinet meeting is not the place for arguments and rows, though the notion of what passes for peaceful behaviour can differ greatly.

APPLYING DECISIONS

Cabinet can have little effect upon everyday life unless its decisions are implemented. Whoever controls the mechanisms for recording and circulating decisions can exercise substantial power, at least negatively. In most countries the conclusions of cabinet are the binding decisions of government. Consequently how those decisions are expressed, to whom they are communicated, and how and by whom the application of these decisions is monitored, become important matters. Civil servants play the main part in fulfilling these tasks.

How decisions are expressed

As already noted, the decisions of cabinet are usually formulated orally in the meetings by the prime minister. This is important as the prime minister can crystallise the outcome of the discussion and this formulation constitutes the decision of the cabinet which in most cases is expressed in the form of a minute or conclusion. This is the general pattern, but there is one exception and some variations. The exception is France where no summing up is made; in Finland, the prime minister sums up only in informal meetings of the cabinet, while in formal meetings the written proposal of the minister in question is usually accepted; in Italy the prime minister's summing up is not fully established as an accepted practice and in Austria the prime minister formulates the conclusions but only occasionally is this done in the cabinet meeting.

Recording and circulating decisions

In terms of writing up minutes and conclusions of cabinet, a distinction must be drawn between eight countries where the responsibility lies solely with the cabinet secretariat, and three in which the prime minister's staff play an important part, although only in Germany are they solely responsible. The overall exception is Sweden where no minutes are taken in cabinet, though an informal record is kept for the prime minister. The allocation of this task to the prime minister's staff and the fact that the prime minister also sums up the conclusions orally in cabinet meetings obviously gives the prime minister and his or her advisers considerable discretion to shape the authoritative decisions of the cabinet.

The opportunity for cabinet members to alter and query the minutes and conclusions of cabinet is restricted in all systems by time factors and by the extent to which minutes and conclusions are circulated. In Germany, Ireland, and the Netherlands, an extra opportunity is provided by the fact that the cabinet minutes and the conclusions of the previous meeting are approved at the following meeting. In all other countries this never or very rarely happens.

In terms of the circulation of cabinet minutes and conclusions, there are three sets of practices. In most countries circulation is highly restricted. In Sweden and Italy, minutes are usually not circulated at all; in France and Finland the record of cabinet meetings is circulated only in the cabinet secretariat, to the prime minister and the head of

State, though cabinet ministers can consult these documents at the relevant offices; in Belgium and Austria minutes have a similarly restricted circulation, though in Belgium conclusions are circulated more widely – to all government members; in Ireland minutes and conclusions are never circulated as a complete document, though the conclusions to specific areas are specially forwarded to the ministers concerned. Second, in Britain and Germany, circulation is broadened to include all cabinet members, though in Britain those ministers who are not in the cabinet and senior departmental civil servants are usually shown only those parts of the cabinet conclusions that are relevant to their responsibilities. Finally, in the Netherlands and Norway, cabinet minutes enjoy the widest circulation and are sent to all ministers.

A further distinction can be drawn amongst those countries in which cabinet minutes and conclusions are circulated relatively widely – Britain, Germany, Belgium, Austria, Netherlands, Norway – in terms of who exercises the discretion to circulate minutes and conclusions, especially in cases where there is some ambiguity about who should receive these documents. Discretion is most reduced in the Netherlands where circulation is determined by a clearly established rule laid down in the standing order of the council of ministers. In Austria, Belgium, Britain, Germany, and Norway the scope of circulation is a matter of accepted practice, but changes in that practice lie within the discretion of the head of government, though the cabinet may be drawn into these discussions in the Austrian case; in Britain, when it is felt that cabinet decisions may need to be more widely circulated than is normally the case, this discretion is usually exercised by the secretary to the cabinet and only very rarely by the prime minister. In France a rule dating from 1947 states that cabinet minutes should be circulated; but, in practice, this rule is not applied.

Monitoring the application of decisions

The monitoring of whether cabinet decisions are implemented is important both in terms of ensuring the effectiveness of cabinet government and as a further indication of the degree to which the system is directed from the centre. The significance of the central coordinating institutions should not merely be gauged in terms of the extent of their involvement in the initiation, shaping, and determination of policy proposals, but also at the level of implementation. In all cases the initial responsibility for carrying out policy decisions rests with the relevant departments. The central machinery comes into play in terms of the extent to which its personnel attempt to oversee and monitor the departments in carrying out their tasks and of the extent to which this role is fulfilled by the prime minister and his staff or some other body such as the cabinet secretariat.

The formal monitoring from within the cabinet system of whether cabinet decisions are carried out is hardly undertaken at all in Britain, Italy, and Sweden; in Finland it only applies to policy decisions made in informal cabinet meetings, formal policy decisions being the sole responsibility of each minister. In Britain, under Thatcher and Major, the prime minister's policy unit has begun to monitor the carrying out of decisions, though on an intermittent and somewhat uncoordinated basis. In Sweden most decisions are implemented by agencies and not ministries and the prime minister's staff have an overall responsibility for formulating the instructions for the agencies and for detailing how they should carry out cabinet decisions. In Italy, the cabinet secretariat has some monitoring responsibility, but this is neither very developed nor very effective.

In the majority of countries, formal monitoring of implementation is carried out within the cabinet system. In Austria, Ireland, and the Netherlands this function is specifically undertaken by members of the cabinet secretariat, either the secretary to the cabinet secretariat or one of his officials. In France and Norway, monitoring is shared between the prime minister's staff and the cabinet secretariat, though it is the latter that is most significant. Information is passed on to the prime minister who in France can give instructions to the minister if decisions have not been carried out or have been delayed. Belgium and Germany are the most centralised systems with the power to monitor implementation formally being placed in the hands of the head of government and his staff.

As far as the publicity given to the decision reached is concerned, in many countries, cabinet decisions are not announced at all or made officially public. Publicity is regularly given to these decisions in only five countries: Sweden and Finland, as one might have expected given the openness of their political systems, as well as France, Belgium, and Austria. In all the countries a communique is issued about the decisions of the cabinet.

Who has the best opportunities to shape the flow of business?

Three sets of actors play a key part in organising the flow of business in Western European cabinets: ministers, either collectively in cabinet and committee or as individual departmental heads, prime ministers (as well as the French and the Finnish presidents), and officials, primarily from the cabinet secretariat and/or from the prime minister's office, but also from the departments. The fact that these three groups are involved to different degrees and in different ways in different countries makes it difficult to generalise about clear-cut patterns with respect to the manner in which cabinet business is handled. Nevertheless, while there are variations at the margin, a clear distribution of responsibilities arises in most cases, notably the key position of the prime minister and of senior officials in the secretariat and prime minister's office. In none of the countries studied here are the tasks relating to the management of the flow of business fully vested collectively in the cabinet.

Before proceeding to explore these patterns in more detail, it is worth noting that two of the three broad factors that are analysed in this volume (and may be expected to give shape to cabinet decision-making), namely coalitions and the party composition of the cabinet, appear to have little, if any, impact on the processes that are adopted to handle business. Variations can be more adequately explained through country idiosyncrasies. In general the rules about business and the ways in which it is handled tend to remain stable from cabinet to cabinet within each country and in each case the civil service plays the central part in ensuring continuity and stability.

It is valuable to summarise broadly the way in which the three sets of actors are able to influence the flow of business in Western European cabinets. Cabinet ministers, individually or collectively, have an important part to play at the points where significant and major proposals originate and at the points where decisions are formally determined – in either cabinet or cabinet committee. They have generally little influence upon the procedures for collecting materials, circulating them, and timetabling business, though in some countries some ministers, particularly those concerned with business management, are more involved in these tasks than their colleagues. Moreover, as we saw, in Belgium, Britain, and France cabinet ministers do not even receive the papers and/or the minutes of cabinet committees of which they are not members. In the majority of countries individual ministers are involved in the formulation of papers for cabinet and cabinet committees. They are either closely involved in the drafting or are extensively consulted by the civil servants responsible for writing up the documents. Ministers play no part at all in the distribution of cabinet papers nor in the recording and distribution of cabinet and cabinet committee decisions. They can, of course, challenge the record of these decisions (with some difficulty in France, however, where no records are distributed), but the circumstances surrounding the way in which business is recorded and the timetable developed make it difficult to do so.

The part that ministers play collectively as members of the cabinet in helping to develop the rules that organise business is also varied. In a number of countries, they are involved at least to an extent in the elaboration and the alteration of the rules; this is the case in two of the largest countries, France and Germany, in two of the Scandinavian countries, Norway and Finland, and in Ireland. But even in these countries ministers are constrained: in part because in two of these five countries, Germany and Finland, the more important rules are determined by statute or even laid down in the constitution; in part because, as in Ireland, the prime minister also intervenes; and in part because, in the end, rules are rarely changed and existing procedures tend to be maintained and are only added to at the margins.

As ministers individually or collectively in cabinet or committees are typically not the main actors in the organisation and management of cabinet business, the onus of responsibility falls appreciably more on prime ministers and senior officials. While ministerial actors tend to exercise their influence early in the process during which materials come to the cabinet and while ministers meeting in committees tend to be influential at intermediate points (and may indeed be, as in Britain, France, Italy and Belgium, decisive at that juncture), the influence of prime ministers tends to be exercised principally at what might be regarded as the two most crucial points. First, together with ministers in some countries (notably Ireland), alone in others, though usually subject to the advice of officials (Britain, Sweden, Belgium, and Italy), they have the power to alter most of the rules under which the cabinet conducts its business. There is here a direct contrast between groups of countries, for those noted above can be clearly distinguished from the others in that the cabinet collectively is empowered to make such changes.

The role of prime ministers is also often critical during many of the processes involved in the handling of business. When difficulties arise, they are often consulted about matters to do with the timetabling and distribution of business and the recording of decisions. In effect, they have therefore some say in the extent to which papers are distributed, at least in Belgium, and they have some say in cases of uncertainty or disputes over the content and the distribution of records. In committee-based systems they have an important say in the chairmanship, composition and terms of reference of committees. They have a major say in the drawing up of the cabinet agenda in most countries (indeed probably at least indirectly in all), though only in Germany do chancellors have a clear statutory power to establish priorities on these agendas. Finally and above all, they have a substantial say in the outcome of cabinet deliberations by virtue of the power to sum up 'the sense of the meeting', and also by helping to build a consensus or at least producing a decision acceptable to all, as is notably the case in Ireland. These powers of prime ministers have clear limits, some of which have to do with the nature of the cabinet: we shall examine them in Chapter 10. Yet the rules and traditions that prevail in each country serve not only to limit, but also to provide opportunities for the heads of governments to exercise influence. The 'arbitrating' power of French prime ministers and the role of German chancellors in agenda prioritising, for instance, are characteristics that, among others, give these heads of governments opportunities that can have a marked effect on the way business is transacted.

Meanwhile, the actors whose role appears to be most pervasive at every point are the members of prime ministers' offices or of cabinet secretariats. In every country, they are the 'guardians' of the rules and indeed the transmitters of these rules to those ministers who enter cabinet for the first time. They are closely involved in the initiation process in some countries (Germany, Austria, Belgium, and Ireland) and they compete with the ministers in the presentation of matters that will come to be discussed in the 'cabinet system'. They are also involved in the collection of the information needed by the committees in some countries (France, Britain, Germany, Norway). Everywhere they handle – and handle alone – the collection of cabinet papers, which they then distribute to cabinet members; they often adjudicate on possible disputes about who is to receive papers in Britain, France, Germany, and Ireland; they prepare in detail the longer-term timetable of the cabinet as well as the agenda of the coming meetings and they ultimately record and issue minutes and conclusions. Where central monitoring of the application of decisions takes place, these officials have the primary and substantive role. Thus the handling of decision-making within the 'cabinet system' truly extends appreciably beyond cabinet members. Members of prime ministers' offices and of cabinet secretariats, small or large, have a presence and visibility at most key points of cabinet decision-making: we need therefore to return to the matter and see, in Chapter 6, whether, given their strategic position between departments, ministers, and cabinet, these officials can be regarded as in some sense taking over, in part at least, the role that, in theory is usually accorded to ministers or the whole cabinet.

The formal features shaping the handling of business in cabinet systems are not rigid: although they are relatively stable, they are open to change and do indeed change. As far as rules are concerned, those cabinet systems that are most institutionalised are the least amenable to alteration by particular individuals. Beyond these confines the determination of cabinet practices is often in the hands of prime ministers, and above all of the members of the secretariat or its equivalent. Officials have thus a considerable opportunity to play a part in the process of cabinet decision-making, a part that is substantial even though it may not reflect a deliberate desire to determine policy and may in part be a consequence of the requirements that follow on from the necessity of dealing with the large and complex amount of business that cabinets in the modern age are subject to. Whatever the motive, their handling of business can shape the basis, the timing, and the pattern of involvement in – and, consequently, the outcome of – decision-making.

Overall, country distinctions can be sharp, but they are also somewhat eclectic. For the procedures used by the cabinets largely result from traditions and practices that have emerged somewhat independently in each of the countries concerned. There are some regularities which come from the need to handle matters as speedily as possible, but the variation in the processes is such, especially in conjunction with the relative rigidity of the formal structures that we examined in the previous chapter, that only in a marginal sense do the broader factors that we examine in this volume affect the main ways in which cabinet business is handled.

Notes

1. T. T. Mackie and B. W. Hogwood (1985), p. 1. Dunleavy and Rhodes use the expression 'core executive', though this defines the area of interest more widely to cover, among others, finance ministries. See P. Dunleavy and R. A. W. Rhodes (1990).
2. G. T. Allison (1971), pp. 83 and 169. See also J. Pfeffer (1981), especially Ch. 5.
3. C. Hood (1986), Chs 2 and 3.

4. S. A. de Smith, 4th ed. (1981). P. Hennessey (1986), pp. 8–14. Cabinet Office (1992).
5. Hall, P., Land, H., Parker, R. and Webb, A. (1975), pp. 35–8.
6. M. Isberg (1982).
7. Between 30 and 40 percent of ministers in these five countries specifically mentioned the role of the prime minister's office in developing policy suggestions for the cabinet (Ministerial Question 6(b) variable 73).
8. In Norway and Belgium, the figures are respectively 38 and 34 per cent (Ministerial Question 6(b), variable 71).
9. See, for example, R.H.S. Crossman (1972), pp. 55–75.
10. B. Donoughue (1987), pp. 27–8. A. Seldon (1990), pp. 110–1.
11. See T. T. Mackie and B. W. Hogwood (1985).
12. In Austria, Finland, and Sweden the cabinet meets on a regular basis informally, in the case of Austria about four times a month and in Sweden about 20 times. These effectively count as cabinet meetings as decisions are reached, even if they require to be ratified in the subsequent, formal cabinet meeting. P. Vinde and G. Petri (1978), p. 30; J. Nousiainen (1988a), p. 221 and P. Gerlich and W. C. Müller (1988a), p. 143.
13. M. Burch (1988b), p. 41.
14. See Chapter 4, p. 82.
15. J. Nousiainen (1988a), p. 221.
16. S. Eriksen (1988b), p. 188.
17. M. Burch (1988b), p. 46.
18. B. Castle, vol. 2 (1974–6) (1984), *passim*.
19. P. Gerlich and W. C. Müller (1988), pp. 139–40. W. C. Müller (1992), p. 109. K. Steiner (1972), p. 115.
20. T. Larsson (1988b), p. 210.
21. R. B. Andeweg (1988a), p. 55.

6 Ministers and the Role of the Prime Ministerial Staff

Ferdinand Müller-Rommel

The personal staff of prime ministers have come to play a large part in Western European governments, a part that is sometimes regarded as excessive in that it appears to have undermined the nature of cabinet decision-making. Cabinet government may no longer be collective and collegial in most Western European countries for a variety of other reasons, but the existence of prime ministerial staffs seems to have contributed to a substantial extent to the phenomenon.[1]

Admittedly, prime ministers have appointed advisers to help rather than hinder the process of cabinet decision-making. No doubt the existence of this staff was made necessary, as cabinet government would almost certainly not have been able to function without at least a cabinet secretariat: this was shown to be the case in Britain when such a body was set up during the First World War.[2] Yet it is equally obvious that, by managing the flow of business in and around the cabinet, prime ministerial staffs can – and obviously often do, deliberately or otherwise – influence markedly the substance of decision-making. This situation is, of course, largely a post Second World War development: before 1939, prime ministers often only had one or very few private secretaries; since the 1970s and 1980s, the secretariat has become large, in some countries at least. This is why the expansion of prime ministerial staffs can be regarded with some justification as indicating that in Western European countries there is a move away, not just from parliamentary government, but even from cabinet government *stricto sensu*.[3]

In fact, the political part played by prime ministerial staffs remains unclear: there seem to be major variations across countries in the extent to which, and the manner in which, they intervene in cabinet decision-making, but the systematic comparative analysis of their role is still not very advanced. The question is complicated by the fact that what is meant by prime ministerial staffs is ambiguous: in some countries, two different bodies advise and help the head of the government. One of these is composed of the *personal staff* of the prime minister (and, in the French case, by the personal staff of the president as well); the other body is usually regarded as being – and indeed typically labelled as – the *cabinet secretariat*. The distinction between these two organs does not exist everywhere: in particular, it does not exist in the country where the prime ministerial staff is most developed, Germany; yet the fact that two bodies may exist to advise and help the prime minister adds to the complexity of the analysis, since the functions exercised by each of them may not always be entirely clear and may indeed overlap.

These functions range between two poles, administrative and political. At one extreme, prime ministerial staffs act administratively in that they organise the meetings of the cabinet and in particular the flow of business between the prime minister and the ministers. They are concerned with gathering, circulating, and to an extent controlling, ministerial proposals; they deal (at least in many cases) with the cabinet agenda; they record and monitor cabinet decisions and supervise the implementation of these decisions; and they often play a part in the development of longer-term ideas about cabinet activity. In doing so, prime ministerial staffs can be said to exist in order to improve the efficiency of the cabinet: indeed, it is difficult to see how a modern cabinet could operate without them. Yet this type of activity is never entirely administrative; moreover, the prime ministerial staff – whether labelled cabinet secretariat or not – is of necessity primarily at the disposal of the prime minister. Thus the prime minister is helped by the very existence of these officials.

Meanwhile, the prime minister is also helped in another way, namely because members of the prime ministerial staff can – and often do – act as the personal, private, and direct advisers to the head of the government. They then act in an essentially political manner: they make suggestions to the prime minister on policy questions; they may even develop their own policy proposals. This type of behaviour is so political that it is likely to affect the political image of the prime minister and even to influence the leadership style of the head of the government at cabinet meetings or elsewhere.

The main aim of this chapter is to explore how prime ministerial staffs are viewed by the principal 'users', namely the ministers, and in particular to see to what extent the somewhat negative views sometimes expressed about the role of these staffs are shared by those who are directly subjected to their actions. To undertake this analysis, we shall first briefly survey the situation as it exists in Western European cabinets and in particular examine the size and apparent role of prime ministerial staffs on the basis of country-by-country descriptions which can now be found in the literature. We will then turn to the judgement that Western European ministers pass globally on the role and value of these staffs. Finally, we shall look at a number of variables that may account for differences in the views expressed by ministers. Specifically, as in other chapters of this volume, we shall look at the impact of the distinction between single-party and coalition cabinets, at the effect of the party composition of the government and at possible country variations; we will also examine whether the nature of prime ministerial leadership tends to shape the character and role of prime ministerial staffs. This part of the study will be confined to nine countries, as the inquiry into the views of ministers on prime ministerial advisers was not undertaken in the Netherlands, Sweden, or Finland.[4]

PRIME MINISTERIAL STAFFS IN WESTERN EUROPEAN GOVERNMENTS

Prime ministerial staffs are relatively new everywhere in Western Europe; they are at least appreciably more recent than cabinet government. The position and role of these groups differ appreciably, so does the size of these bodies. Also, the distinction between 'cabinet secretariats' and 'prime ministerial staffs *stricto sensu*', which was mentioned earlier, makes it sometimes difficult to decide exactly who belongs to the staff of the prime minister.

Even if one takes both cabinet and personal secretariats into account, variations in size are large across Western European cabinets. Admittedly, differences in the population size of the countries concerned can account for the fact that the staff of the head of the government is much larger in Germany (450 members) than in Norway and Ireland (less than twenty), while Britain and France occupy intermediate positions. Yet differences in the size of the prime ministerial staffs also reflect differences in the functions that we described earlier. The staff of the German chancellor is not only the largest of all; it also has a very broad remit and is manifestly very involved in regulating and even in supervising the activity of government departments.

Even if the cabinet secretariat is taken into account, the size of the prime ministerial staff of most countries is closer to the Norwegian or Irish figures than to the German figures. To begin with, there are four countries, Denmark, Ireland, Austria, and Norway, where the prime minister's office is small and relatively uninvolved in the cabinet decision process. In Denmark, the prime minister's office consists of sixteen relatively senior officials, three private secretaries and two permanent secretaries: none of these are political appointees and they restrict their activities to collecting information and monitoring departmental policy-making; in addition, they help the prime minister to evaluate the implications of the cabinet agenda from the prime minister's point of view.[5] In Ireland, the prime minister's office consists of three or four personal advisers who are political appointees and a small number of professional full-time civil servants who collect information on policy issues from the departments and coordinate as well as prepare the cabinet meetings for the prime minister. In Austria, the office is also very small and has no major impact on the decision process: the agenda is set by the chancellor and the official cabinet meetings are preceded, as we noted in Chapter 4, by unofficial meetings during which the main decisions are taken.[6] In Norway, there are five political appointees and nine civil servants employed in the prime minister's office. They prepare the cabinet meetings but have apparently no influence on the content of the cabinet agenda; nor do they exercise any control over the policy suggestions coming from the ministries.[7]

In most other countries, the private secretariat of the prime minister is small, but the cabinet secretariat can be relatively large. This is the case in Britain, for instance. The private secretariat is new and not large, but it plays a strong political role. Thus Mrs Thatcher's personal staff consisted of between twelve and thirty people: five private secretaries, a personal assistant, a secretary concerned with appointments, a foreign affairs adviser, a political secretary, an eight-person strong Policy Unit, two press secretaries, a parliamentary private secretary, a parliamentary clerk, and a small group forming an Efficiency Unit.[8]

In Belgium, France, and Italy, the prime minister's office is somewhat larger than in Britain, though it is still not very large. The offices in Belgium and Italy consist of between fifteen and twenty highly political civil servants who administer matters in a political manner while enforcing the collective decisions taken by the cabinet. In the French case, there are two sets of advisers, those to the prime minister and those to the president. Members of both offices are involved in the same policy questions and compromises have to be thrashed out between them; both groups also have to discuss matters with the (more administratively inclined) members of the cabinet secretariat. This cabinet secretariat is relatively large; it includes about one hundred civil servants whose task is to prepare the cabinet agenda and to keep an eye on policy suggestions coming from the different ministries.

It is in Germany that the staff of the head of the government is the largest and appears to wield the greatest influence. The office of the German chancellor has a staff of 450, only a small minority of whom, however, are political appointees. These are the head of the office, the heads of the six divisions in which the office is divided, and three State secretaries. These political appointees direct between fifty and sixty higher civil servants as well as their supporting and technical staff, who are spread over forty-one policy units. Each one of these policy units 'mirrors' a policy field in one of the departments of the government: there are as a result strong links between the civil servants in the chancellor's office and their opposite numbers in the various ministries. The members of the chancellor's office discuss proposals with the civil servants in the departments before they reach the cabinet; if there is conflict, they attempt to elaborate compromises. If and when an agreement is reached, the outcome is usually accepted by the ministers concerned and by the political appointees at the top of the chancellor's office. The proposal is then sent directly to the cabinet for approval. Such a procedure may therefore have the effect of reducing the extent of discussion taking place at cabinet meetings.[9]

Since, in most countries, prime ministers' offices are relatively small, they might be expected to have only a limited impact on the overall process of cabinet decision-making. This conclusion does not necessarily follow, however, as these relatively few prime ministerial advisers may have considerable seniority and political influence and thus be able to direct and even alter the flow of business. Numbers may not be a satisfactory indicator of power: this is why it is essential to find out from those who are likely to know to what extent and in what ways advisers to prime ministers affect the character of cabinet decision-making.

THE IMPORTANCE AND CHARACTER OF THE ROLE OF PRIME MINISTERS' ADVISERS: THE ASSESSMENT OF THE MINISTERS

The assessment and the measurement of the role of prime ministerial advisers raise difficulties. Ideally, one would wish to devise truly objective indicators of this role. As these do not exist, the best alternative is to rely on the judgement of those who are close to these advisers; no one is closer than the cabinet minister who can see, sometimes at the expense of his or her own ideas, what members of prime ministers' offices are able to do. Admittedly, the account given by ministers may not always be entirely accurate or impartial; there may be underestimates or exaggerations. Some ministers may not even be in a position to assess fully the part played by prime ministerial advisers. Yet these problems would be serious only if we were to rely on the assessment of a very small number of cabinet ministers: given that those who were interviewed form a substantial group, even at the level of each country, the overall picture is likely to be accurate – underestimates and exaggerations will tend to cancel each other out. Moreover, cross-country variations, if any, can also be examined as well as differences resulting from the distinction between single-party and coalition governments or differences resulting from ideological distinctions among ministers and among governments.

Let us thus first consider generally the way in which ministers assess the role of prime ministerial staffs. Respondents were asked to answer five questions aimed at determining this role. First, they were asked to say whether, in their opinion, prime ministerial staffs played an important political part. Second, they were asked to specify what was the precise nature of the role of prime ministers' offices in cabinet government: in this respect, respondents had to state whether the members of these offices gave personal advice to prime ministers, whether they prepared the cabinet agenda, whether they controlled policy proposals coming from the ministers, and whether they developed their own policy proposals. As Table 6.1 shows, a large proportion of interviewees, but not a majority, consider prime ministerial advisers to be generally important in the policy-making process. Very large majorities of those who answered feel that prime ministerial staffs do give personal advice to prime ministers and do prepare the cabinet agenda; on the other hand, only a minority, however substantial, among those who answered feel that prime ministerial advisers control ministerial proposals or put forward their own policies.

The differences are thus substantial in the reactions of respondents with respect to the first two and the last two of the specific questions put to them about the role of prime ministerial staffs. The first two points – personal advice to prime ministers and preparation of the cabinet agenda – seem to be regarded as 'natural' and as the *raison d'être* of prime ministerial staffs. The other two points are obviously not routine and most ministers do not believe that prime ministerial

Table 6.1   The role of prime ministerial staff (percentages)

	Yes	No	N
Administrative role:			
– Prepare cabinet agenda	72	28	(260)
– Control ministers' proposals	43	57	(234)
Political role:			
– Advise the prime minister politically	92	8	(255)
– Develop own policy proposals	36	64	(236)

advisers are involved in this way, a finding that is worth stressing, given the rather widespread view that prime ministerial advisers tend to exercise control over the government. Indeed, interestingly, for many ministers at least, the 'importance' of advisers is connected to the assessment that they make of the involvement of these advisers in policy 'control' or in policy 'making'. Many of those who say that prime ministerial staffs give personal advice to prime ministers or prepare the cabinet agenda also state that the advisers do not generally play an important part. On the contrary, only one interviewee in each case both claimed that prime ministerial staffs were not important and stated that these staffs were involved in controlling ministerial proposals or in putting forward their own policies. Thus almost all the ministers who feel that prime ministerial staffs control or make policy proposals also conclude that these advisers are important in cabinet decision-making: indeed, they typically say that these advisers are 'important' and not only 'somewhat important'.

A kind of hierarchy thus emerges among the activities that ministers see prime ministerial staffs involved in. There is indeed a scale, at any rate among the respondents who replied to all four questions relating to the specific activities of those advisers. These form only 62 per cent of the ministers interviewed from the nine countries in which the respondents were asked these questions, admittedly, but the large majority of these (153 out of 188) in effect ranked these four activities, from the most widespread (advising the prime minister politically) to the least common (prime ministerial advisers putting forward their own proposals), with agenda-drawing and controlling proposals coming from the ministers occupying intermediate positions.[10] Only thirty-six respondents did not give answers that fit this ranking: nine of these stated that prime ministerial advisers only drew the cabinet agenda, seven that they both advised prime ministers and controlled ministerial policies (but did not draw the cabinet agenda), and fourteen that they both advised prime ministers and put forward policies of their own (but neither drew the cabinet agenda nor controlled policies coming from the ministers). Without claiming that this ranking is universally accepted, it is clearly the case that most ministers relate the 'importance' of the role of prime ministerial advisers to two activities only, which they consider to have much greater impact than the other two, as can be seen from Table 6.2.

There is thus a ranking suggesting that ministers view the four activities that we have discussed here as based on a single scale; there is also a tendency for the four questions to correspond to two different characteristics. These characteristics can be regarded as being based on a distinction, which has been already referred to, between what seems to be primarily the 'political' role and what seems to be primarily the 'administrative' role of prime ministerial staffs. For, at any rate to an extent, respondents link their answers in two pairs. Those who state that prime ministerial staffs are concerned with the cabinet agenda also tend to state that they are involved in supervising proposals coming from ministers, while those respondents who say that prime ministerial staffs advise prime ministers personally are also likely to be those who state that these staffs put forward their own proposals. These two pairs of responses are somewhat different in character, even if they cannot be

Table 6.2   The importance of prime ministerial staffs in relation to their activities (absolute numbers)

| Activities | *The prime ministerial staff is regarded as:* | | |
	important	*of some importance*	*not important*
None	–	1	4
Advising PM only	4	17	13
Advising PM and agenda preparing	10	18	8
Advising PM, preparing agenda and controlling proposals	30	12	1
All four activities	32	1	0

regarded as being totally distinct: one can therefore describe them as giving at least a picture of two different tendencies among the activities of prime ministerial staffs. Prime ministerial advisers who are predominantly viewed by ministers as preparing the cabinet agenda and as controlling proposals from ministries can be described as having principally an *administrative* role; those who are predominantly viewed by ministers as giving advice to the prime minister and as developing their own policy proposals can be described as having principally a *political* role. There are of course many mixed cases, corresponding to those when ministers consider the prime ministerial staff to be involved in both of these types of activities.

There is indeed evidence suggesting that, to an extent at least, ministers associate cabinet agenda-drafting with the supervision of proposals coming from departments and that they associate the personal advice given by prime ministerial staffs with these staffs putting forward their own proposals. This is to say that, to an extent, prime ministerial staffs are regarded as being more administrative or more political. The evidence is provided by the fact that, if one correlates the answers to each of the four questions with those to all the other three, the only two tables that show any association at all are the one that links the two 'administrative' questions and the one which links the two 'political' questions: even if this association is weak, it is less weak than that which can be found when considering the other four possible types of relationships.[11]

Although such an association does therefore exist and one can speak of prime ministerial staffs as being more 'administrative' or more 'political', one should also remember that this is a tendency only and that we have here a continuum rather than a dichotomy. For, while it is true that 39 per cent of the respondents answer positively to the two 'administrative' questions and 34 per cent to the two 'political' questions, some of the respondents in each of these two groups are the same (if they answered positively to all four questions or even if they gave a positive answer to both questions of one 'pair' *and* to one of the two questions of the other 'pair'): this is principally because, as we saw earlier, a large majority of ministers answer that prime ministerial staffs advise prime ministers personally *and* help to draft the cabinet agenda. Yet the distinction corresponds in part to the views of the ministers: while many among them – indeed most – have a conception of the role of prime ministerial staffs as being of a mixed politico-administrative character, while, as we saw, they also tend to rank the activities of these offices and feel that two of these activities are markedly more

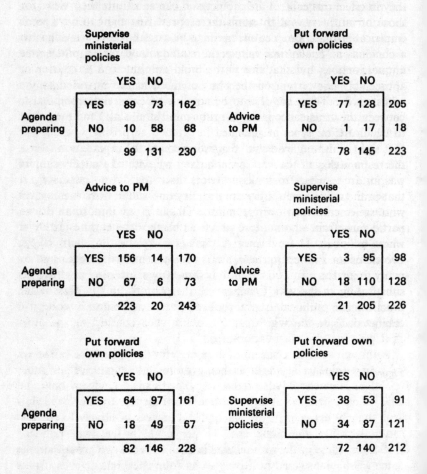

Figure 6.1   Association between the four activities of PM staffs (absolute figures – yes/no answers only)

important than the other two, they also often divide these activities into those that appear to be more concerned with the life of the cabinet in general (which we have labelled as more 'administrative') and those that are more concerned with the personal role of these staffs (which we have labelled as more 'political').

Thus, in the eyes of the ministers, prime ministerial staffs fulfil in many cases a set of important functions which seem to give them a special role in the development of the cabinet decision-making process: the criticisms that are sometimes levelled against these advisers – that they in effect can control the cabinet and can substitute their views for those of ministers – might seem therefore at first sight to have some empirical justification. Yet one needs to be careful before drawing such a conclusion. That prime ministerial staffs should play a part seems unquestionable; but that this part should amount to a 'take over' is appreciably less certain on the basis of the evidence provided by the ministers. For what has also to be noted is that no relationship exists between the importance given to prime ministerial staffs and the extent to which major issues get debated in cabinet: surprisingly perhaps at first sight – although we shall discover elements of explanation later – the respondents of the ministerial survey who stated that the cabinet was an arena where major issues were discussed did not also suggest that prime ministerial staffs were not very important; nor are ministers who see members of prime ministerial staffs as important drawn particularly from among those who feel that the cabinet is not an arena where major issues are discussed: there is no relationship between the two elements. Prime ministerial staffs may be regarded as important by many ministers: but this is not because they are also regarded as substituting their views for those of the cabinet. In the eyes of the practitioners, prime ministerial staffs do not therefore impede collective cabinet decision-making.

Figure 6.2   Cabinet as arena for issues *v.* importance of PM staff (absolute figures)

		Important	Of some importance	Not important	
Cabinet as an arena for issue date	Yes always	36	39	17	92
	Yes somewhat	77	42	27	146
	No	11	19	6	36
	NR/NATC	9	5	2	16
		133	105	52	290

The prime ministerial staff is regarded as:

Note: NR = no reply.
         NATC = not able to cover.

DO VIEWS ABOUT PRIME MINISTERIAL STAFFS VARY ACCORDING TO SOME GENERAL PARTY OR COUNTRY CHARACTERISTICS?

Coalition *v.* single party cabinets

It seems reasonable to expect the ministers' views on prime ministerial staffs that we have thus examined to be coloured by, if not necessarily to result from some general political characteristics of governments or by country idiosyncrasies. To begin with, the coalition or single-party nature of the cabinet seems likely to affect these views. As a matter of fact, the distinction between coalition and single-party government does appear to have a marked impact, with single-party majority governments and coalitions being at both extremes and single-party minority governments being in the middle.

There is little difference with respect to the question of the personal advice given to ministers by the prime ministerial staff: 90 per cent of the respondents who answered this question answered it positively, whether they were ministers in coalitions, in single-party majority cabinets or in single-party minority cabinets. That there should be no difference on this point is no surprise, since, as we noticed earlier, this question constitutes the 'base of the pyramid', so to speak, in terms of the part played by ministerial staffs in the process of cabinet decision-making: if a difference is to appear, it is unlikely to emerge or to be very marked in the context of answers about an activity that nearly every minister appears to believe is the most natural function of prime ministerial staffs.

With respect to the other three questions that are discussed here, on the other hand, differences are large between coalitions and single-party governments. There are, first, marked discrepancies among respondents in relation to the preparation of the cabinet agenda. The view that prime ministerial staffs are involved in this activity is held above all by ministers from coalition governments (90 per cent of them) and by members of single-party minority governments (68 per cent of them), while only one-third of the ministers belonging to single-party majority governments have the same opinion. Second, the majority of ministers from coalition governments and one third of the ministers from single party minority governments believe that prime ministerial staffs control proposals coming from individual departments; only 10 per cent of the ministers from single-party governments share this view.

is

This means that members of coalition governments tend to feel that prime ministerial staffs are primarily concerned with helping the process of cabinet decision-making as a whole. This is confirmed by the fact that, on the last of the four questions, that which asks whether prime ministerial staffs put forward their own proposals, there is little difference between ministers from coalitions and ministers from single-party majority governments (41 *v.* 33 per cent), ministers from single-party minority government being those among whom such a view is least widespread (16 per cent).

Not surprisingly, too, in view of the connection that we saw between the importance given to prime ministerial staffs and the positive answers to the questions relating to the involvement of these staffs in supervising ministerial proposals and in putting forward their own, prime ministerial staffs are indeed viewed as appreciably more important by ministers from coalition governments than by ministers coming from single party majority cabinets. In coalition governments, prime ministerial staffs are involved in coordination between the political allies and in managing the overall governmental policy administratively and, to a more limited extent, politically as well.

Figure 6.3   Party structure of government and the role of prime ministers' staff

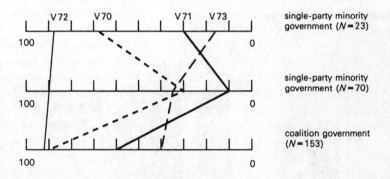

Answers in percentages; yes, prime minister's staff:

V 70 = Prepare cabinet agenda
V 71 = Control ministers' proposals
V 72 = Advise prime minister politically
V 73 = Develop own policy proposals

The 'administrative' *v.* the 'political' character of prime ministerial staffs thus appears in large part related to and indeed consequential on the fact that governments are based on a coalition, on a single majority party, or on a single-party cabinet that is in a minority. For members of single-party majority governments, prime ministerial staffs tend to have primarily a political role; for members of coalition governments, on the other hand, they tend to have primarily an administrative role, at least in the sense that we have used these terms here. Members of single-party governments are in the middle and seem therefore to regard prime ministerial staffs as having a mixed role.

This thus further suggests that prime ministerial staffs do not necessarily reduce the collective character of cabinet decision-making. By getting involved more in the fields of agenda-drawing and in the supervision of proposals coming from individual ministers, especially in the context of coalitions, prime ministerial staffs are likely on the contrary to increase the collective character of cabinet government: the autonomy of individual ministers diminishes and the rest of the cabinet becomes more involved in what each member does. This role of prime ministerial staffs in coalitions goes some way towards explaining the earlier finding that prime ministerial staffs do not appear to have any negative effect on the involvement of the cabinet in major debates. At least to the extent that they have an 'administrative' role, prime

Figure 6.4   Party structure of government and political and administrative role of prime ministers' staff

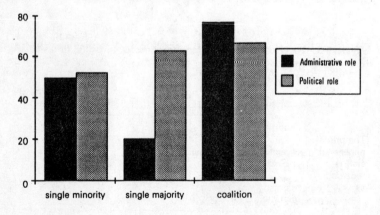

ministerial staffs may well be a help to the cabinet decision-making
process.

Party composition of cabinets

The character of prime ministerial staffs, as seen by ministers, appears
markedly related to the party composition of cabinets. By and large,
and perhaps somewhat surprisingly, socialist ministers are appreciably
less likely than other ministers, and in particular than christian
democrat ministers to give prominence to prime ministerial staffs.
First, socialist ministers are somewhat less likely than christian
democrat ministers to consider these as important in policy-making:
22 per cent of the socialist respondents state that they are not
important while only 17 per cent of their christian democrat colleagues
have the same views.

Second, there are pronounced differences among ministers of the
different parties about the forms of involvement of prime ministerial
staffs, except, but not surprisingly, with respect to the question of the
personal advice given by members of prime ministerial staffs to prime
ministers. Thus, while nearly all (96 per cent) christian democrat
ministers state that prime ministerial staffs are involved in the
preparation of the cabinet agenda, only 47 per cent of their socialist
colleagues feel the same; while 61 per cent of the christian democrats
say that prime ministerial staffs supervise ministerial proposals, only 27
per cent of the socialists react in the same way; finally, on the question
of whether prime ministerial staffs develop their own proposals, only a
quarter of the socialist ministers give a positive answer while 45 per

Figure 6.5   Party of the minister and importance of prime ministerial staff
(percentages)

		Socialist	Liberal	Christian	Conserv.	Other
The prime ministerial staff is regarded as:	important	40	18	25	4	13
	of some importance	44	11	16	21	8
	not important	56	21	15	4	4

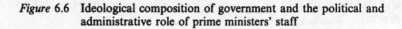

Figure 6.6   Ideological composition of government and the political and administrative role of prime ministers' staff

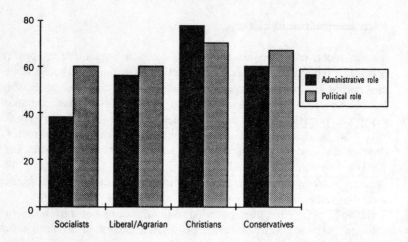

cent of the christian democrats do so. Overall, party differences are most pronounced towards the 'administrative' pole of the role of prime ministerial staffs: while only 37 per cent of the socialist ministers feel that prime ministerial staffs act in an 'administrative' capacity, 78 per cent of the christian democrats feel the same; but there is also a tendency for socialist ministers to give less prominence to the political role of prime ministerial staffs than ministers from other parties, and in particular than christian democrats.

This finding is also rather remarkable: contrary to what might have been expected, it is among the ministers of the Right and Centre that greater importance is given to prime ministerial staffs, not among ministers of the Left. That this should be the case suggests in turn two reflections. The first is that the suspicion about the possible 'dangerous' role of prime ministerial staffs is clearly not widespread among the *ministers* of the Left, to say the least, even if this view may be shared among other sections of the Left. Second, since it is the Right and Centre that, on balance, recognise the importance of prime ministerial staffs, it is not surprising that these advisers should be regarded as playing a managerial part and as being primarily concerned with expediting business efficiently: the fact that they are a help to cabinet decision-making comes out appreciably more vividly than the fact that they might be a hindrance.

Figure 6.7 Ideological composition of government and the role of prime ministers' staff

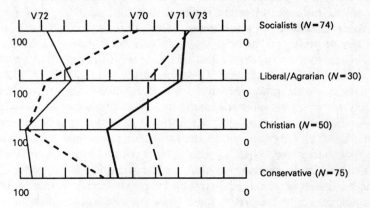

Answers in percentages; yes, prime ministers' staff:

V70 = Prepare cabinet agenda
V71 = Control ministers' proposals
V72 = Advise prime minister politically
V73 = Develop own policy proposals

The leadership of the prime minister

Prime ministerial leadership can be expected to affect the role of prime ministerial staffs. We will examine prime ministerial influence on cabinet decision-making in general in Chapter 10, but it seems appropriate to consider here the specific influence that this leadership may have on the part played by prime ministerial advisers; this is in order to see, in particular, whether this part is truly very different if the prime minister is more or less 'active'. In principle at least, one might expect very active prime ministers to want their personal staff to help them in every possible way, including acting against the rest of the cabinet. Less active prime ministers, on the contrary, for example those who are more anxious to 'arbitrate' than to 'initiate', seem likely to let members of their staff prepare compromises; indeed, they may want them to follow the proposals of ministers and ensure that these do not conflict with one another or, if a conflict cannot be avoided, that the problem is resolved as quickly and as painlessly as possible. Clearly, these are two extreme poles and many prime ministers will fall at some point between them, but the extreme positions are likely to be revealing: in this study, the matter can be examined by using the answers given by respondents to a question designed to assess how broad the influence of prime ministers is. This makes it possible to discover the extent to which prime ministers make a large mark on policies or prefer, on the contrary, to be somewhat more 'laid back'.

The questions that were asked of ministers with respect to prime ministerial staffs do not make it possible to test directly whether these officials do what prime ministers want them to do; but at least the autonomy of prime ministerial staffs from the cabinet can be assessed by looking at how far this staff puts forward its own proposals. On the other hand, an indicator of the extent to which prime ministerial staffs are watchdogs on behalf of the cabinet and attempt to prevent difficulties from emerging in the open is provided by considering whether these personal advisers supervise ministerial proposals. A positive answer to the first of these questions would seem likely to be associated with an assessment that the prime minister is active; a positive answer to the second would seem likely to be associated with an assessment that the prime minister is less of an 'activist'.

The trend is indeed in the expected direction, even if it is not very strong. Only 29 per cent of the prime ministers who are reputed to be more 'active' had prime ministerial staffs who were regarded as supervising proposals from individual ministers; this proportion is of 44 per cent among the prime ministers who are not reputed to be as 'active'. Conversely, while, among this last group, only 22 per cent of the prime ministerial staffs are said to put forward their own proposals, the proportion is of 40 per cent among prime ministers who are regarded as more 'active'.

It is not possible to go further, admittedly, and to claim that, in general, 'active' prime ministers are frequently associated with 'political' prime ministerial staffs and less 'active' prime ministers with 'administrative' prime ministerial staffs. Such a conclusion might appear to follow from the answers to the two questions that we have just examined; but it does not hold for the other two specific questions relating to the role of prime ministerial staffs that we have examined in this chapter. For 'active' prime ministers are primarily associated with prime ministerial staffs involved in preparing the agenda (although this can be regarded as an 'administrative' function that helps the whole cabinet); less 'active' prime ministers, on the other hand, are somewhat more associated with prime ministerial staff who give them personal advice (although this can be regarded as a 'political' function). Thus

Figure 6.8   Leadership style of the prime minister and the role of prime
ministers' staff

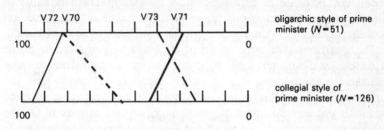

Answers in percentages; yes, prime ministers' staff:

V 70 = Prepare cabinet agenda
V 71 = Control ministers' proposals
V 72 = Advise prime minister politically
V 73 = Develop own policy proposals

the conclusion that can be drawn with respect to the possible influence
of the style of prime ministers' leadership is only that an
'administrative' role corresponds to less 'active' prime ministers and
that a 'political' role corresponds to more 'active' prime ministers with
respect to those aspects of the role of prime ministerial staffs that are
regarded by respondents as *more important*.

Country characteristics

As we saw earlier, the size of prime ministerial offices varies
considerably across Western Europe: presumably, the functions and
responsibilities of the members of these offices tend to vary as well.
Indeed, as we also saw, the analysis of ministerial responses suggests
that some prime ministerial staffs play a more 'political' part, others a
more 'administrative' part, while the role of yet others is more mixed.
Since the size and characteristics of prime ministers' offices vary across
countries, country variations would also seem to affect the part played
by the members of these offices in cabinet decision-making.

The nine countries for which the ministerial study provides an
indication of the role of prime ministerial staffs do indeed divide into
four groups, these groups corresponding by and large to the scale that

we found earlier to exist with respect to the four types of activities of prime ministerial staffs: it will be recalled that personal advice given to prime ministers by their staff is at the bottom and these advisers putting forward proposals on their own is at the top. In the first group, which includes France, Italy, and Belgium, prime ministerial staffs have almost the maximum role possible: they are concerned with all four activities. The second group consists only of Germany and is characterised by highly positive answers with respect to three types of activities, but not to the fourth, as few ministers from that country believe that prime ministerial staffs put forward their own proposals. Third, in Austria, Denmark, and, in a more erratic manner, Norway, prime ministerial staffs are considered by respondents to be essentially involved only in the two less 'important' types of activities, namely advising the prime minister and preparing the cabinet agenda; in Norway, however, interviewees state that prime ministerial staffs are not involved in cabinet agenda preparation, but are involved to an extent in supervising proposals coming from ministers: the Norwegian cabinet is thus one in which the four-item scale that we found to exist in general does not fully obtain. Finally, in the last two countries in which the questions on prime ministerial staffs were asked – Britain and Ireland – responses are also at variance from this four-item scale. In both cases, prime ministerial staffs are regarded as advising prime ministers personally, though the point is only partly accepted by Irish

Table 6.3   Country characteristics with respect to the activities of prime ministerial staffs

	F	I	B	D	A	DK	N	GB	IRL
Advising PM	H	H	H	H	H	H	H	H	M
Preparing cabinet agenda	H	H	H	H	H	MH	L	L	H
Supervising ministerial proposals	H	H	MH	M	L	L		M	L	L
Putting own proposals	M	M	MH	L	L	L	L	M	M

H = high
MH = medium high
L = low

respondents. Meanwhile, most British respondents judge prime ministerial staffs to play little part in the preparation of the cabinet agenda and in supervising proposals coming from ministers; on the other hand, many feel that prime ministerial staffs put forward their own proposals. So do Irish respondents, but they also think that prime ministerial staffs have a substantial part to play in preparing the cabinet agenda.

There are thus manifest country idiosyncrasies that are likely to be based on structural characteristics of the prime ministerial offices, on traditions, and on the part played by other advisers to the prime ministers, whether from the party or parties in power or from the civil service: this is manifestly true for Britain, where the preparation of the cabinet agenda is probably regarded as a civil service matter, not as one that is to be handled by the personal staff of the prime minister. Furthermore, variations in the role of prime ministerial staffs do not even follow the distinction between more parliamentary and less parliamentary countries, a distinction that helps to account for a number of aspects of cabinet decision-making: with respect to the role of prime ministerial staffs, on the other hand, there are both more parliamentary and less parliamentary countries at the top and at the bottom of the scale of 'importance' of prime ministerial staffs. Thus Britain and Italy are at the top of this scale, together with France, while Austria and Denmark are at the bottom, together with Ireland. Alongside the coalition or single-party character of the cabinet, alongside the party composition of that cabinet, and alongside the style of the prime minister, truly specific elements of the political life of each country thus play an important part in determining the nature of the role of prime ministerial staffs.

In their majority, ministers believe that prime ministerial staffs are an important feature of the process of decision-making of Western European cabinets. This must mean that the influence of these advisers is somewhat independent of the size of the offices concerned, even though the smallest of them appear to play less of a part than those who are larger. A number of other factors affect the importance of prime ministerial staffs. Traditions about what is the 'proper' relationship between ministers, civil servants, parties, and other political actors all have a part to play – as have the coalition or single-party structure of the cabinet, on the one hand, the party composition of the government, and the type of leadership characterising the prime minister.

Thus prime ministerial staffs are more or less involved in the life of cabinets: they personally advise the head of the government in nearly all cases; they often help to prepare the agenda; and on many occasions they supervise the proposals coming from the ministers – and even put forward some of their own policies. Yet while prime ministerial staffs are engaged in these activities, it is remarkable to note that ministers, whether from the Right or from the Left, do not regard this involvement of prime ministerial staffs as detrimental to the collective life of the cabinet. These advisers are viewed as helpful elements in cabinet life; they do what they are expected to do – namely, provide a means of smoothing the process of cabinet decision-making. This process may no longer be collective, but prime ministerial staffs do not seem to share the blame – if blame is to be shared – in such a development.

Notes

1. See for instance G. W. Jones (1991), pp. 1–17.
2. The cabinet secretariat was set up in Britain in 1916 by Lloyd George.
3. The question of 'prime ministerial government' was referred to earlier. See Chapter 1.
4. Included are Gemany, France, Italy, Belgium, Ireland, Norway, Denmark, Austria, and Britain.
5. J. Vahr (1991).
6. P. Gerlich and W. C. Müller (1988), p. 143.
7. S. Eriksen (1988b), p. 189.
8. A. King (1991), p. 41.
9. F. Müller-Rommel (1992), *passim*.
10. A number of responses have had to be excluded as they did not cover all the questions.
11. Differences in numbers result from the fact that some respondents answered only two or three of the four questions.

7 The Links between Cabinets and Parties and Cabinet Decision-Making

Lieven de Winter

Almost as soon as parties emerged, the assessment of the impact of these bodies on the composition, functioning, structure, and output of cabinets was a subject of concern and controversy. This impact is so marked that cabinet government is indeed often described as being party government:[1]

> The battle between cabinet and parties is a battle to occupy the centre of the political terrain. The traditional (British) view suggests that the cabinet is central; yet, even in Britain, when Labour is in power, this 'axiom' becomes a mere postulate about which there is some doubt. The validity of the postulate is even more questionable when one considers Belgium, Finland, Italy, Germany, or the Netherlands.[2]

As a matter of fact, the nature of parliamentary government entails that parties play a key part in the life of the government if the system is to function effectively, since the very survival of the government depends on its enjoying the continuous support of a majority of the legislature.[3] This means that parties need to control MPs, but, in exchange, that these can and will exercise a considerable supervision over the cabinet.[4]

There are three main ways or modes by which parties can have an impact on ministers (and indeed ministers can have an impact on parties). The first of these is the most direct: party leaders may attempt to influence ministers face to face during formal or informal occasions (while ministers can attempt during these occasions to influence party leaders as well); second, the relationship can be indirect in that the parliamentarians of a party may attempt to influence the ministers of that party (and reciprocally ministers can attempt to influence parliaments); finally, in coalition governments, there can be discussions among the party leaders, both inside and outside the cabinet, in order to influence government policy.

The extent of impact can vary within each of these three modes. At one extreme, there can be almost no relationship at all; at the other, there can be a very close connection; this connection can be positive or negative, depending on whether the relationship is one of collaboration or, on the contrary, of conflict and competition. We need therefore to look at the 'temperature' as well as at the mode of this impact: this examination will be the object of the first section of this chapter.

We will then examine in the second part how far these modes of party impact appear related to one or more of the three general explanatory variables whose influence is monitored throughout this volume, namely, the single-party or coalition basis of the cabinet, the nature of the party or parties in power, and the specific 'cultural' traditions of each country. Finally, we will consider in the third part to what extent the various modes of party impact – direct, parliamentary, interparty – affect the character of cabinet decision-making processsses and specifically their centrality, their collegiality, their collective nature, and their level of conflictuality.

MODES AND EXTENT OF THE IMPACT OF PARTIES ON CABINETS

Direct forms of party–cabinet relationships

The direct influence of parties on governments can take two forms, a policy form and an appointment form. In terms of policies, parties can go as far as wanting to dictate what the cabinet must do; however, they may be less ambitious and merely put pressure on ministers. In terms of appointments, parties can – and indeed most commonly do – send to the government some of their top people; as a weaker type of influence, parties may ask cabinet ministers to report to party leaders periodically to explain what they do.

Respondents to the ministerial interviews were asked to state how far such practices occurred in the context of the cabinets to which they had belonged. The answers show a clear ranking: a large majority of interviewees said that they attended party meetings at least

Table 7.1 Party–cabinet links (absolute figures)

	Yes	No	Missing	% Yes
Attended party meetings	242	95	73	59
Party position influential in cabinet	156	209	45	38
Referral to party for decision	111	238	61	27
Briefing by party	89	269	52	22

occasionally (59 per cent); but only a minority gave a positive answer to three other questions: 38 per cent stated that parties sent their influential leaders to the cabinet; 27 per cent said that decisions were referred to party headquarters when matters could not be solved in cabinet; and 22 per cent indicated that they were briefed by their party about issues coming up for deliberation by the government.

Although these answers fall along one dimension and only one, they do not constitute a scale in the full sense of the word, as only about half the responses can be incorporated in this scale. What the ranking reveals, however, is that the four types of party–cabinet interaction are not ordered entirely in an expected manner: briefings by parties are mentioned less frequently than the referral of matters to the party hierarchy for decision, for instance; what also emerges is that direct party–cabinet relationships are more often concerned with personal contacts than with the imposition of policy lines.

While the direct relationship between parties and cabinets tends therefore to be more at a personal than at a policy level, it is also both sustained and cooperative rather than distant and competitive. Thus, not surprisingly in what are ostensibly regarded as 'party governments', only 8 per cent of the ministers interviewed stated that they had no contacts at all with their party, although a fifth said that these contacts were infrequent. About half – but only half (49 per cent) – said that there was close cooperation between party and cabinet; 70 per cent said that there was no competition between party and cabinet, against 13 per cent who said that there was. In many cases, however, cooperation and competition go together: nearly two-thirds of the respondents who experienced competition also referred to cooperation (34 out of 53 answers).

Table 7.2　Cooperation or competition between party and cabinet

| | Party–cabinet | | Parliament–cabinet | |
	N	%	N	%
Both cooperation and competition	34	8	65	16
Cooperation only	165	40	233	57
Competition only	19	5	15	4
Neither	120	29	39	9
Missing data	72	17	58	14

Indirect party-cabinet interaction through parliament

Much party–cabinet interaction does not take place directly from and to the party headquarters, but indirectly through parliament. This is the way in which, traditionally, influence was exercised on governments and this channel remains the proper constitutional one in parliamentary systems. As a matter of fact, it is sometimes difficult to distinguish the direct party route from the indirect parliamentary route of party–cabinet interaction as well as from the pressure put by individual MPs on ministers and especially on the ministers of their own party.

On the basis of the same distinctions as the ones adopted earlier for the direct form party–cabinet interaction, 4 per cent of the respondents stated that they had no contact with MPs and 10 per cent that they had infrequent contacts, while almost three-quarters said that they had close contacts of a cooperative character and a fifth experienced competition (also often alongside cooperation). If one excludes the one-sixth of the interviewees who did not answer these questions, one minister out of nine did not experience either close cooperation or competition with parliament: this is a markedly smaller group than the equivalent one in terms of direct party–cabinet interaction (a third). Moreover, as in the case of direct party-cabinet interaction, but only more so, the large majority of those who experienced competition also experienced cooperation (65 out of 80 or over four-fifths): thus 85 per cent of those who answered this question – and as many as 70 per cent of all the ministers in the sample – stated that they experienced close cooperation with parliamentarians, a proportion that confirms the widely held view that ministers work closely with their parliamentary supporters.

Direct party–cabinet interaction and parliament–cabinet interaction are broadly associated. Two-thirds of the (admittedly small number of) ministers who stated that there was neither cooperation nor competition at the parliamentary level also stated that this was the case at the level of direct party–cabinet interaction; nearly four-fifths of the respondents who described party-cabinet interaction as cooperative and, *only* cooperative, made exactly the same comment about parliament-cabinet interaction.

The interparty mode of party–cabinet interaction in coalitions

In coalitions, the parties supporting the government can interact both within and outside the cabinet. There can be formal meetings as well as informal contacts between the leaders of the parties supporting the government, these contacts leading ultimately to decisions that are binding on the coalition, even if members of the government did not, or did not fully, take part in these decisions.

Table 7.3   Cooperative and competitive styles of party–cabinet relationships compared with parliament–cabinet relationships (absolute figures)

	PARLIAMENT				
	Both cooperative and competitive	Cooperative only	Competitive only	Neither	Total
Both cooperative and competitive (PARTY)	14	15	2	1	32
Cooperative only	22	128	5	9	164
Competitive only	7	8	2	2	19
Neither	20	69	4	25	118
Total	63	220	13	37	333

Of the interviewees who answered this question (which naturally excluded those who had not taken part in any coalition), very few thought that there were no contacts at all (seven cases); about a fifth thought that 'party summits' were the main form that these interparty relationships took and a tenth referred to other types of formal collaboration; but the largest group – 40 per cent – believed that the collaboration was informal, while only 14 per cent of the respondents thought that there was primarily competition. There is little association between the responses given by ministers about forms of direct party–cabinet and parliament–cabinet interaction and responses given about forms of interparty interaction in coalitions, except that those who mention party summits tend to be drawn primarily from among those ministers who mentioned the existence of close cooperative links in direct party–cabinet and in parliament–cabinet relations (24 and 25 responses out of 26), while those who emphasised the existence of informal collaboration among coalition parties tended also to be those who stressed the existence of cooperation and of cooperation only in parliament–cabinet relations (77 out of 97).

Table 7.4   Types of interaction among parties in coalitions

	N	%
Party summits	58	14
Formal collaboration	28	7
Informal collaboration	100	24
Informal competition	36	9
No contact	16	4
No reply, not entered	101	25
Missing	71	17

The interaction between cabinet members and their party is thus rather close; it is still closer with the parliamentary party. This interaction tends to be informal and cooperative. There are also more than traces of competition, often associated with cooperation, while ministers who do not interact directly with their party are prone to note the existence of competition among the coalition parties. Having thus described the structure of the party–cabinet relations, we can now turn to an examination of the way in which this interaction is affected by the single-party/coalition distinction, by the character of the party in power, and by the 'cultural' specificities of each country.

THE ROLE OF GENERAL FACTORS IN ACCOUNTING FOR THE MODES OF MODES OF CABINET–PARTY INTERACTION

The single-party/coalition distinction and cabinet–party interaction

We have already noted one way in which the single-party/coalition distinction affects cabinet–party interaction: interparty relationship arises almost exclusively in coalitions. Although some negotiations among parties have to take place in single-party minority governments if the cabinet is to survive, and although formal discussions among parties occur occasionally in single-party majority governments, when it is felt valuable to enlarge the majority for a specific purpose, interparty interaction is essentially a coalition characteristic.

The single-party/coalition distinction does also have an effect on the two other ways in which parties and cabinets interact. First, as far as the direct interaction between parties and cabinets are concerned, there are marked differences in the effect of the single-party/coalition distinction on the forms of interaction. Almost all ministers from single-party majority governments state that they attended meetings of their party at least occasionally; nearly two-fifths (38 per cent) of the ministers from coalition cabinets said that they did not do so. Conversely, half the respondents from coalition cabinets said that party influentials were appointed to the cabinet, but only a little over a quarter (28 per cent) of the respondents from single-party majority governments said the same. On the other hand, the style – cooperative, competitive – of party–cabinet interaction does not seem related to the single-party/coalition distinction: the only difference appears to be that ministers from single-party minority governments overwhelmingly cite cooperation as the style to which they have been accustomed.

Conversely, the single-party/coalition distinction appears to have little effect on the forms of interaction between parliament and cabinet, but some effect on the style of this interaction. Nearly all the ministers from single-party governments, whether based on a minority or on a majority, refer to close contacts – cooperative or competitive – with parliament; but 15 per cent of the ministers from coalitions deny the existence of such contacts. If we relate this answer about cabinet–parliament relations to the styles of cabinet interaction with party headquarters, it seems possible to conclude that ministers from single-party minority cabinets cannot afford to have no links with parties in parliament and that ministers from single-party majority cabinets need

Table 7.5   The single-party/coalition distinction and styles of cabinet party and parliament relationships (percentages)

Party–cabinet styles	Single-party minority	Single-party majority	Coalition	N
Party–cabinet styles				
Both cooperative and competitive	9	12	9	(34)
Cooperative only	81	40	48	(165)
Competitive only	–	9	5	(19)
Neither	9	40	38	(119)
Total percentage	99	100	100	
N	(33)	(81)	(223)	(337)
Parliament–cabinet styles				
Both cooperative and competitive	18	36	12	(65)
Cooperative only	72	59	68	(232)
Competitive only	–	–	7	(15)
Neither	9	5	13	(38)
Total percentage	99	100	100	
N	(33)	(88)	(229)	(350)

to have links with parliamentarians in order to ensure that the proposed legislation is passed smoothly. Only among ministers from coalitions does one find respondents who mention competition *alone* as the main style of parliament–cabinet interaction, while they do not describe direct party–cabinet relationships in the same way. Single-party governments appear therefore closer to parliament and coalition governments closer to party headquarters.

Type of party and party-cabinet interaction

The type of party appears to be closely related to modes of party–cabinet interaction. Surprisingly perhaps, ministers from christian democrat parties are those who mention most not only the presence of party influentials in the cabinet, but the fact that ministers are briefed by their party and the fact that decisions are taken at party headquarters. Conservatives are those who stress most that they attend party meetings. Christian democrats thus appear to be those for whom the direct party-cabinet link is the deepest and the most policy-oriented.

Meanwhile, the style of direct party–cabinet links also differ according to the party in power. This link is weakest among conservatives and liberals: nearly half the ministers from these parties state that there is neither close cooperation nor competition; on the other hand, while about a fifth of the respondents from christian democrat and socialist parties speak of competition with the party as well as cooperation (17 and 21 per cent respectively), socialists alone state in substantial numbers that competition is the *only* form that this interaction takes.

Ministers from the various parties also have different opinions with respect to the links between parliament and cabinet: no conservative interviewee, for instance, stated that there was neither collaboration nor competition, while 10 per cent of the ministers from other parties said so; conservatives also tend to emphasise competition more than

Table 7.6 Party composition of governments and styles of cabinets–party and cabinet–party and cabinet–parliament relationships (percentages)

	Socialist	Liberal	Christian	Conservative	N
Party–cabinet styles					
Both cooperative and competitive	10	6	17	10	(34)
Cooperative only	47	58	49	41	(150)
Competitive only	11	–	1	–	
Neither	32	36	32	48	(91)
Total percentage	100	100	99	99	
N	(147)	(53)	(77)	(29)	(306)
Parliament–cabinet styles					
Both cooperative and competitive	20	9	15	55	(62)
Cooperative only	67	76	61	45	(204)
Competitive only	3	5	7	–	(13)
Neither	10	10	17	–	(34)
Total percentage	100	100	100	99	
N	(151)	(58)	(75)	(29)	(313)

other parties: over half stated that it took place, admittedly alongside collaboration, while the equivalent proportions for the other parties was between 13 and 23 per cent. Thus the respondents who stress the parliamentary link are the conservatives, while members of other parties tend to stress the direct party link; but, for conservatives, this close link with parliament is not always cooperative: to an extent at least, it is competitive.

Finally, there are very few cross-party differences with respect to the interparty coalition mode. Conservatives appear not to recognise the existence of formal collaborative arrangements (except party summits); but, in other parties, less then 10 per cent of the interviewees refer to *formal* collaborative arrangements outside party summits. Overall, socialists, christian democrats, liberals, and conservatives report in practically the same proportions the existence of a variety of forms of interparty relationships. That there should be uniformity in this respect is not surprising. In coalitions, interparty forms of interaction are necessarily identical since what is described here is the way in which a number of parties relate to each other: when party summits exist, ministers from all the parties concerned must recognise the existence of these summits. Parties can have an effect on direct party–cabinet and on parliament–cabinet relations; they can have an effect on interparty interaction only to the extent that some parties may not easily become partners of some others because of differences arising from their conception of what interparty relations should be: but, when a coalition between some parties has been set up, ministers from all the parties in the coalition will naturally describe in the same manner the interparty relations taking place in that coalition.

COUNTRY TRADITIONS AND PARTY–CABINET RELATIONSHIPS

Direct party–cabinet interaction

The effect of specific country traditions on party-cabinet interaction appears substantial. To begin with, at the level of direct party–cabinet relations, differences in the forms taken by these links suggest that there are distinct country patterns. Thus, first, the large majority of the interviewees said that they did occasionally attend a party meeting; this was true of all countries except France, where over three-quarters said that they did not attend any such meetings. Second, overall, 44 per cent of the ministers who responded (from eleven countries, as the question was not asked in Germany) mentioned the importance of party influentials in cabinets; but this score was markedly lower in Britain, Ireland, and France (25 per cent of positive answers in the first case, 6 per cent in the last two). Third, while 32 per cent of the ministers stated that parties settled issues when the cabinet could not do so, again, in France, Britain, Ireland, and in this case also in the Netherlands, the score was markedly lower, with no positive answers at all in France and Britain and only 13 and 4 per cent of such answers in Ireland and the Netherlands respectively. Thus the Dutch cabinet may be a key source of decision-making, but in part because party influentials are in the cabinet. Finally, while 23 per cent of the ministers from eleven countries (Swedish ministers having not been asked this question) claimed that ministers were briefed by their party on cabinet agenda issues, France, Britain, Ireland, and the Netherlands score again very low (between 0 and 12 per cent), although this was also the case of Italy and Norway (respectively 5 and 12 per cent).

The direct party involvement in cabinet life thus varies markedly: it is typically large in Scandinavia and in Central Europe, very limited in Britain and Ireland, and almost non-existent in France. In the Netherlands, it exists only to the extent that party leaders are in the cabinet and exercise influence as a result. Admittedly, in Britain, too, and indeed probably in Ireland and France as well, many prominent party men and women are in the cabinet: yet their colleagues do not

Table 7.7   Sources of ministers briefing about cabinet agenda issues (1965–85) (% affirmative answers)

Country/ Sources of cabinet agenda briefing	DK	BRD	NL	B	F	GB	IRL	I	A	SF	N
Cabinet secretariat	18	8	0	41	0	10	13	48	11	7	0
Dep. civil servants	82	92	92	18	100	95	78	76	93	21	88
Personal staff	14	17	4	100	100	48	52	71	90	34	82
Party	18	58	12	61	0	8	9	5	24	48	12
Outside advisers	4	58	16	2	0	8	23	11	25	7	0
Other	33	100	4	15	35	8	55	17	4	66	9

Note: The question was not asked in Sweden.

seem to regard them as cabinet influentials *as a result*. The question
that arises is whether they still act as *party* influentials; the answers
given seem to suggest that this is not quite the case.

Some of the more detailed country differences are also revealing. In
Belgium, nearly all ministers attend the weekly meeting of their party
executive. In the christian democrat and liberal parties, ministers have
the upper hand: they inform their party colleagues about developments
and only on some crucial matters can the executive exercise real
influence; in the socialist parties, on the contrary, ministers often
receive their 'marching orders' after fierce discussions: for important
matters they have generally to sound their executive. There are also
informal and formal meetings of the ministers of each party, and in
particular formal meetings with the party chairmen on the day before
cabinet meetings, other party influentials and sometimes parliamentary
leaders being also present; the agenda of the cabinet meeting is
scrutinised and party positions are defined. Party chairmen are key
figures, especially in the socialist parties; this is less the case in the
christian democrat parties, in part because the turnover is relatively
high.

In the Netherlands, similar contacts between ministers and party
leaders take place, but their impact is more limited. In the 1950s and
1960s, there were weekly party lunches before cabinet meetings;
parliamentary leaders then began to attend together with the
secretaries of State. 'Occasionally party discipline is enforced and the
decision taken by cabinet differs from the one that would have emerged
had all ministers followed their individual judgement'.[5] There are
variations across parties, however. Socialist ministers do not normally
attend the weekly meetings and enjoy substantial autonomy; the same
occurs in the Liberal party while, among christian democrats – at any
rate under Lubbers – the party chairman did attend weekly meetings of
the ministers of the party and ministers sometimes attended the
meetings of the party executive, but continued to enjoy substantial
autonomy.

The difference between Belgium and the Netherlands is thus very
large: Austria is an intermediate case, with party–cabinet meetings
being held both in the context of coalitions and single-party cabinets,
the most important issues being discussed at these meetings. Populist
and socialist ministers attend weekly party meetings, but these are
primarily sounding boards for the ministers; rather than giving power
to party leaders, these give an opportunity to cabinet members to
consult and inform the party.[6]

In Scandinavia, links between party and cabinet exist, but, rather as in Austria, they do not result in binding decisions. In Finland, ministers attend regular weekly meetings of the party executive: the discussion ranges from genuine joint discussion to mere consultation. In Norway, the executive of the Labour Party is only attended by those ministers who are members of this body, while other ministers participate when an issue that concerns them is discussed. The party executive is not primarily a policy-making body, however, as it is concerned mainly with organisation; its influence has also gradually declined. Meetings with the leaders of the trade unions are more important with respect to economic policies: thus, in the 1978–81 Nordli cabinet, a 'liaison' committee was established to give advice on the preparation of the legislative programme: it comprised representatives of the Labour party, of its youth organisation, of the parliamentary party, and of the Labour federation.

The Italian situation is characterised by strong party influence, but not through clear institutional channels: power is located in the headquarters of the coalition parties as well as in the factions of these parties, admittedly, but it does not manifest itself through formal and regular contacts between party executives and ministers; rather, party leaders exert their influence on ministers through their collaborators and by public statements, although these are typically made only on issues vital to the cabinet's survival. On the whole, the cabinet is not strong enough to take decisions independently from the general secretaries of the political parties and from the leaders of the factions. Some decisions are taken outside the cabinet by party representatives who may or may not be members of the cabinet: these decisions can become party policy without further discussion.[7]

The Italian case contrasts sharply with that of the three other large Western European countries that are studied here. In all three, there is a marked distance between party and cabinet, especially when the government is of the Right or Centre. Germany is perhaps the one of these three countries in which the link is least vague. Although ministers rarely attend meetings of their party executive, whether they are social democrats or christian democrats, there is some relationship between SPD ministers and the party executive and even occasionally almost joint decision-making; on the other hand, the CDU is consulted by ministers in specific cases only: this leaves members of the cabinet with a large amount of autonomy.[8]

In Britain, the Conservative party has no formal part at all in shaping policy, though ministers have frequent informal contacts with the parliamentary backbenchers and with a few party leaders in the country. In the Labour party, links are closer, but they take the form of a tug of war between the executive, the annual conference, and the cabinet: ministers and prime ministers have oscillated between efforts at compromise and declarations of autonomy. In practice, however, the Labour party's opposition to the cabinet tends generally to be symbolic, unless the ministers are divided or unless there is considerable feeling in the *parliamentary* party.

Finally, in France, ministers are often truly cut off from their party organisation, especially on the Right: this is in part due to the fact that many ministers are technicians. There are differences, however: while all the ministers from the Gaullist and Centre parties stated that they did not attend party meetings, nearly half the socialist ministers who answered stated that they had done so. Moreover, in the socialist governments, weekly meetings have taken place between the prime minister, the president of the Republic, and the first secretary of the party: some degree of coordination is thus assured between party and cabinet.

Interaction through parliament

Country variations with respect to parliament–cabinet interaction are also substantial, contacts being particularly limited in France and relatively limited in Austria, the Netherlands, Belgium, and Italy: in France and Austria, the political system is government- (or government and party-) centred; one might have expected a closer parliament–cabinet relationship in the Netherlands, given the large role of parliamentary leaders in that country; in Belgium and Italy, there is a clear division between party–cabinet and parliament–cabinet interaction.[9]

Table 7.8   Relation between ministers and their parliamentary party (1965–85) (% affirmative answers)

Country/ type of relation	DK	BRD	NL	B	F	GB	IRL	I	A	SF	N
Close cooperation	96	83	64	70	92	100	69	70	93	95	84
Competition	21	8	16	11	8	70	31	14	7	30	19
Little or no contact	0	4	28	33	39	3	6	31	20	3	3

Note: The question was not asked in Sweden.

Moreover, while a large majority of ministers from all countries state that they work in close collaboration with their parliamentary party, this does not mean that they really negotiate with these parliamentarians; the cooperation may be rather superficial. Finally, at the opposite extreme, levels of competition are relatively high in Britain, Ireland, and Finland; they are lower, though not negligible, in the other Scandinavian countries, in the Netherlands, and in Italy.

We noted earlier that the single-party/coalition distinction did not have any relationship with the forms of parliament-cabinet interaction. This matter can be considered in greater detail at the country level, both among countries that have had single-party governments (and coalitions) and countries that have had only coalition governments. First, among the countries that have had single-party governments (and, in all cases but one, coalition governments as well), Austria and Ireland appear to be those where the parliamentary party has the least influence. In Austria, although ministers attend the meetings of the groups, they do so only to inform and not to consult.[10] Parliamentary parties essentially implement the will of the party or of the government, though more in the Socialist party than in the Liberal and People's parties (and indeed more in single-party governments than during coalitions):[11] parliamentary parties are highly disciplined and follow nearly always the intraparty line.[12] Ministers refer to 'cooperation' and not to 'competition', except to an extent among the Populists, in part because of the factionalised nature of that party. In Ireland, on the contrary, competition is reported to be high between parliamentarians and ministers by half of the Fine Gale ministers, two out of five of the Labour party ministers, but only by a small minority of their Fianna Fail colleagues; ministers have also to consult backbenchers regularly if they wish to avoid problems. Overall, though, government MPs rarely succeed in promoting or altering the shape of new policies and the parliamentary party has little more than a ceremonial role.[13] Secrecy often leaves MPs uninformed and discipline ensures that backbenchers will toe the government line.

In Britain, the parliamentary parties are unquestionably the most important sources of party influence. This is true of both major parties, even if, as we already noted, extra-parliamentary influence does play some part in the Labour case. Ministers attend regularly the meetings of their parliamentary party or of its subcommittees. Three-quarters of the Labour ministers interviewed and two-thirds of their Conservative colleagues mentioned the existence of some competition between themselves and their parliamentary group; while, in the early postwar period, the Conservative backbenchers' committee (the '1922 committee') had relatively limited influence, the role of this body has grown (in part because of the power that Conservative MPs acquired in the 1960s to elect the leader). Moreover, beyond the formal relationships that take place through the parliamentary parties as such, many informal contacts exist between individual MPs and ministers, for instance in the corridors of the House, in the bars, or during the divisions.

In minority Danish cabinets, parliament plays a considerable part in defining cabinet policy: cooperation is high.[14] Cabinet committees discuss proposals with the relevant committees of the parliamentary party;[15] in the Liberal party at least, ministers attend the policy committees of the parliamentary party. Indeed, an inner cabinet is often established which includes the prime minister and two influential ministers, alongside the chairman of the parliamentary party of the government party as well as representatives from this parliamentary party. The parliamentary party does not dominate, however, as, in a minority government, ministers can point out to their parliamentary party that the policy standpoints of other parties have to be taken into account. Since the late 1960s, agreements between minority governments and some of the opposition parties have indeed been struck. Moreover, the cabinet often accepts seeing its bills defeated without feeling that it needs to resign.[16]

In Norway, cooperation is mentioned by all, except some Liberals and Socialists, while competition is reported by all Centre ministers and by a third of the Conservatives. In order to reduce tension between party in government and party in cabinet, parliamentary leaders have sometimes been coopted to the cabinet: thus the leader of the Conservative parliamentary party regularly attended cabinet meetings in the 1981–3 period; when the Christian People and Centre parties entered the government, their parliamentary leaders joined the cabinet for the initial budget discussions and the preparation of the programme.

There are thus considerable variations in the extent of interaction between parliament and cabinet among the countries that have had both single-party and coalition governments; the same is true if we examine the countries where coalitions have been the rule. France and Germany are those where this interaction is lowest; it is higher, but still relatively limited, in Belgium and Italy, largely as a result of the strength of party headquarters that we noticed earlier; it is most developed in Finland and the Netherlands.

In France, where ministers are not or no longer members of parliament, they do not attend the meetings of the parliamentary parties. The prime minister holds a weekly meeting with the parliamentary leader of his or her party in the National Assembly and more irregular meetings with the leaders of the other parliamentary parties supporting the government; there is also a minister dealing with relations with parliament. In Germany, ministers rarely attend meetings of the parliamentary parties, the 'state secretary' being in charge of this task. Yet cooperation is reported by respondents to be high: only a small minority of the socialist ministers state that the interaction has a competitive character.[17]

Parliament–cabinet interaction is somewhat closer in Belgium and Italy, although it takes place alongside highly developed direct party–cabinet relationships. In Belgium, the parliamentary mode appears to play a part among christian democrats only, and indeed, in recent years, only among the Dutch-speaking christian democrats: the parliamentary party can occasionally challenge the ministers who tend to come regularly to meetings. In the francophone christian democrat party, relations are more easy going, while, in the Liberal parties, attendance is infrequent and the autonomy of the ministers is large. In the Socialist parties, the strength of the presidents is such that parliamentary parties are reduced to being mere sounding boards. The party presidents are, ultimately, the true influentials.

In Italy, the parliamentary majority is less cohesive than the cabinet majority, given in particular the strength of the committees and, until recently, the existence of the 'secret vote'.[18] Contacts between ministers and parliamentary parties are fragmented and limited to each minister's departmental questions. Compromises have often to be made with the parliamentary parties, including those of the opposition – for instance, the Party of the Democratic Left (ex-Communist); if the cabinet does not do so, it risks defeat in parliament. Overall, Italian ministers, in particular those from the small parties, do not experience a marked cooperation with the parliamentary parties.

The two countries in which the parliament–cabinet mode of interaction is the most developed are Finland and the Netherlands. In Finland, ministers are not fully autonomous and have to consult MPs about policies. In the two largest parties, the Centre and Socialist parties, parliamentary committees are influential: thus competition between ministers and parliamentarians of these two parties is relatively large, as well as between ministers and parliamentarians of the Communist party, but not among Liberals.[19] Yet cohesion is high and discipline is strict. Moreover, ministers have gradually attended parliamentary party meetings rather less over time: this is partly compensated for by the fact that leaders of the parliamentary groups can join informal cabinet meetings.

In the Netherlands, parliament–cabinet interaction is substantial, although ministers are not members of parliament. There are variations across parties, however. Liberal ministers never attend the meetings of their parliamentary party, but the leader of the parliamentary party in the lower house occasionally comes to lunch meetings of Liberal ministers: this does not prevent these ministers from acting autonomously. This is not the case in the Labour party where, occasionally, genuine joint decision-making occurs, and where ministers confer weekly with the leader of the parliamentary party of the lower house;[20] such meetings also occur among christian democrats and have a marked impact. Since ministers report relatively infrequent relations with the parliamentary party as a whole, especially among christian democrats, but also mention close cooperation, it follows that the leaders of these parliamentary parties are key intermediaries.

Interaction through the interparty mode

With respect to the interparty mode of interaction, variations are also substantial. Thus formal party summits are regarded as normal in Germany, Italy, and Finland; they play some part in Belgium and Denmark, but they are not important in the Netherlands, Norway, and France, and they play no part at all in Austria and Ireland (while the question does not arise in Britain, since there were no coalitions in that country during the period under consideration).

As in relation to parliament–cabinet interaction, the coupling of Austria and Ireland in the same group seems rather surprising. In Ireland, the British model applies and the leadership of the government party (or parties) tends to be in the cabinet; in Austria, interparty collaboration is the order of the day, especially during periods of grand coalitions; but it is so fundamental that it takes place routinely and informally. The same appears to be broadly the case in Norway, where coordination among the parties tends to take place in the cabinet or in parliament. Only in Finland is collaboration reported to be primarily formal.

Party summits take different forms and are more or less regular. In Germany, they emerged during the grand coalition of 1967–9, when power was transferred from the cabinet to a small informal group of politicians: the Kressronner Kreis was thus effectively in charge of

Table 7.9   Relations between coalition parties (% affirmative answers)

Country/ Type of relation	DK	BRD	NL	B	F	IRL	I	A	SF	N
Summits	35	50	11	35	9	0	50	0	70	5
Informal collaboration	32	35	35	34	42	30	40	100	0	64
Informal competition	12	0	35	15	36	21	28	0	0	9
No contacts	0	0	3	8	0	9	0	0	0	27

Note: The question was not asked in Sweden. There were no coalitions in
Britain during this period.

decision-making.[21] Since 1969, governments have tended to resort to
informal groups to steer coalitions: these include representatives of the
chancellor's office, of the relevant ministries, and of the parliamentary
parties of the majority.[22] In Italy, meetings of top party leaders
together with the prime minister take place when difficulties occur.
Similar practices have been found to exist elsewhere, as in Norway
during the Willoch cabinet and in the Netherlands, during the Den Uyl
cabinet, when ministers of the Labour party, of D-66, and of the PPR
met weekly with the parliamentary leaders: the christian democrats
were absent from these meetings, however. In Belgium, party summits
have taken place occasionally over some crucial problems, especially
over linguistic issues: this was the case in particular during one of the
Tindemans governments; yet experience suggested that it was better to
appoint the party presidents to the cabinet and this turned the cabinet
into a true decision-making arena.

THE EFFECT OF THE INTERACTION BETWEEN PARTY AND
CABINET ON CABINET DECISION-MAKING

Since there are important variations among Western European
countries in the modes and extent of interaction between cabinets
and parties, it becomes necessary to ask: how far do these variations
affect the characteristics of cabinet decision-making processes? In
particular, how far do variations in party–cabinet interaction lead to
variations in the centrality of the decisions taken by cabinets, in their
collective character, in their collegiality, in particular with respect to
the role of the prime minister, and in the levels of cabinet conflict?

The centrality of the cabinet and the modes of party interaction

One might perhaps have expected that the more developed the interaction between cabinet and supporting parties, the more the cabinet would play a central part in decision-making. As a matter of fact, the difference is non-existent at the level of cabinet–parliament relations and small at the level of direct party–cabinet relations. While 27 per cent of the ministers with no (or only infrequent ones) contacts with their party executive stated that the cabinet was the place where major issues were debated, 34 per cent of those who have frequent contacts said the same. While 40 per cent of those who had a competitive relationship with their party executive stated that the cabinet was a place where major issues were debated, the proportion was 30 per cent among those who did not experience such competition.

The collective character of the cabinet and the modes and extent of party interaction

The collective character of the cabinet appears to be a little enhanced by the fact that ministers are in a competitive relationship with their party, either directly or in parliament: 47 per cent of the respondents who were in competition with their party executive also intervened frequently on matters outside the jurisdiction of their department, as against 33 per cent of those who did not behave in such a manner; 41 per cent of the ministers who intervened often outside the jurisdiction of their department were in competition with parliament, as against 34 per cent of those who did not behave in such a manner.

The collegial character of the cabinet, the role of the prime minister and the modes and extent of party–cabinet interaction

The collegial character of the cabinet might be expected to be affected by levels and forms of party–cabinet interaction, in that, if this level of interaction is high, the role of prime ministers would seem to be more to seek consensus than to force issues. This hypothesis is in part confirmed: 83 per cent of the ministers who attended party meetings regularly were also ministers who worked under a prime minister who was consensus-seeking, as against only 21 per cent of the ministers who did not attend such meetings. Some 83 per cent of the ministers who had a competitive relationship with their party executive had served under prime ministers who had a consensus-seeking role, as against 69 per cent of the ministers who were not in competition with their party.

Yet a competitive relationship between cabinet and party executive does not appear to affect the extent to which prime ministers may be forceful rather than, or as well as, being consensus-seekers. The only relationship that emerges is that linking a competitive relationship between cabinet and party executive, on the one hand, and prime ministerial influence based on consensus-seeking rather than on approaching ministers individually, on the other. Meanwhile, the competitive character of the party-cabinet relationship is more closely associated to a consensus-seeking role on the part of the prime minister in coalition governments than in other types of cabinets: there is a difference of twenty-one points between competitive and non-competitive situations in coalitions while it is only of five points in single-party governments, whether of a majority or of a minority character. Almost certainly, in single-party majority governments, little competition between party and cabinet means that the prime minister is the unchallenged leader of the party; conversely, a situation of competition between ministers and party executive pushes the prime minister towards a consensus-seeking role, not just in coalition governments, but in single-party cabinets, as, in this case, such a role tends to discourage the prime minister from wanting to play a forceful part as well. ·

Meanwhile, there is no association between prime ministerial style and the nature of the relationship between cabinet and parliamentary party. This is perhaps because prime ministers can deal with MPs by

Table 7.10 Styles of cabinet-party relationships and prime ministerial action (absolute figures)

Party–cabinet style	Consensual			Forceful		
	Yes	*No*	*% Yes*	*Yes*	*No*	*% Yes*
Both cooperative and competitive	29	5	85	12	22	35
Cooperative only	139	22	86	60	98	38
Competitve only	15	4	79	4	15	21
Neither	54	65	45	30	89	25
Total	237	96		106	224	

other means and in particular because they can exercise direct influence on parliament more easily than on the party.

Levels of cabinet conflict and the modes and extent of party-cabinet interaction

Finally, conflict levels can be expected to be related to the modes and extent of party interaction, as the more ministers are subordinated to their party, the more there might be conflict in the cabinet; if ministers are subordinated to their party, they will come to the cabinet as delegates and will therefore tend to oppose each other strongly rather than seek compromises. On the other hand, there will be less tension when ministers are trustees who have infrequent contacts with their parties, who are not bound by party directives, and who can reach compromises based on their own views.

The answers given by the ministerial respondents broadly support this expectation. In the context of direct party–cabinet relations, both the form and the style of party interaction appear to have an effect on levels of conflict. As many as 60 per cent of the ministers who did not attend party meetings normally felt that there were few or no conflicts in cabinet, while this view was shared by only 22 per cent of the ministers who attended party meetings. Some 44 per cent of the ministers who did not have any contact with their party executive experienced little or no cabinet conflicts, as against 24 per cent of those who did have such contacts. In terms of the style of party–cabinet interaction, 13 per cent of the ministers who were in competition with their party executive experienced conflicts in cabinet, while this was the case of 29 per cent of those who were not in competition with their party. The interaction with the parliamentary party leads to contrasts of the same kind.

Parties affect cabinet decision-making to a different extent, through different channels and at different periods. Three modes of interaction are particularly important in this respect. The intraparty mode refers to direct contacts between cabinet ministers and leaders of party organisations. There are considerable variations in the extent to which these contacts are institutionalised and in the extent to which they lead to binding decisions. In general, ministers tend to cooperate more closely with their party executives in coalitions than in single-party governments, and in christian democratic parties more than in conservative parties, in Finland and Norway, Ireland, Belgium, Austria, and Germany. Meanwhile, there is also competition for political power between ministers and party executives in socialist parties in general and in particular in Norway, Belgium, and Britain, while in France and the Netherlands there is neither competition nor collaboration.

Influence at the level of the relationship between cabinet and party through parliament is manifest, as specific features of the political system account for the existence and prominence of this type of link. There are more parliamentary contacts in single-party cabinets than in coalitions, as well as more among conservatives than those in other parties. In a number of countries, parliament–cabinet interaction is limited, not merely in France, but in Belgium and Italy as well (in these last two countries seemingly because direct party–cabinet links are strong); the ties are closer in the Netherlands, while the party–cabinet link operates essentially through parliament in Britain and to a lesser extent in Ireland.

Finally, the interparty mode is the mechanism by which the various parties decide about cabinet policy 'above' the government, so to speak, the party summit arrangement being the clearest manifestation of this mode of behaviour; there are variations in the spread of this mechanism across countries: party summits are important in Germany, Italy, and Finland; they occur occasionally in Belgium; they are almost unknown in France, the Netherlands, Norway, and Austria, the Austrian situation being one of close but informal cooperation among coalition partners.

These modes of relationship seem to have some limited effect on processes of decision-making in cabinets. Where cabinets are more closely influenced by the supporting party or parties, the cabinet is perhaps a little more central, and the collective character of the cabinet is a little more pronounced; collegiality is rather more marked in that prime ministers are more induced to to adopt a consensual rather than a forceful role, but conflicts are also more widespread. The nature and strength of the party–cabinet link has thus an impact on the characteristics of Western European cabinet governments.

Notes

1. See Chapter 1, note 3, for a reference to the literature on 'party government'. See also the bibliography on p. 320.
2. J. Blondel and F. Müller Rommel (1988), p. 11.
3. See Chapter 1.

176 *The Link between Cabinets and Parties*

4. Or in the case of a minority government the cabinet must be at least able
  to rely on a positive attitude on the part of a majority of MPs.
5. R. B. Andeweg (1988a), p. 62.
6. P. Gerlich and W. C. Müller (1988), p. 146.
7. M. Cotta (1988), pp. 135–6.
8. F. Müller-Rommel (1988a), p. 166.
9. About three ministers out of ten report to have no, or infrequent, relations with their parliamentary party.
10. Less than weekly but at least once a month.
11. W. C. Müller (1990), pp. 16–19.
12. Ibid., p. 20. Parliamentary parties have become less disciplined and also more influential.
13. B. Farrell (1988), p. 41.
14. Yet competition between ministers and party groups was reported to be significant by conservative ministers only (60 per cent).
15. D. Arter (1983), pp. 102–3.
16. E. Damgaard (1990), pp. 6–7.
17. On the other hand, decision-making processes within parliamentary parties are also closely connected to, and sometimes determined by, policy decisions of the party organisation. See T. Saalfelf (1990), p. 4.
18. As is well known, Italian parties are often divided into factions: the system of preference voting also strengthens the tendency towards rebellious behaviour on the part of individual MPs.
19. D. Arter (1983), pp. 204–5.
20. Ministers from Democrats '66 did not attend regular meetings of the parliamentary party, but the leader of the parliamentary party in the Second chamber did meet weekly with the ministers of his party; these ministers did enjoy a substantial autonomy *vis-à-vis* the backbenchers.
21. F. Müller-Rommel (1988a), p. 163.
22. Ibid., p. 158.

Part III

The Role of Individuals in Cabinet Decision-Making

8 Individual Ministers and their Role in Cabinet Decision-Making

Jean Blondel

The assessment of the role of political actors is notoriously difficult: there is still no truly conclusive evidence that 'leaders do make a difference', let alone what the extent of this difference is.[1] The question of the role of ministers in cabinet decision-making therefore poses major problems. There are practical obstacles: only detailed participant observation would reveal fully how each minister behaves. There are methodological difficulties as well: students of political leadership have for instance not been able so far to discover indicators that would measure the respective contribution made by individuals and by the environment.[2]

Yet it is valuable to explore what the role of individual ministers might be in Western European cabinets as there are a number of reasons for believing that the extent to which the government is collective or collegial is influenced by the behaviour of these ministers. It was suggested in Chapter 1 that these may be more or less inclined to participate in the affairs of the whole cabinet because of their background. Even without considering the impact of the personality characteristics of the respondents, as this would require a type of approach with which most respondents would have been uneasy, three characteristics come to mind that suggest that the behaviour of ministers may well affect substantially collective decision-making processes in cabinets. First, background characteristics are indeed likely to play a substantial part. At one extreme, ministers who are technicians are less likely to be concerned with issues that do not relate to their departments, especially if they have been appointed in order to solve a particular problem; this situation occurs less frequently in cabinet-type systems than in presidential systems, but it does happen. It seems, on the contrary, that ministers who have a less specialised background – lawyers, teachers, for instance – are more likely to be interested and involved in matters that go beyond their department. Second, and more generally, some ministers may have broad interests and indeed be competent in a number of fields. This may be a result of their past careers and, in particular, of the fact that they have previously occupied a number of ministerial posts as well as positions of junior ministers in other departments. To an extent, this is an accidental occurrence that relates to the specific characteristics of the life of some cabinet ministers; but, to an extent too, this development affects some countries more than others. Third, ministers may also be more competent to discuss matters outside their department if they are briefed in advance about the implications of matters that are to be debated. By and large, in Western Europe, it does not seem that such a briefing is very common but, on this point too, there are variations from country to country.

It is not possible in this study to assess directly the possible impact of these factors on collective decision-making, but the interviews that were conducted enable us to examine a number of parameters of this impact. Specifically, ministers who state that they have been involved in the affairs of departments other than their own would appear likely to play a larger part in the collective process than those who concentrated on their own ministry. The morale of ministers also deserves to be investigated, since levels of frustration are likely to reveal whether government members wish to extend their action but feel prevented from doing so. By analysing what makes ministers 'tick', whether they are satisfied or dissatisfied, and indeed what skills they feel they need in order to be successful, one can build gradually, albeit in a roundabout way, a picture of the part they play and of the part they want to play in the cabinet decision process.

The interview schedule administered to Western European ministers in the context of this study was naturally better able to tap attitudes than to assess behaviour, though many questions were designed to elicit from ministers information about how they had acted when they were in office. The reliability of these answers is somewhat open to question, admittedly, not so much because respondents might deliberately not tell the truth, but because, with the passage of time, memories become blurred and impressions may be therefore in part false. Yet it seems reasonable to assume that the responses given correspond broadly to the reality, with respect to both attitudes and behaviour: the conclusions of this chapter will be based on this broad picture.

The interview data make it possible to explore the part played by cabinet ministers in three main ways. First government ministers can be classified in terms of the extent to which they regard themselves as having been active, both as departmental heads and as members of the cabinet: from this examination emerges an impression of the proportions of ministers who fulfil their function in a manner approximating the model of parliamentary government. It might be thought that respondents would tend to embellish the part they played; this seems not to be the case. Second, we can observe the extent to which ministers are satisfied with the whole cabinet machinery and with the relations that they had with those who were close to them, civil servants, party leaders, parliamentarians. Third, we can examine what ministers say about the type of background that they regard as helpful for a governmental career: do they feel, for instance, that technical expertise is truly valuable? Do they believe that it is useful to have been an MP? By analysing reactions to these three elements, one can get at least a partial impression of the manner in which ministers feel that they contributed to the cabinet decision process.

This composite picture of ministerial role and of ministerial assessments about cabinet decision-making processes can be related to the single-party or coalition structure of the governments, to the nature of the party or parties in the government, and to the general characteristics of the cabinet in the different countries in order to see how far ministerial attitudes may be shaped by these factors. After having described, in the first part of this chapter, how ministers assess their role and the qualities that they feel are required to make a good minister, we shall therefore examine how far the way in which ministers see their involvement and that of others in the cabinet appears to be fashioned by the cabinet party structure, by aspects of the nature of the party or parties in the government, and by specific country characteristics.

HOW INCLINED ARE MINISTERS TO PARTICIPATE IN GOVERNMENTAL AFFAIRS?

Extent and levels of activity: from 'activists' to 'spectators'

The extent to which members of political elites participate in the activities of the bodies to which they belong varies appreciably, as has been established by many studies. For instance, Headey suggests, in his study of *British Cabinet Ministers*, that these differed markedly in the way they approached their tasks: he describes them as ranging from 'policy initiators' to 'minimalists'. In an earlier work on Connnecticut legislators, *The Lawmakers*, Barber found that these ranged from real 'lawmakers' to 'spectators'.[3] Similarly, members of Western European cabinets are not equally involved in the affairs of the governments in which they participate: indeed, the candour with which the respondents described the level of their own involvement was remarkable.

In parliamentary governments, the involvement of ministers has two distinct aspects which can be regarded as being almost contradictory since governments' members are in charge of a department, on the one hand, and elaborate cabinet policy jointly with their colleagues, on the other. This is the direct consequence of the fact that the heads of at least the most important departments form a collective cabinet. Indeed, the role of ministers could be regarded as extending more broadly into the life of the parties, the life of parliament, and indeed public life in general, as Headey points out;[4] but these activities should be viewed as extensions of ministerial tasks: they are consequential on the part played by ministers in their department or in the cabinet, for instance to explain or defend their policies. Departmental and cabinet activities are different: they are part of the definition of the ministerial job; yet they are distinct as well as complementary. They are complementary to the extent that ministers may need to use the cabinet arena to press for departmental policies and then be, as Headey puts it, 'departmental battle axes';[5] but these activities are also distinct in that ministers may be involved in matters that are not related to their department: such ministers are the 'all-rounders' who devote some of their time and energy to extra-departmental matters.

The existence of these two broad types of ministerial activities leads to the conclusion that there are two dimensions according to which cabinet members may be more or less active. To simplify, one can reduce these dimensions to a four-fold division, ministers being regarded as 'active' or 'inactive' (in relative terms) with respect to their department and with respect to non-departmental matters at cabinet level. One can therefore speak of 'fully active ministers', of 'spectators', of 'departmentalists', and of 'generalists'.

Active and less active departmental ministers

The 'activism' of ministers with respect to their departmental tasks can be assessed here on the basis of answers to four questions that were put to respondents. These four questions were designed to ascertain whether ministers were prepared to act on their own even when they were confronted with problems of an innovative character, with problems that were politically 'hot', with problems that involved heavy costs, or with problems requiring coordination (a fifth question – 'on other grounds' – resulted in a variety of answers which it is difficult to bring together under one rubric). The answers to the four questions reveal who has wanted to be truly active and who has not and who is and who is not prepared to act without being overconcerned with the reactions of colleagues.

Taken separately, the answers to each of these questions suggest that a minority of ministers only, but a substantial minority, can be regarded as 'departmental activists': between a quarter and 40 per cent of all the ministers interviewed replied that they were not prevented from acting alone because they were confronted with a situation falling into one of the categories that we listed. This is a substantial proportion, indeed probably larger than might have been expected, though it corresponds broadly to the proportion of 'policy initiators' identified by B. Headey (23 out of 50 or 46 per cent).[6] Moreover, only on two of these questions (matters that are politically 'hot' and matters involving coordination) was the number of those who stated that they could not act on their own markedly larger than that of those who said they could; there were more 'active' than 'inactive' ministers in the context of matters requiring innovation while the numbers of 'active' and 'inactive' were almost the same with respect to matters involving high expenditure.

The answers to these questions can be taken together, moreover, and provide the basis for a complex measure of ministerial 'activism' at the departmental level, for these answers appear to proceed from a single underlying factor. There is therefore a general dimension of ministerial 'activism' with respect to departmental matters.[7]

Ministers as more or less active members of the cabinet

Constitutionally at least, a minister's role in cabinet government is not merely to be the head of a department: it is also to be involved in the life of the government as a whole. One can participate in the life of the government in two different ways, however, as was pointed out earlier: one can be a 'departmental battle axe' or an 'all-rounder'. In the first case, the minister's main contribution consists of fighting for the department of which he or she is the head: this is not truly a form of collective participation, but rather a different way of being a departmental head. Only 'all-rounders' are genuinely involved in collective decision-making. Thus, if we are to measure the activism of ministers as members of the cabinet, we have to concentrate on the extent to which they are involved in matters that extend beyond the jurisdiction of their department: this is the object of one question of the interview schedule, the matter being underlined by a subsequent question in which respondents were asked to state how far, in general, other members of the cabinets to which they belonged did or did not also act beyond the jurisdiction of their departments.

The responses to both questions, both separately and jointly, are revealing. Very few ministers (5 per cent) claimed that none of their colleagues went beyond their jurisdiction in the cabinet, while over half – indeed 57 per cent of those who answered the question – claimed that ministers did so occasionally and nearly two-fifths suggested that it was a common occurrence. As far as their own behaviour was concerned, ministers responded broadly in the same manner, except that the proportion of those who said that they never went beyond their jurisdiction was appreciably higher (15 per cent) and the proportion of those who said that they did so occasionally was correspondingly lower (52 per cent). The correlation between the two answers is high, as was to be expected: indeed, only one respondent stated that he or she participated beyond his or her jurisdiction while also stating that other ministers never did so. By and large, the group of those who stated that they never participated is drawn from among those who said that ministers in general only acted occasionally beyond their own departmental jurisdiction. Meanwhile, while 87 ministers claimed that they had participated less than the rest of the ministers, 53 stated that they had participated more: this last group is, differentially at least, the most active of all in terms of cabinet decision-making.[8]

Activists, spectators, departmentalists and generalists

Ministers in cabinet government are expected to be both active heads of their departments and active members of the government; it is the second capacity which makes, as we know, the originality of cabinet government since, by being active government members, ministers contribute to the collective character of the cabinet. Yet the answers given by Western European ministers show that many of these are not very active, neither as heads of their departments nor as collective members of the government. The cut-off point between 'more' and 'less' activity is naturally somewhat arbitrary; the distinction is therefore relative, but it reveals substantial differences. At one

extreme there are the ministers who are fully active: they fulfil entirely
the requirements of the job; they look after the interests of their
departments and undertake initiatives in that capacity; yet they are also
involved in the affairs of the whole government. This group forms
about one in ten of the respondents (9 per cent): on the basis of this
evidence, it would seem that the requirements of cabinet government
are somewhat theoretical, especially since the ministers at the opposite
end of the range, those who can be regarded as being 'spectators', are
four times more numerous and form two-fifths of the total.

It may be somewhat one-sided to draw too rapidly the conclusion
that ministers are rather inactive, however, if one considers the other
two groups, the 'departmentalists' and the 'generalists'. The first of
these includes those ministers who take their job as head of a
department to heart, but who do not or only marginally fulfil the task
of membership of a collective cabinet: they form a sixth of the total. If
one adds to these the fully active, one therefore finds that only a little
over a quarter of all the ministers are fully engaged in their role as
departmental heads. This is an appreciably smaller proportion than
that of those who take a substantial part in the collective life of the
government as these include, on top of the 9 per cent who are fully
active, 30 per cent who are 'generalists'.

Table 8.1   'Departmentalists' and generalists (absolute figures)

| | | Active in departments | | |
		Yes	No	
Active in cabinet	Yes	Activists 25	Generalists 81	106
	No	Departmentalists 48	Spectators 118	166
		73	199	272

Many cabinet ministers can thus be regarded as 'spectators' as they
appear to play, by their own recognition, a limited part in the life of the
cabinet and take few initiatives with respect to their department; but
about as many cabinet ministers are also involved in the collective life of
the cabinet as a whole. This seems to provide support for the view that
cabinets constitute genuine groups whose members often interact.

Indeed, perhaps it is the 'ideology' of the cabinet itself that contributes indirectly to the proportion of 'departmentalists' being relatively low, as ministers may well consider that they would be going against the spirit of collective government if they were to take too many initiatives. On balance, therefore, the conclusion must be mixed: while many ministers seem by their attitudes to contribute to a moderate extent to the collective character of the cabinet, many also must contribute to a reduction of this collective process, either because they are strong 'departmentalists' (as if they were members of a presidential government) or because their commitment to their job is relatively limited.

Contentment with the *status quo* and the participation of ministers in cabinet affairs

By and large, cabinet government has functioned relatively smoothly in Western Europe since the Second World War, though there have been notable exceptions, such as France before 1958, Italy, and perhaps Belgium and Finland, at various points during the period. There have been complaints about the process, often voiced by academics; yet the system has functioned. One can perhaps expect as a result that the practitioners of politics, the ministers, might be broadly satisfied with the *status quo*. On the other hand, the collective character of the cabinet is rather limited: while this may be, as we saw, the result of the fact that many ministers remain 'spectators' and some others are 'departmentalists', these modes of behaviour may in turn be the result of the fact that ministers do not want – or do not feel able – to change the *status quo*. They may therefore accept to operate decision-making processes in which the collective element is limited; but they might still consider such a situation as far from ideal. An examination of the degree of satisfaction of respondents should make it possible to assess the extent to which there are traces of frustration.

Criticisms have not merely been levelled at the less than perfect nature of collective cabinet decision-making, however; they have also been voiced, both by observers and by insiders, at the conditions under which ministers are able to exercise their jobs as departmental heads. This has sometimes been said to be due to the fact that ministers were not competent to handle the particular department that they were running; but this has also been regarded as being the consequence of too high a turnover or of the fact that those who were close at hand – the civil servants, the party leaders, the members of parliament – were not always as helpful, to say the least, as they might have been.[9] Such comments have been made so widely that one might expect to find substantial levels of dissatisfaction among ministers about the way in which they are able to run their jobs as heads of a department as well as with respect to the overall conduct of the affairs of the government.

Ministers were asked to express their views about cabinet decision-making in a number of ways. To test the extent to which they might be uneasy about the general character of cabinet decision-making, they were asked whether they were generally satisfied with the process; to assess what they felt about their own position, they were also asked whether they had been happy with the particular post that they had held; finally, to discover whether they felt hindered in their own activity, they were asked about their views about the relationships that they had with civil servants in their departments, with their party, and with parliament. We are concerned here not so much to discover the substantive content of the answers, but to obtain an impression of the extent to which ministers are satisfied with the help they receive from those around them.

At first, it seems that the satisfaction of ministers is high on all counts: between twice and four times as many ministers express contentment as express discontentment. Yet there are appreciable differences. There is a substantial minority of discontented in relation to the general working of the cabinet (60 per cent satisfied, 26 per cent dissatisfied, with 14 per cent not replying); discontentment is much lower, indeed usually low on the more specific aspects of ministerial life: those who are satisfied constitute on three questions out of six 80 percent or more of those who give an answer.

The various forms of satisfaction and dissatisfaction are not closely related, however. Specifically, dissatisfaction with the general process of decision-making is not linked to dissatisfaction with detailed aspects of that process. The only forms of dissatisfaction that are correlated to each other are those referring to relationships with party leaders and

Table 8.2 Levels of satisfaction of ministers (percentages)

Satisfied with	Yes	No	Missing
– cabinet decision-making	60	26	14
– post(s) occupied	46	21	32
– with civil servants			
a) (not overselling)	59	11	30
b) (not blocking)	61	16	23
– with party executive	51	13	36
– with parliamentary party	51	20	29

with parliamentarians: ministers who thought that they were in 'competition' with one group also tended to feel that they were in 'competition' with the other; but those who felt that they were in some way ill-served by civil servants in their department were drawn from another group: statistical analysis shows that this form of discontentment corresponds to a different factor. Nor do either of these forms of discontentment relate markedly to dissatisfaction expressed about the particular job that the minister held or with dissatisfaction with cabinet decision-making in general. There was only a limited relationship between answers expressing discontentment about the particular job held and discontentment about relations with party leaders or parliamentarians, while there was no relationship at all between any of these forms of discontent and overall dissatisfaction with cabinet decision-making.[10]

The discontentment felt by at least some ministers has thus four different and unrelated objects and it is remarkable that these should be unrelated. In the first instance, there are the ministers who are unhappy about the cabinet decision-making process as a whole. They form a quarter of the respondents and a third of those who gave an answer to that question: to a limited extent, this form of dissatisfaction appears related to the fact that there are few opportunities to debate major issues in the cabinet; it is perhaps *prima facie* surprising that this relationship should be so small. It cannot truly be said that, as a general proposition, those who belonged to governments where there was a substantial amount of debate were markedly happier than other ministers.

Table 8.3   Levels of satisfaction and debates in cabinet

	Debates in cabinet						Total
	Always		*Sometimes*		*Rarely or never*		
	N	%	N	%	N	%	
Very satisfied	24	47	119	37	8	16	51
Satisfied	60	33	100	54	24	13	184
Dissatisfied	30	35	43	51	12	14	85
Very dissatisfied	3	21	5	36	6	43	14
No reply/ not able to cover	12	28	28	65	3	7	43
Total	129	34	195	52	53	14	377

Note: Missing 33.

What is clear, however, is that general dissatisfaction relates to the life of the cabinet as a whole and not to the specific experience of the respondents. This general dissatisfaction is not triggered by the fact that, for instance, the ministers had not received the post that they had asked for or because their relations with their party, the parliamentarians, or the civil servants of their department were not excellent: since none of these forms of discontentment correlates with the discontentment expressed at the general level, it seems at least reasonable to conclude that it is the way in which ministers interact that is being criticised. What is not clear is whether the origin of the discontentment stems from too high or too low a level of interaction.

The answer to this last point may be partly given indirectly by considering the relationship between general levels of satisfaction or dissatisfaction and levels of 'activism'. This relationship is difficult to interpret, admittedly: those who are most dissatisfied with general cabinet decision-making processes are the 'departmentalists', 35 per cent of whom are dissatisfied as against 26 per cent overall; those who are least dissatisfied are the 'generalists', only 17 per cent of whom are dissatisfied, while both the very active and the 'spetatators' are close to the average. This result suggests that 'generalists' feel able to participate in collective deecision-making while 'departmentalists' are less able to undertake the activities that they would wish to develop on behalf of their ministry. Although the difference is not very large, it seems therefore that the cabinet is 'too' collective in the eyes of those who want it to be a departmental machine, but collective enough in the eyes of those who wish the government to decide collectively. This finding leads in turn to the tentative conclusion that ministers would marginally

Table 8.4 Activism and ministerial satisfaction

| | General satisfaction | | | | |
| | Yes | | No | | |
	N	%	N	%	
Activists	17	77	5	23	22
Departmentalists	26	60	17	40	43
Generalists	59	81	14	19	73
Spectators	75	69	33	31	108
	177	72	69	28	246

Note: No reply/not able to cover/other missing 164.

welcome less collective cabinets; it can also be inferred that the attitudes of ministers are a contributory factor to the relatively limited extent to which many contemporary governments are collective.

How ministers view the importance of technical and political preparation and the impact of these views on the collective character of cabinets

Since the 1960s, a substantial literature, particularly in Britain, has extolled the virtues of the technical training of ministers and stressed the dangers of maintaining traditional ideas of amateur government. Headey discussed the matter at some length; he noted that 'half the ministers he interviewed believed that the attributes of the intelligent layman and parliamentary politician are no longer ideal qualifications for holding office'.[11] Yet this conclusion was drawn on the basis of answers given by ministers in the late 1960s in one country (Britain) where the tradition of the 'intelligent layman' in government has long prevailed. Since Headey wrote, the view that technicians should be in charge has gained some ground, especially during the 1970s, though the question did not seem to be as high on the agenda in the 1980s: Kellner's and Crowther-Hunt's work on *The Civil Servants* is perhaps the last time that a strong emphasis was placed on the need for specialisation in government.[12]

Ministers were asked four questions designed to discover what background seemed to them to be of value for a governmental career. Two of these aimed at assessing whether technical competence in general or a prior specialised knowledge of the affairs of the department were regarded as central; the third inquired of those who had been MPs whether a parliamentary experience was regarded as having been helpful; and the fourth aimed at assessing how far those who had been junior ministers felt that this had been valuable for their cabinet career.

Overall, ministers answered positively to all four questions by substantial majorities. About three-fifths of those who replied and indeed somewhat over half of all the interviewees felt that a technical background was important and the same proportion said that expertise in the field of the department of which they were the head was helpful: these findings confirm the apparent trend towards an increase in the importance given to a technical or specialised background in the course of the last decades. Among those who had been MPs and among those who had been junior ministers, even larger majorities stated that the experience was valuable for the cabinet career (70 per cent in both cases). Thus ministers would seem not just to want to have a technical background, but wish to benefit from both a specialised and a 'general-political' background. Indeed, when all four variables are correlated, they emerge as belonging to one factor only.[13]

There are differences among types of ministers, however, and in particular between the 'generalists' and the 'departmentalists'. 'Generalists' are far more anxious to have both more specialisation and more political experience than 'departmentalists'; on the whole, these stress the value of a technical training rather than that of political experience. This confirms the impression that ministers are more anxious to be better departmental heads than to be part of a collective decision-making process in the cabinet, as if, for many at least, to participate truly in collective decision-making was a kind of luxury while the 'real' activity with which they have to be concerned is that of their department.

Table 8.5 Political and technical qualities looked for by ministers related to level and form of activism (percentage)

	Political qualities only	Technical qualities only	Both	Neither	Total
Actvities	–	25	66	9	12
Departmentalists	30	45	25	–	40
Generalists	17	19	64	–	42
Spectators	31	26	42	–	87
Total	25	29	45	1	181

Note: No reply/not able to cover/other missing 239.

Western European cabinet ministers are thus moderate, but only moderate supporters of the collective character of the government. A substantial proportion does become involved in the affairs of departments other than their own, but an even larger proportion does not do so or does so only rarely; an appreciable minority is dissatisfied with cabinet decision-making processes and this minority is greater among the 'departmentalists' than among the 'generalists', as if the former wanted to have more room for manoeuvre for ministerial initiatives, while the latter were contented with the (somewhat limited) amount of collective government that exists. Finally, there is more demand and more praise for specialist training than there is for a good political background, the 'generalists' being as anxious as the 'departmentalists' to press for specialisation. Thus, while there appears to be relatively little discontentment about the level of collective decision-making, despite the fact that we know that it is generally low, there seems to be at least some desire on the part of ministers to increase departmental involvement. This does suggest that, if only to an extent, the impact of the views and patterns of behaviour of ministers on cabinet life is to reduce rather than to increase the collective character of governments.

MINISTERIAL ATTITUDES AND BEHAVIOUR AND THE ROLE OF STRUCTURAL CHARACTERISTICS OF CABINETS

Yet these views and these patterns of behaviour could be a result largely, if not wholly, of the structural characteristics of cabinets and, in particular, of the single-party or coalition composition of these cabinets. For instance, if it is the case, as was suggested earlier, that ministers with a technical training are more likely to be primarily concerned with the affairs of their own department than ministers with a training in subjects such as law or teaching and if it is also the case that there are more specialists in coalition governments than in single-party governments, at least the size of the 'departmentalist' group of ministers might be regarded as being in part the consequence of the existence of coalition governments. The question of the possible impact of the single-party/coalition dimension on the attitudes of ministers needs therefore to be examined; but this is not the only structural aspect that can have an impact: two other factors, the party composition of governments and the general rules and practices that cabinets adopt in the various countries need also to be investigated to assess the part that they play.

The impact of the single party-coalition dimension on the views and patterns of behaviour of ministers

There is indeed a relationship between the single-party/coalition distinction among cabinets and the attitudes and patterns of behaviour of ministers who compose these cabinets. The difference is not very large, but it leads to the general conclusion that ministers from single-party governments are more supportive of the collective character of cabinet decision-making than are ministers from coalition governments. First, ministers from coalition governments are a little more active as departmental heads than are ministers from single-party governments. There are less active ministers in coalition governments in terms of their willingness to undertake innovative actions on their own, but there are more 'active' ministers in this type of government with respect to two questions (politically 'hot' and coordination), while there is no difference on the fourth question (high cost). Ministers in coalition governments are therefore overall somewhat *more* likely to be active than their colleagues in single-party governments. Conversely, ministers from single-party governments are, to an extent at least, more involved in departments other than their own than ministers from coalition governments. The proportion of those who intervene frequently is about the same (approximately two-fifths) in both cases, but about a fifth of ministers from coalition cabinets never ventured outside the field of their department while in single-party cabinets only 10 per cent were in this situation. This contributes to the building of a picture of more 'generalist' ministers in single-party cabinets and of greater 'departmentalism' in coalition cabinets. Moreover and perhaps more surprisingly, members of coalition cabinets are also more frequently 'activists': this means that the 'generalists' among them are also more likely to be 'departmentalists' as well, than is the case of ministers in single-party governments.

These behavioural characteristics are underlined by the views expressed by ministers with respect to the quality of cabinet decision-making. On the one hand, there is less general dissatisfaction in single-party governments, especially in minority governments, than there is

Table 8.6 Party structure of government and types and level of activity of ministers

	Single-party minority		Single-party majority		Coalition		Total	
	N	%	N	%	N	%	N	%
Activists	3	12	3	12	19	76	25	100
Departmentalists	2	4	7	15	38	15	47	100
Generalists	12	15	25	31	43	54	80	100
Spectators	11	9	42	36	65	55	118	100
Total	28	10	77	29	165	61	270	100

in coalition governments. The difference may not be very large but it is appreciable: while only 15 per cent of the respondents in single-party minority governments are dissatisfied and while they are 22 per cent (somewhat below the average of 26 per cent) in other single-party governments, they are 30 per cent in coalition governments. Although overall satisfaction is high in all cases, the decision-making process is viewed as somewhat less satisfactory in the coalition system. This dissatisfaction is clearly directed at the way overall decisions are taken by the cabinet, as, on the other hand, there is more satisfaction among respondents from coalition governments than among respondents from single-party governments with respect to the relationship with civil servants, party leaders, and parliamentarians: while the proportion of those who were interviewed and who stated that civil servants tended to block policies is about the same, except for members of minority cabinets who were the least satisfied with civil servants, 15 per cent of members of single party cabinets as against 5 per cent of members of coalition cabinets felt that civil servants were inclined to oversell the policies they wished to see pursued; 31 per cent of the members of single-party governments as against 17 per cent among ministers from coalition cabinets also felt dissatisfied with their relationships with parliamentarians; finally, a quarter of the members of single party governments as against a fifth of the members of coalition governments felt dissatisfied with the post or posts that they held, as if ministers of single-party governments were more often appointed from above to the departments that they ran. There is thus an overall picture of greater contentment in the specialised activities of the government on the part of members of coalition cabinets which reinforces the impression that these ministers are, by and large, less inclined to give a high premium to the collective character of the government.

Finally, members of coalition governments also believe rather more than members of single-party governments that specialisation should be greater than it is, although differences are relatively small. There are also rather more ministers from coalition governments than ministers from single-party cabinets who feel that it is important to have acquired expertise in the department that one is appointed to run (52 per cent of all the respondents among ministers from coalition governments *v.* only 39 per cent among ministers from single-party governments). It is true, admittedly, that coalition government ministers also give more importance to having had parliamentary experience than do members of single-party cabinets and that the former appear therefore to feel the need for more general political experience; but they do not seem to value quite as much the managerial experience that a junior ministerial job gives: while 66 per cent of the members of coalition governments who had previously been junior ministers said that the experience was valuable, this was the view of 87 per cent of their colleagues from single-party governments.

Members of coalition governments are thus less inclined to press for collective forms of decision-making and are more inclined to praise departmental initiative and specialisation. It is of course not permissible to claim that the distinction between single-party and coalition government is the cause of the difference, but this distinction is likely to play a part in that ministers with a greater inclination to be specialists are more likely to be selected in a coalition context. Coalition governments could not function effectively if all members wanted to be markedly involved in all the affairs of the cabinet: to say the least, the selection of ministers of coalition governments does reflect this reality; departmental and specialist attitudes are also probably likely to be fostered in coalition governments even among those ministers who might otherwise have been inclined towards a more collective view of cabinet decision-making.

Party characteristics and ministerial views and patterns of behaviour

Alongside the single-party/coalition dimension, the specific character-istics of parties might be expected to be related to the views and patterns of behaviour of ministers: in reality, however, this impact remains limited. Indeed, rather remarkably, ministers from all parties (at least from all the parties that had sufficient numbers of representatives in the sample to be analysed – that is to say, conservatives, liberals, christian democrats, and socialists), divide almost exactly in the same manner on most issues relating to cabinet decision-making processes. There are, for instance, few interparty differences among ministers in terms of levels of satisfaction with the behaviour of civil servants: the relationships are uniformly regarded as good. Thus the view, sometimes expressed on the Left, that civil servants systematically block or adulterate proposals from socialist governments, is not shared by socialist ministers, a point that had already been made for Britain by Headey.[14] It must also be noted that a minority of ministers from the Right and Centre believe that civil servants are likely to block their proposals.

There is also little to differentiate ministers among the parties in terms of their approach to their role. Indeed, levels of departmental activism are equally spread across the ideological spectrum. The only difference that can be noted concerns a slight tendency for conservative and liberal ministers to be, perhaps surprisingly, somewhat less concerned to take part in the general affairs of the government than socialists and especially christian democrats. As a result, there are somewhat fewer less active christian democrats and socialists than members of the other parties, but the difference is also slight.

Table 8.7   Party of ministers and types and levels of activity of members

| | Party of minister | | | | | | | | | |
| | Socialist | | Liberals (+ Agr) | | Christian democrats | | Conserv. | | Total | |
	N	%	N	%	N	%	N	%	N	%
Activists	13	57	2	9	7	30	1	4	23	100
Departmentalists	26	58	9	20	7	16	3	6	45	100
Generalists	39	53	11	15	18	25	5	7	73	100
Spectators	49	50	22	22	14	14	13	13	98	100
Total	127	53	44	18	46	19	22	9	239	100
No reply, NATC	47	36	24	19	45	35	13	10	129	100
Grand total	174	47	68	18	91	24	35	10	368	100

Note: Other parties, missing 42.

There are some differences in levels of satisfaction among ministers of the various parties, but these are on the whole not very large. Conservatives are those who are most satisfied with cabinet decision-making in general, the most dissatisfied being the liberals, while christian democrats and socialists are in the middle. It may be that liberals are the least satisfied because, on the whole, they are the junior partners in governments and feel that they cannot have a sufficient say (though this may not be objectively the case).[15] Why conservative ministers are more satisfied is not clear, however. They are also those who are the happiest with the post or posts they hold, together with the christian democrats, while liberals and socialists are the most discontented on this point. We noted already that there were no differences with respect to the relations between ministers and the civil servants of their departments. On the other hand, there are some differences in the responses of ministers of the various parties with respect to the extent to which they experienced difficulties with their party leaders or with parliamentarians. Perhaps not surprisingly, given what is known of the relationship between socialist governments and socialist parties, socialist ministers display a higher level of discontentment than liberals and christian democrats in this respect; if conservatives do not appear to have had much difficulty in dealing with their party 'apparatus', they record a markedly low level of satisfaction with respect to their relations with parliamentarians (45 per cent claim not to be satisfied): this is indeed the only group in which the proportion of discontented ministers is larger than is that of the contented. Thus conservative ministers are happy with their job and with the nature of cabinet decision-making; they would like to be freer to 'get on with it' and they resent the interference of their backbenchers. This, as we shall see, may be partly a result of the reaction of British ministers, who form a large part of the contingent of conservative ministers and who are particularly dissatisfied in terms of their relationship with their parliamentary party.

Table 8.8   Party of minister and level of satisfaction with cabinet decision-making (percentage of dissatisfied)

		Party of minister		
Dissatisfied with	*Socialist*	*Liberal (+Agr)*	*Christian democrats*	*Conserv.*
General cabinet decision-making	28	37	20	14
Post held	24	25	14	17
Civil (a) not overselling	13	6	15	17
service (b) not blocking	17	16	13	11
Party	18	4	15	9
Parliamentary colleagues	20	13	18	45
Total N	174	68	91	35

Note: Other parties, missing 42.

Except on the matter of the ties between ministers and the parliamentary backbenchers, levels of satisfaction are thus relatively similar; in particular, there is little difference in the reaction of christian democrats and socialists who form the two largest groups of ministers interviewed. The same conclusion can be drawn from responses relating to attitudes about the value of specialisation and of a previous political experience. Surprisingly perhaps, socialists do not appear to feel the need for greater expertise: they emphasise specialisation even less than ministers of other parties, while the liberals are those who emphasise it most. The conservatives, also perhaps surprisingly, do not claim that there is less of a need for technical training than other ministers, although they are less concerned than the rest of their colleagues with expertise in the department of which they are the heads. By and large, there is consensus among ministers of all parties with respect to the value of a technical background. There is also a broad consensus among all parties with respect to the value of a parliamentary background. It is really only on the value of a junior ministerial experience that differences emerge among the parties: conservatives are particularly convinced of the value of such posts for a subsequent cabinet career, while this is less the case of members of other parties; but only half the christian democrats and a third of the socialist and liberals had such an experience, while this was the case with 86 per cent of the conservatives, among whom, as was pointed out, the British contingent constitutes a large element.

Thus national party characteristics appear not to have a marked relation with (nor arguably an impact on) the attitudes of ministers with respect to the relative importance of departmental initiative and expertise, on the one hand, and collective cabinet decision-making, on the other. This may indirectly provide evidence for the point, often repeated, that ministers become socialised to the government and to their job while in office and are in some ways closer to each other than they are to the leading members of their parties who are not ministers: the difficulties that socialist ministers state that they experienced with their party and that conservative ministers record with respect to their parliamentary backbenchers are part of this evidence. Party members and parliamentary supporters may be essential if ministers are to maintain a link with the rank-and-file in the country: yet, despite or indeed perhaps because of this situation, they seem also to be sometimes a source of dissatisfaction for at least a number of cabinet members.

COUNTRY CHARACTERISTICS AND MINISTERIAL VIEWS AND PATTERNS OF BEHAVIOUR

While party idiosyncrasies ostensibly play a very limited part and while the single-party/coalition distinction plays a significant but modest part in shaping the views and patterns of behaviour of ministers, country differences seem on the contrary to have a large effect. We noted in Chapter 1 that many cabinet characteristics were in reality based on arrangements and practices common to all the cabinets in a given country, irrespective of their single-party or coalition structure. Moreover, the study of ministerial careers also shows that an important distinction has to be made between countries in which cabinet has a truly 'parliamentary' base and those in which specialists are more numerous.[16] This may have definite effects, for instance on the mobility of ministers who might consequently tend to be 'generalists' or 'departmentalists'. In Britain, Belgium, Italy and to a lesser extent France, ministers are relatively 'mobile' in that a substantial percentage move from post to post; in the Netherlands, Germany and Austria, on the contrary, the percentage of one-post ministers is high or very high. It would therefore seem to follow that, on this ground, the potential for collective decisions in the cabinet is greater in the first group of countries than in the second. Other characteristics, for instance the presence of a substantial personal staff at the disposal of ministers, may also have an effect on the extent, and type, of influence of ministers: in this respect, ministers from France or Belgium are potentially better placed than ministers from other countries.

There are other more precise and more systematic distinctions, moreover. First, substantial country variations can be noted in the extent of ministerial 'activism'. Ministers appear most willing to act on their own in France, Germany, Sweden, and Norway: the German situation may well be a reflection of the fact that ministers have legally a substantial area of independence; French 'activism' may indirectly compensate for the hierarchical character of the semi-presidential governments of the Fifth Republic. At the other extreme are Belgium, the Netherlands, and Ireland; Britain, Denmark, Finland, Austria, and Italy are intermediate cases. In several countries, there are substantial variations from one answer to another in the proportion of 'active' ministers. On this aspect, therefore, it is difficult to draw the conclusion that country specificities are more than idiosyncratic differences, since, however large, these differences do not seem to fit any particular pattern.

This is not the case with respect to the involvement of ministers in the affairs of the cabinet as a whole. While, in France, not one minister interviewed claimed to have acted frequently beyond his or her departmental jurisdiction, this was the case of about half the respondents in Italy, Denmark, Belgium, and Ireland, of about a third of the interviewees in Norway, Britain, and Germany, and of a quarter or somewhat less of their Finnish, Dutch, Austrian, and Swedish colleagues.[17] The broad distribution of these countries corresponds to the distinction between the countries where the 'parliamentary' base is large and those in which specialists are numerous, except for the fact that one might have expected more ministers to state that they had acted frequently beyond their jurisdiction in Britain and Sweden.

If one then looks at the overall country distribution of ministers among 'activists', 'departmentalists', 'generalists', and 'spectators', fully active ministers are proportionately mostly found in five countries (Belgium, Germany, Italy, Denmark, and Finland) while 'spectators' are most numerous in France, Britain, Austria, Ireland, and Norway, a division that is difficult to interpret. On the other hand, 'generalists' tend to be more numerous in countries where cabinets tend to be truly 'parliamentary' (Britain, Ireland, Belgium, Italy, Denmark, and Norway – Norway being the only case that does not fit this pattern), while 'departmentalists' are more numerous where there are also more specialists (France, Austria, Finland, and Sweden, Sweden being perhaps surprisingly located in the group).[18] There is thus a broad relationship between the country traditions with respect to the 'parliamentary' or 'specialist' background of ministers and a greater or lesser emphasis on the collective aspects of cabinet government.

The same distinction can be found with respect to the level of satisfaction of ministers with cabinet decision-making in general. This level is very high in Austria, Germany, Denmark, and Norway, medium in Britain, the Netherlands, and Finland, rather low in Belgium, Ireland, and Italy, and very low in France. Only France does not fit the expected pattern since, elsewhere, ministers are more satisfied in the less parliamentary countries (Austria, Norway) than in the more parliamentary countries (Belgium, Ireland, Italy), with Britain, the Netherlands, and Finland being intermediate cases. The lower level of satisfaction in the more 'parliamentary' countries does not appear to be a result of the fact that the collective character of the cabinet is too low, however, but seems to result, on the contrary, from the impression that ministers have that their impact on their department is not as large as they would have liked, as we noted earlier; in the less parliamentary countries where specialisation is greater, on the other hand, satisfaction is higher. The very low level of satisfaction of French ministers may therefore be the only example of the opposite view: in a country that used to be highly 'parliamentary' before 1958 and in which ministers seem to have almost no say in collective decision-making, frustration may consequently be high.

The contrast between countries where cabinets are strongly parliamentary and those where ministers are often specialists does not affect levels of satisfaction with particular aspects of governmental life – for instance, in terms of the relationship of government members with their parties, the parliamentarians, or the civil servants. Differences in this respect do not appear to follow any general trend but rather to correspond to particular country situations. Thus satisfaction is on the whole relatively low in the Netherlands and in Britain, while it is high in Austria and France.

Finally, there are also large differences from country to country with respect to the attitudes of ministers to the value of a specialised training or of a general political background. *Prima facie*, the differences that can be found are rather difficult to interpret, however. For instance, it is not immediately clear why four-fifths of the Norwegian and German ministers should feel that expertise in the department of which a

Table 8.9   Level of ministerial satisfaction per country (percentages of dissatisfied)

	Total country numbers of cases	Dissatisfaction with:				
		General cabinet decision-making	Post held	Civil service	Party	Parliamentary colleagues
Austria	28	14	0	10	14	7
Belgium	44	34	32	9	30	11
Britain	40	38	50	15	27	70
Denmark	28	18	18	25	7	21
Finland	42	29	29	5	7	29
France	29	52	21	3	0	8
Germany	24	4	–	–	12	8
Ireland	33	45	42	45	6	30
Italy	23	43	39	42	9	13
The Netherlands	24	33	17	33	8	17
Norway	36	17	6	11	31	17
Total	359					
Missing *	61					

Note: * Sweden is excluded because of missing data.

minister is the head is important, while less than a third of their British colleagues and less than two-fifths of their French colleagues have the same view. There are similarly large and somewhat puzzling differences on the other questions: while two-thirds of all respondents from Denmark, Germany, and France think that a parliamentary background is valuable, this is the case of only about a third of their British and Austrian colleagues; while nearly all the British respondents feel that a junior ministerial background is a bonus, only two-fifths of their Finnish colleagues react in the same manner.

Yet a closer examination of the differences suggests that there are three distinct patterns. In four countries, the Netherlands, Finland, Denmark, and Ireland, responses follow broadly the same trend as they do in Western Europe on average across the four questions relating to matters of background, whether specialised or general-political, though the responses are markedly more positive in Denmark and Ireland, somewhat more negative in Finland, and about average in the Netherlands. In four countries, Belgium, Italy, Austria, and Norway, ministers insist on the need for technical and departmental expertise, while they are relatively lukewarm about a parliamentary or junior ministerial background. French and British ministers have the converse attitude, except that in this last country great stress is placed on the part played by junior ministerial positions in the development of a cabinet career, but not on a parliamentary background. Only Germany can be said to be somewhat erratic, the emphasis being placed on both departmental and parliamentary experience, but not on either a technical or a junior ministerial background. Although the attitudes of Swedish ministers cannot be fully ascertained in this respect, because no information was available on two questions, less stress is placed, as in France, on the value of a specialised background and more emphasis is given to the value of a parliamentary background. While responses of British ministers are broadly along the expected lines, even if the limited importance given to parliamentary experience is surprising, the responses of French ministers are consistent with the apparent frustration that was noted earlier: these ministers seem to feel that the cabinets to which they belonged were overtechnical or over-specialised and did not allow as a result for much, if any, collective decision-making.

There is thus some division of opinion among the ministers of the various countries as to what background is most suited for cabinet members. This division of opinion does not altogether follow the cleavage between countries where cabinets include many specialists and countries where this is not the case, however: the distinction is more complex. In some countries, cabinet members appear to wish to have what they do not have, while in other countries ministers appear satisfied with the type of background and training that exists. The first situation corresponds primarily to the cases of Belgium, Italy, Denmark, and France: in Belgium, Denmark, and Italy, ministers want cabinet members to be better prepared technically with less emphasis being placed on political experience; this is consistent with the view, which was noted earlier, that 'generalists' are far more anxious than 'departmentalists' to have both forms of training. The only country that does not fit this pattern is France, where the converse is true. On the other hand, Austrian, Norwegian, and Dutch ministers appear satisfied with the type of background from which cabinet members are currently drawn; British ministers have broadly a similar attitude, but the stress placed on the importance of a junior ministerial experience suggests that they feel that a managerial training is also valuable.

These findings can be summarised in a different way: with the exception of France, ministers of countries in which technicians are numerous praise technical training, while ministers from countries in which technicians are relatively rare also emphasise the need for a technical background rather than for a political experience, Ireland and Britain being the only exceptions among these: Irish ministers wish to benefit more from both types of experience, while British ministers seem only to want a greater emphasis to be placed on management training.

Therefore, country characteristics apparently play a substantial part in shaping the views and practices of ministers, a part that seems indeed larger than that which is apparently played by the single-party/coalition distinction. This impact takes two forms. One of these can be regarded as idiosyncratic, perhaps because only one country has had a given type of experience. Thus only French cabinets have moved suddenly, indeed almost overnight, from a fully 'parliamentary' to a rather technocratic government; thus Britain is the country in which junior ministers have played the greatest part for the longest period.

The other form that the impact of country characteristics takes suggests a marked influence of the distinction between more 'parliamentary' and more specialist cabinets. There is greater stress on collective government in the first case than in the second; yet more collective government does not mean greater satisfaction on the part of the ministers, their colleagues from the less 'parliamentary' cabinets being, on the whole, more contented with patterns of decision-making; finally, and somewhat perversely given the aims of cabinet government, ministers from the more 'parliamentary' countries appear to wish they had had a more specialised background. Whether the distinction between countries where cabinets are more 'parliamentary' and those where cabinets are more specialised plays overall a larger part in shaping the character of contemporary Western European governments than does the distinction between single-party governments and coalition governments is not altogether certain: what is certain is that both distinctions need to be taken into account in an analysis of the reasons why ministers participate more or less in collective cabinet decision-making.

Western European ministers display large differences in the way in which they interpret their role; they also vary appreciably in the beliefs that they hold about what makes a 'good' or an influential minister. This was to be expected, in view of the basic dilemma between more or less collective or collegial and more 'hierarchical' forms of cabinet government. Thus the countries in which governments are more collective tend also to be those in which ministers are more anxious to become involved in matters outside their departmental brief; but differences among ministers also relate to other dimensions: perhaps the most striking case is that of French cabinet members who appear frustrated because of the relatively limited role of cabinet deliberations and because of the rather technical and streamlined character of the governments to which they belong. A similar, though less pronounced, feeling of frustration appears to exist in other countries: British ministers seem to feel the need for more managerial training; Belgian and Italian ministers wish to have had more technical experience.

Yet, overall, Western European ministers seem broadly happy with the general context in which they operate. How far this general satisfaction is in part a recognition that little can be done to change the system or how far it is the result of a socialisation process is difficult to tell, though the finding that 'departmentalist' ministers are more satisfied than are 'generalists' seems to suggest that, at least among some cabinet members, there is little pressure for an increase in collective decision-making. Most ministers are transient; most have also spent a substantial part of their adult life – at any rate, their political life – hoping to reach the cabinet: it is perhaps not surprising that there should not be a widespread desire to entertain the idea of major changes in the *status quo*. As long as this is the case – and the situation is unlikely to alter significantly – the ratio between collective and departmental aspects of ministerial life is also likely to display little change.

Notes

1. From the title of the work of V. Bunce, *Do New Leaders Make a Difference?* (1981).
2. See J. Blondel (1987), pp. 80–114, for a discussion of ways in which the analysis of the respective role of leaders and of the environment might be undertaken.
3. B. Headey (1974), pp. 23–4. J. D. Barber (1968), in particular pp. 19–21.
4. B. Headey (1974), p. 50–5.
5. Ibid., p. 49.
6. Ibid, p. 60.
7. The four components are related in forming an underlying factor. The figures are:

	Factor matrix
Var 03	.67546
Var 04	.58849
Var 05	.68467
Var 06	.62326

8. Fifty-three respondents stated that they acted themselves beyond their jurisdiction, often while also stating that the bulk of ministers did so occasionally.
9. The question of the relationship between ministers and civil servants has been often discussed, in many cases to suggest that ministers were not obeyed or had their proposals blocked. This was said in particular by R. H. S. Crossman in his *Diaries of a Cabinet Minister*. Most ministers do not appear to share this viewpoint: see below.
10. The factor loadings are:

	F 1	F 2
Var 37 (Gen satisfaction)	.20524	−.03220
Var 78 (Posts occupied)	.50278	.02639
Var 80 (Oversell)	.11806	−.82940
Var 81 (Blocking)	−.10500	−.88106
Var 86 (Party exec.)	.73636	−.06670
Var 90 (Parl. party)	.79903	.13268

11. B. Headey (1974), p. 62ff.
12. P. Kellner and Lord Crowther-Hunt (1977). J. D. Aberbach *et al.* (1981) place no emphasis on the problem.

13. The factor loadings are:

	F 1
Var 74 (Expertise)	.62921
Var 75 (Specialisation)	.70410
Var 76 (Parl. experience)	−.55006
Var 77 (Jun. minister)	−.63058

14. B. Headey (1974), p. 14.
15. It was found that, in reality, at least the German liberals did gain appreciably from their pivotal position, however small they were. See R. Hoffebert and H. Klingemann (1990), *passim*.
16. J. Blondel and J.-L. Thiébault (1991), chs 5 (L. De Winter, 'Party and parliamentary pathways to the cabinet') and 6 (W. E. Bakema, 'The ministerial career').
17. We had occasion to note in Chapter 4 the relatively limited extent to which discussion takes place in the French cabinet: the fact that it is not larger may have some relationship with the low level of satisfaction of French ministers which we shall examine shortly.
18. In Germany, the proportions of the two groups are identical and, in the Netherlands, some questions on 'activism' had not been asked.

9   The Role and Position of Ministers of Finance

Torbjörn Larsson

The collective and collegial leadership of the executive branch is a basic principle of parliamentary systems, as we know; but, as we also noted, this principle is flouted for many structural reasons as well as because the ministers themselves are far from being always eager to participate, or at least to participate fully, in collective and collegial decision-making.

Moreover, another characteristic of contemporary cabinets reinforces the tendency towards oligarchical rule – namely, that some ministers hold a position that enables them, indeed typically forces them to play a key part in the life of the cabinet. On the one hand, inner groups sometimes appear to control decision-making, although, as was pointed out in previous chapters, the general extent to which this trend exists remains clouded to some extent in mystery. On the other hand, and more explicitly, a dual leadership has been a recurrent feature of many governments both in the past and in the contemporary world: parliamentary government can indeed be said to have started in the form of dual leadership arrangement between King and prime minister.[1] Such an arrangement has typically given way to the single leadership of the prime minister in Western Europe, although the dual leadership of president and prime minister continues to be a characteristic of French and to an extent Finnish, governments. Meanwhile, another form of dual leadership has emerged in many Western European cabinets, as a result of the part played by ministers of finance alongside the heads of governments. By the very nature of the position that they occupy, ministers of finance interfere in a vast number of decisions taken by other cabinet members; for very few governmental decisions of any significance do not have financial implications.

As ministers of finance have such a key role, they are bound to develop a special relationship with prime ministers. It is also a relationship that has no equivalent: to an extent, the minister of finance can even be regarded as a second prime minister, since no other minister is involved in all the aspects of the life of the cabinet in the way the minister of finance is. There may be a special relationship between prime ministers and ministers of foreign affairs, but such a relationship touches only one aspect, however important, of governmental life; as a matter of fact, foreign affairs questions primarily play a major part in large countries. Meanwhile, ministers of finance relate to prime ministers everywhere and on almost every issue. Thus, if there are cabinet members who can be expected to be 'above' the others and who are likely to belong to an inner group where such a body exists, ministers of finance are those most likely to be among them. Other ministers recognise this situation well: the large majority of those who answered a question designed to find out who were the two most important ministers mentioned the minister of finance; indeed, those who did not, cited special reasons (such as newness of the incumbent) to account for the fact that the minister of finance was not regarded as one of the two top ministers in the particular case.[2]

The power and influence of ministers of finance stem from their relationship with three kinds of actors. We have just mentioned their link with the prime minister; a second type of link relates them to all ministers in the cabinet; and the third type of relationship is with the civil servants in the ministry and, through these, with economic and financial influentials. Although we concentrate in this volume on the role of ministers within the cabinet and the government, the part played by such a key external factor as the ministry of finance needs to be recorded: both the strength of ministers of finance in cabinets and the constraints imposed on these ministers depend to a large extent on how they interact with officials of the ministry and, beyond these, with the economic and financial community at large.

THE MINISTRY OF FINANCE AND THE CONSTRAINTS ON ECONOMIC POLICY

Economic decision-making is of manifest significance for a nation's prosperity. This means that economic constraints on the government are likely to be severe. Not only does the government not have real control over the economy, but it has to consider standpoints taken by a variety of interests, to a large part private, that play an important part in economic decision-making processes. These interests are typically articulated in both formal and informal bodies, which markedly reduce the room for manoeuvre of all governments, including those that are elected with large majorities.

Independently from the constraints imposed by the many private interests, a number of institutions may, and indeed often do, restrict the freedom of action of ministers of finance. One major constraint is constituted, in many countries at least, by the central bank. Central banks appear to have strengthened their position in the course of the last decades and thus to have recovered a large part of the prestige that they lost immediately after the Second World War.[3] The role of the central bank is reinforced by the fact that, as has often been pointed out, there is a close relationship in many countries between the officials of the ministry of finance – who are the arms of the minister – and those of the central bank. This relationship spills over to the banking system in general and to large businesses, both at the national and at the international level.[4] Treasuries have normally a vast network of contacts with banks and other financial institutions, though who influences whom in each case is not entirely clear. What is clear is that ministers of finance cannot ignore this network and that they are often confronted as a result with a vast lobby in which it is difficult for them to make their voice felt.

Indeed central banks, such as those of the United States and of Germany, have independent power in the economic field since they have the right to take decisions that the cabinet cannot control. Collaboration rather than conflict may develop as a result and, for instance, the governor of the German Bundesbank has typically participated in cabinet discussions about important economic issues: although he does not have a vote, his arguments naturally carry great weight.[5] Influence by consultation, as this type of arrangement might be called, has not been restricted to Germany: it is a factor of some significance in Italy, for instance.[6] In Britain, several important economic decisions have been taken by the prime minister, the chancellor of the exchequer, the head of the Bank of England and small groups of civil servants: the rest of the cabinet did not know that the meetings had taken place.[7]

Rumours of the treasury and the central bank plotting together are also common. The goal can either be to get rid of a minister of finance who is not performing in ways that these economic decision-makers like or to prepare the cabinet for 'economic realism' by holding back vital information. It is difficult to know how much real substance these conspiracy theories have, however.[8] Moreover, to add to the web of bodies that constrain ministers of finance, international organisations constitute increasing constraints on governmental economic policy.

Overall, it is worth distinguishing between micro- and macro-economic matters when looking at the role of the minister of finance. Admittedly, the dividing line between micro- and macro- is somewhat blurred: the size of the budget may result in inflation and this may in turn lead to a decision to make substantial cuts in government spending. Yet a large part of the preparation of the budget is regarded as being of little or of no general political importance to most ministers and to the whole cabinet, in contrast to macro-economic decisions such as whether there should be an increase in interest rate or a devaluation of the currency. It is to be expected that different procedures will therefore be used with respect to micro- and macro-economic issues.

PRIME MINISTER AND MINISTER OF FINANCE: PARTNERS OR COMPETITORS?

The type of relationship existing between the formal leader of the cabinet and the minister in charge of economic policy is critical to the cabinet decision-making process. At one extreme, there can be severe competition and, at the other, there can be partnership. In general, although prime ministers may have particular areas of interest, they are unlikely to spend a large amount of time or effort on micro-economic issues: their power and efforts will be mostly directed towards macro-economic matters. They may occasionally be drawn towards a micro-economic problem, however, if a conflict emerges within the cabinet itself, with the opposition, or with an interest organisation; they are then forced to devote their attention to the problem.

In fact, how much attention the prime minister pays to macro-economics is to some extent determined by background factors. A head of government who is an ex-minister of finance is more likely to maintain a keen interest in economics, both micro- and macro-, as was the case with Callaghan or Schmidt, who displayed more interest in economic matters than their respective predecessors.[9] More generally, a prime minister with a background in economics or who dealt previously with economic matters is more likely to be concerned with economic issues that come up in the cabinet. Such a career background is rare for prime ministers in Western Europe, however: in the period studied here, only twenty-five prime ministers had been ministers of finance before becoming heads of the government: that is to say, about one in nine of all ministers of finance and about one in ten of all prime ministers. It is in Finland that ministers of finance appear to have the highest probability of becoming prime ministers.[10]

Background is of course not the only important variable in this respect. To begin with, where the head of State is very influential, as in France and to a more limited extent in Finland, the relationship between prime minister and minister of finance may be affected because the president may occasionally want to use the minister of finance against the prime minister, even if, by and large, the president tends to concentrate on foreign affairs.

Coalitions may also affect the relationship between ministers of finance and prime ministers. There is a risk of tension between them if they come from different parties. Moreover, as we know, important matters may be dealt with by party leaders in coalitions. Thus the effect may be a reduction of the power of both the prime minister and the minister of finance. This may happen because many questions of an economic character are regarded as sensitive and are therefore dealt with by party leaders rather than by the minister of finance. The conduct of macro-economic policy may also be regarded as more of a political process in a coalition government than in a single-party government where the expertise of economists may be given greater leeway.

The relationship between prime minister and minister of finance is also affected by the extent of specialisation of the bodies that serve them. Ministers of finance have very large administrative machines at their disposal: whenever they need advice on economic issues, this advice can be readily given; as we saw in Chapter 6, prime ministers' offices are typically much smaller than ordinary government departments, even where, as in Germany, they are substantial: heads of governments can therefore afford only a limited number of economic advisers. Indeed it is not unusual for prime ministers not to have any economic advisers at all, even if this is less the case currently: prime ministers' offices are so small in Sweden and Norway, for instance, that special economic advisers to heads of governments are very few. Even in Britain, where the prime minister has the formal title of 'First Lord of the Treasury' (a title with no practical significance), economic advisers without ties to the chancellor of the Exchequer are few. Yet, recently at least, the group has increased and indeed notorious clashes occurred in the 1980s: the departure of Nigel Lawson from the chancellorship in 1989 can be attributed in large part to a conflict with a member of the prime minister's office. However, prime ministers may not always be prepared to follow the advice given to them by their special advisers: Harold Wilson installed a unit in the prime minister's office in the 1970s but he did not back this unit: much of the work that this unit did was not used because of the lack of support of the head of the government.[11] Moreover, prime ministers may not find specialists who do not agree with the views of treasury officials and are truly competent or carry sufficient prestige:[12] their chances of receiving alternative economic advice on a permanent basis are therefore rather slim.

Overall, there appear to be substantial differences in the extent to which prime ministers exercise influence in economic matters, according to Western European ministers. While almost all the British respondents felt that they were most influential, only about a quarter to a third of their colleagues from Austria, Italy, Germany, and Finland felt the same, and about two-fifths of their colleagues from Denmark. The only other countries where a majority of cabinet ministers felt that prime ministers were influential in economic matters were France, Ireland, and Norway.

Table 9.1 Prime ministers judged as being most influencial in economic matters (percentages)

Britain	98
France	73
Norway	61
Ireland	61
Denmark	39
Finland	32
Germany	29
Italy	27
Austria	23

Note: Answers to this question are not available for the Netherlands and Sweden.

THE MINISTER OF FINANCE *v.* THE CABINET AND OTHER MINISTERS

In the previous chapter, we saw that individual ministers often did not wish to play a major part in decision-making outside their own departmental area. The question of the role of the minister of finance goes deeper: what is at stake is how far ministers are willing to accept that the treasury or its head will effectively supervise the activity of their own department.

The distinction made earlier between micro-economic and macro-economic matters applies here. With respect to micro-economic policies, it is probably generally the department, rather than the minister, that plays the largest part. Issues are discussed at official level. Thus the treasury checks the proposals in advance: this procedure is well known to all and is basically accepted, both by the officials in the departments and by the ministers. In this respect, the game played by the spending ministries and the spending ministers, on the one hand, and the treasury and the minister of finance, on the other, tends to be the same everywhere. The spending ministries want to receive more; the treasury protects the budget by contesting much of what is being proposed by way of increased expenditure. Unless a department wishes to turn the issue into a major political conflict, the haggling will take place at the level of officials and therefore will involve the treasury rather than the ministers.

Behind the haggling lies a continuous struggle to find ways of allocating limited resources. The idea is not that one side should always win and the other lose, but rather that both sides should be strong and that the strength should be evenly distributed, thus enabling the best possible allocation of the resources to different public demands. If the spenders become too powerful, some sectors will be neglected and there will eventually be an outcry. The type of crisis management that will inevitably follow is not in the interest of the government as a whole nor indeed of the minister of finance or the treasury who prefer controlled and planned expansion or contraction of public expenditure. It is therefore not in the interest of the treasury to have weak spending departments and weak spending ministers, although, when confronted with such a situation, the treasury will take advantage of it;[13] indeed treasury officials tend to believe that they are the elite of the civil service and that they therefore would run other departments far better and more efficiently.[14] Yet, despite these problems, it is not in the interest of the spending departments to have a weak minister of finance, since too much giving-in by the treasury will only result in crises later on.

If a conflict arises and a minister wishes to fight an issue, two alternatives are open. One consists of trying to bring the question to the cabinet: such a strategy is not very common, however, as the minister knows that colleagues will only give reluctant support, since an increase in one minister's estimates will lead to cutbacks or smaller increases elsewhere. Moreover, colleagues regard a minister as weak and indecisive if problems with the minister of finance are brought too often to the cabinet meeting by that minister.

The second route consists of going to the prime minister: this brings us back to the special relationship between prime minister and minister of finance. The prime minister cannot allow himself to support spending ministers too often, because, if the minister of finance is not generally backed, the prime minister will be inundated with requests for re-discussion of matters turned down by the minister of finance. The prime minister would find that he or she is filling two jobs, with disastrous results for the economy.[15] Moreover, a minister of finance who is constantly overruled by the prime minister will soon grow tired of his position and quit. Thus the survival instinct will normally prevent the prime minister from overruling the minister of finance, especially with respect to micro-economic issues. Yet the role of the minister of finance in micro-economics is rather passive, as the initiative to change policies in an area comes, to a large extent, from the spending minister concerned.[16]

Thus, overall, individual ministers will not necessarily gain much by battling with the ministry of finance over micro-economic issues; but it is not clear that this should be regarded as a sign of influence of the *minister* of finance as such, as distinct from the department as a whole. The fact that the ministry can often impose its views on other departments is part of the somewhat hierarchical structure of governments which was referred to earlier and which gives the treasury a superior status. It is probably none the less true that, at any rate in the last resort, the fact that the minister of finance is able to impose the view of the treasury when matters come exceptionally to the cabinet or are referred to the prime minister indicates that he or she is not a minister as any other.

THE MINISTER OF FINANCE AND OTHER ECONOMIC MINISTERS

With respect to macro-economics, the minister of finance often plays a more active part; yet, even there, the influence of the minister can be restricted. This power is limited by the power that a few important ministries may have. This is true for instance of agriculture, labour and employment, social security, and health; but this is particularly true when a ministry of economics or of economic affairs exists alongside the ministry of finance. This practice has tended to develop, though typically with mixed results at best. There are now many countries in which a ministry of economic affairs exists alongside the ministry of finance, but there are substantial variations in the relative influence of these economic departments and of the ministers who head them. In some countries, such as Sweden, Norway, Britain, and Italy, one minister is always regarded as senior; on the other hand, in Belgium, the Netherlands, and Denmark, it is more difficult to discover who is the leader in the field.[17]

If economic responsibilities are split, conflicts between ministers and between ministries can be multiplied: for instance, there is often tension between ministries with budgetary responsibilities and ministries with responsibilities for macro-economic issues or long-term economic policy. More generally, the nature of the relationship between these ministries and their heads is determined in part by the reasons for the creation of an economics ministry. These reasons are of three types. Sometimes, the ministry of economic affairs is set up as a counter to the ministry of finance, as in Britain in 1964;[18] a similar development occurred in Italy.[19] In some cases, the division is introduced in order to reduce the load of the minister of finance: this seems to correspond to the situation in Austria. Finally, the division may be made in order to solve a problem of portfolio allocation in a coalition government, as was the case in Sweden in 1976 and appears to occur on occasion in Belgium where up to six ministers have been known to be in charge of the area of responsibility of the treasury. Yet whatever the reasons why and despite the ways in which the ministry of finance is split, ministers of finance seem, by and large, to be able to win.

Overall, one finds in Western Europe three main types of arrangements. There can be one minister only, as in Ireland. There can be two ministers, but with the minister of finance clearly on top, as in Sweden, Austria, Norway, Britain, and France. Third, in Belgium, the Netherlands, and Denmark, no one minister among those in charge of treasury affairs dominates the others; this is often, but not exclusively, the case in coalition governments.

Thus the minister of finance may find some opposition within the cabinet, despite the fact that, on balance, the prime minister will provide support in the majority of situations. Ministers of finance can see their position challenged when they are part of a larger inner group in which a number of ministers have or can be regarded as having a part to play in financial or economic affairs. In a somewhat similar manner, the influence of ministers of finance may be to an extent reduced when the cabinet includes other ministers who held similar positions in the past. This situation is relatively frequent in Britain, France, Ireland, Italy, and Norway, less frequent in Belgium, Denmark (perhaps surprisingly in both cases), Germany, and Finland; such occurrences are rare or very rare in Austria, the Netherlands, and Sweden, in the first two of these last three cases because very few ministers occupy successively different positions in the cabinet.

Table 9.2   Ministers of finance having previously held a cabinet post (percentages)

Italy	70
Britain	60
Ireland	54
France	50
Norway	50
Germany (with econ)	36
Belgium (with econ)	28
Finland	27
Denmark (with econ)	26
The Netherlands (with econ)	14
Austria	9
Sweden	0

HOW POWERFUL ARE MINISTERS OF FINANCE?

One way in which the power of ministers of finance in Western European cabinets can be assessed is by examining the conflicts that have taken place in these cabinets. It is then possible to see to what extent these conflicts were concerned with matters of finance and, for these cases, how often ministers of finance won these conflicts. Despite large variations in the number of conflicts analysed for each of the countries, one can at least draw a broad picture. Overall, ministries of finance are involved in a substantial minority of the cabinet conflicts in every country and even in a majority of cabinet conflicts in many of them: only in Belgium and Denmark is the incidence of conflicts involving the ministry of finance very low, while it is relatively low in France; it is on the other hand, very high in Britain. Clearly, some of

Table 9.3   Ministers of finance involved in newspaper reported conflicts
(percentages)

Britain	93
Italy	58
The Netherlands	53
Finland	51
Sweden	36
Ireland	33
Austria	31
Germany	31
France	22
Denmark	8
Belgium	3

these variations result from factors that have little, if anything, to do with finance: the low incidence of conflicts involving the minister of finance in Belgium results from the fact that the problems arising from language divisions are crucial. However, variations must also be affected by the extent to which the minister of finance is influential, though there are no means of assessing precisely degrees in this influence.

It might thus be claimed that the minister of finance is strongest where there are many conflicts, as is the case in Britain. On the other hand, it could be that ministers of finance are so powerful in Sweden, Denmark, Germany, Belgium, France, Ireland, or Austria, that there is no need for them to fight because other ministers rarely oppose what they suggest. This second interpretation is probably closer to the truth. In Belgium and Denmark, and to a lesser extent in Sweden, Germany, Austria, France, and Ireland, ministers of finance are relatively autonomous; in the Netherlands, Finland, Italy, and even more in Britain, they have to fight with their colleagues to establish their control.

The way the cabinet work is organised may have an effect on the influence of the ministers of finance. Cabinet committees can affect relations between these and their colleagues and may be tools that enable them to dominate the cabinet; moreover, the treasury can typically defend its position in any committee where officials are present. By and large, ministers of finance seem able to win by controlling committees and thus do not have to fight in the cabinet: given the importance of committees in the British case, it is therefore somewhat surprising that so many conflicts should be related to financial matters in that country.[20]

The picture is thus mixed. Individual ministers have little say against the ministry of finance on micro-economic issues; on macro-economic questions, there are significant variations from country to country, from time to time, and probably from minister of finance to minister of finance. By and large, the way in which discussion takes place about macro-economics in cabinet is to start with an evaluation of the figures compiled and presented by the minister of finance and the treasury officials: in this context, many of the really important decisions – and typically most of the unpopular ones – are made by very small groups which may include only one or two cabinet members.[21] This seems to enhance the role of the minister of finance; but the question has to be asked: is it the minister or is it the ministry that is then at the origin of such key decisions?

MINISTER OF FINANCE *v.* MINISTRY OF FINANCE

Whatever relationship may exist between the minister of finance and the prime minister and between the minister of finance and the other ministers, one problem remains, namely whether the head of the treasury expresses personal ideas or whether these are the ideas of the financial and economic bureaucracy. It has been pointed out that it is possible for a minister of finance to be unorthodox and a keen spender when new to the job, but after a number of years may become a firm believer in budgetary restraint:[22] the primary concern will then be inflation rather than unemployment and there will be pessimism about the ability to achieve high growth rates.[23]

The position of the minister of finance *vis-à-vis* the ministry will be markedly affected by the duration of the minister in the post: someone who stays for a short period only will be less influential than someone who stays much longer. If rotation is always rapid, civil servants will learn and adjust to the idea that ministers are guests rather than leaders of their ministries. An examination of the average duration of treasury heads across Western Europe shows that there are marked variations.

The average duration of ministers of finance in each country may help to assess the extent of influence of these ministers. However, the matter needs to be considered in the context of the duration of other ministers: as a matter of fact, in general, ministers of finance stay in

Table 9.4 Duration in posts of ministers of finance between 1945 and 1984 (years)

Sweden	5.71
Germany	4.71
Denmark	3.89
The Netherlands	3.76
Austria	3.45
Norway	3.33
France	3.31
Ireland	3.00
Britain	2.66
Belgium	2.60
Italy	2.43
Finland	1.81

office longer than the rest of their colleagues; the only exceptions are Sweden, Germany, Austria, and the Netherlands, but in the first three of these countries the duration of ministers is markedly above the Western European average.

There are two other ways in which ministers of finance are likely to be influential over their department even though they may not stay in their post for very long. One way is to have had previous experience in cabinet, as this suggests that the occupant of the post is a senior politician able to manage successfully a government department. In practice, however, the proportion of ministers of finance with previous cabinet experience is on the whole rather low: surprisingly, only 37 per cent of the ministers of finance had had a cabinet position before heading the treasury. Admittedly, the proportion of finance ministers who had a previous cabinet job is minute in a number of countries where movement from post to post is relatively rare, as in Austria or the Netherlands. Conversely, the highest proportion of ministers of finance with previous cabinet experience can be found in some of the countries where movement from post to post is frequent, as in Britain, Ireland, or Italy. A number of intermediate cases none the less remain difficult to account for.

The other factor that might indicate whether the minister of finance is likely to be able to 'control' the department is constituted by previous specialisation in the field of economics. Ministers of finance who have some specialised knowledge of the area can be expected, other things being equal, to be better able to develop proposals and to

Table 9.5 Ministers of finance having had a cabinet post previously (percentages)

Britain	80
Ireland	62
Italy	59
Sweden	57
Denmark (with econ)	42
Belgium (with econ)	36
France	25
Finland	22
Norway	17
Germany (with econ)	14
The Netherlands (with econ)	10
Austria	9

Table 9.6 Ministers of finance specialised in economics or finance (percentages)

France	100
The Netherlands (with econ)	86
Austria	82
Germany (with econ)	79
Italy	59
Finland	50
Norway	50
Belgium (with econ)	50
Britain	47
Denmark (with econ)	47
Sweden	43
Ireland	23

convince fellow ministers and the treasury about the value of these proposals. Interestingly, the proportions of ministers with some prior specialisation is substantial (60 per cent); indeed, it is often in some of the countries where previous ministerial experience is low (Austria and the Netherlands in particular) that the proportion of ministers with a specialised background is greatest.

There are a number of countries where ministers of finance typically neither have had a previous cabinet post nor have had specialisation in the field: Belgium, Finland, and Norway score below average on both counts, while Denmark is about average in one case (previous cabinet job) and below average in the other. These are therefore the countries where one might expect the officials of the treasury to be able to have the greatest strength, especially if one notes that the average duration of ministers of finance is short in Finland and Belgium and only about average in Norway.

There is therefore scope for officials to exercise more influence in some countries than in others: there are limits to such an opportunity, however. In the first place, the strength of the treasury markedly depends on the extent to which the department is united: the extent of internal conflict within the treasury is not precisely known, but divisions appear to exist; for example, Norway is sometimes mentioned as a country where these occur. Second, one is easily inclined to exaggerate the extent to which differences of opinion exist between ministers and 'their' civil servants, whether in the treasury or elsewhere. We noted in the previous chapter that ministers, by and large, praise the loyalty of their civil servants: the point applies to civil servants in the ministry of finance as well as in other departments. Indeed, it is truly difficult to know who 'socialises' whom in the interchange between ministers and treasury officials. As a matter of fact, treasury officials need a convincing minister in the same way that other departments need strong ministers, as only a convincing minister of finance will inspire confidence in the cabinet and in the nation:[24] the influence is therefore often likely to be two-way.

Ministers of finance are no 'ordinary' ministers: they can and do exercise power over their cabinet colleagues as they have to ensure that the budget constitutes a reasonable package and that a sensible balance is struck between large numbers of interests and of proposals. There do seem to be appreciable differences from country to country, however, in the extent to which ministers of finance are 'above' their colleagues and can exercise their power. These differences do not appear to stem from differences in organisational structure: thus the prime minister plays an important part in economic matters in France, Britain, Ireland, and Norway, although political structures and arrangements are strikingly dissimilar. Overall, ministers of finance may have more power in the larger countries and be more challenged in at least some of the smaller countries; yet in some large countries, and in particular in Britain and Italy, ministers of finance also appear to be frequently involved in conflicts at the cabinet level. Thus it is perhaps in Germany and Austria that ministers of finance succeed most easily in having the upper hand over the rest of the government, though the extremely long duration of some ministers of finance elsewhere, especially in Sweden, also suggests that, there too, a substantial basis for overall control is exercised by finance ministers.

Notes

1. Dual leadership as a general phenomenon has only been examined to a limited extent. See however J. Blondel (1984), pp. 73–91.
2. Out of 410 ministers interviewed, only 28, mostly from Finland and Norway, stated that the minister of finance was not very influential.
3. D. Coombes and S. A. Walkland (eds) (1980), pp. 3–25.
4. N. Johnson (1983), p. 250. A. M. Gamble and S. A. Walkland (1984), pp. 155–69. M. Sexton (1979), pp. 52–5.
5. N. Johnson (1983), p. 249.
6. S. Cassese (1980), pp. 197–8. H. Machin (1987), p. 163.
7. B. Donoghue (1985), pp. 69–70.
8. H. Heclo and A. Wildavsky (1974), p. 172. B. Donoughue (1985), pp. 58–9. M. Sexton (1979), pp. 64–7. N. Johnson (1983), p. 250.
9. B. Donoghue (1983), pp. 65–6. R. Mayntz (1987), pp. 14–16.
10. J. Blondel (1991).
11. B. Donoughue (1985), p. 54.
12. J. Barnett (1982), pp. 124–5. P. Weller in W. Plowden (ed) (1987), pp. 26–7.
13. C. Ponting (1986), pp. 118–19.
14. G. Lord (1973), pp. 131-3. R. Neustadt (1985), pp. 158–9.
15. J. Barnett (1982), Ch. 10. H. Heclo and A. Wildavsky (1981), pp. 181–202.
16. J. Woods (1954).
17. J. Blondel, (1991), p. 5.
18. L. Pliatzky (1982), pp. 62–3. C. Ponting (1986), p. 124.
19. S. Cassese (1980), p. 195.
20. G. Lord (1973), pp. 65–6. J. G. Christensen (1985), p. 136. P. Stenbäck (1981). C. Campbell (1983), pp. 138–9.
21. M. Holmes (1982), p. 132.
22. C. Campbell (1977), p. 10.
23. N. Johnson (1983), p. 249.
24. C. Campbell (1983), p. 155.

10 Prime Ministers and Cabinet Decision-Making Processes

Wolfgang C. Müller, Wilfried Philipp and Peter Gerlich

Of all the components of cabinet life, perhaps the one most likely to give rise to major variations is the prime ministerial component. This is not only because prime ministers are the most visible, most powerful, and most important politicians; this is also because impressionistic evidence suggests that some heads of governments are strong and others are weak; this may be a result of personality differences, peculiarities of the cabinet under consideration, or general characteristics of the political system of the country concerned. Thus one might expect coalitions to be headed more often by less forceful prime ministers than single-party majority governments, although differences among coalitions are large and the impact of prime ministers is likely to vary appreciably as a result.[1] Structural elements and personality traits tend also to be intertwined: the politicians who may become prime ministers in a coalition context will almost certainly have a different personality from those who become prime ministers in single-party majority governments: in coalitions, the main skills required will probably be diplomacy and compromise, while strong leadership may be more at a premium in single-party majority governments.

As a consequence of the visibility and importance of the office, studies of government heads are numerous: they have also given rise, in particular in Britain, to an academic debate about the impact of prime ministers on cabinet decision-making. This has resulted in a number of models, ranging from the concept of 'prime ministerial' government suggested by Crossman to the more balanced presentation of Mackintosh.[2] The ideal-type 'prime ministerial' model has in particular attracted attention by showing that cabinets have lost most of their power to the benefit of heads of governments; this view is exaggerated, to say the least, as the responses to the ministerial interviews strongly indicate: only a minority of cabinet ministers, albeit a large minority (40 per cent), are of the opinion that heads of governments tend to impose their own solutions to problems.

The power of prime ministers is of course a result of a number of political and administrative resources. Political resources vary: prime ministers may or may not be able to appoint freely the members of the cabinet; they may or may not be the leaders of their party. Administrative resources are spread more uniformly: they include the powers of prime ministers over the organisation of the government and the directives to be given to ministers; over the determination of the cabinet agenda and the running of the cabinet meeting; and over the setting up and the role of committees. Heads of governments also have access to more information than their colleagues as a result of the development of prime ministerial offices; they enjoy more publicity in the media; and they typically play an important international role.[3]

These characteristics account for the fact that heads of governments have opportunities to exercise power; they do not help to describe the substantial differences in prime ministerial power from cabinet to cabinet nor do they provide structural reasons for these substantial differences. These matters can be examined only by exploring how far prime ministers intervene in cabinet decision-making as a result of structural characteristics, noting, however, that, as has been seen in the preceding chapters, differences among types of cabinet structures – and in particular between coalitions and single-party majority governments – are not always as crucial as might have been expected, while differences based on country specificities can be highly significant. It is not possible here to examine the psychological underpinnings of prime ministerial behaviour, but the analysis of the ministerial responses does provide a detailed picture of the extent, forms, and styles of influence of these heads of governments.

The bulk of the analysis of this chapter is thus based, as is the rest of this volume, on the answers given by the cabinet ministers who have been interviewed. In the context of the assessment of the involvement of prime ministers, cabinet members were asked to state their experience with respect to three broad sets of questions. One set was aimed at discovering the *fields* of government to which the prime ministers under whom respondents served devoted a special interest: were these heads of governments particularly concerned with foreign affairs, as is often claimed? Were they equally concerned with economic problems or social matters? Indeed, were they perhaps not concerned with any particular aspect of the life of cabinets?

A second set of questions was aimed at identifying the *style* of prime ministers. Did the ministers feel that those under whom they served wanted to achieve consensus? Did they, on the contrary, endeavour to impose their own solutions to the problems that the cabinet faced? Some prime ministers could thus be described as being primarily chairmen wanting to ensure that the atmosphere in the cabinet was as peaceful as possible: these were perhaps not overconcerned as to what the eventual outcome would be; others might be actively involved in shaping decisions, regardless of whether or not these generated conflict in the cabinet.

Finally, a third set of questions related to the *role* of prime ministers – that is to say to the way in which heads of governments are described by their colleagues as intervening in the life of the cabinet. If ministers have a problem, or want to bring an issue to cabinet, or have a disagreement with another minister, would they go to the prime minister or not? Was the prime minister thus seen as a 'facilitator' in the process of decision-making, in some way supplementing and often substituting for the cabinet? Or was the prime minister markedly less involved in the processing of decisions coming to cabinet, thus letting that body retain some of its traditional collegial role?

In the first part of this chapter, we shall examine these three aspects in general in order to see what are the broad characteristics of prime ministerial rule in Western European governments; we shall also examine whether fields of involvement, style, and role are related to one another or not. In the second part, we shall look at the possible effect of the factors that we analysed throughout this book on the fields of involvement, the style, and the role of prime ministers: we will look particularly at the impact of the single-party/coalition distinction, as well as at the part that party differences may play and at the extent to which country variations can be attributed to the peculiarities of the national political culture. Finally, we shall examine whether the characteristics of prime ministers as defined by their fields of involvement, style, and role affect the centrality of Western European cabinets, their collegial and their collective character, and the extent to which they behave in a conflictual manner.

GENERAL DIFFERENCES IN THE FIELD OF INVOLVEMENT, STYLE AND ROLE OF WESTERN EUROPEAN PRIME MINISTERS

Fields of involvement

Prime ministers are often regarded as being, above all, involved in foreign affairs and, increasingly, in economic matters as well: this is broadly confirmed by the ministerial respondents, but some further points need to be made. Interviewees were asked to state whether the prime ministers under whom they had served wished to exercise influence in the fields of foreign affairs, defence, economics, and/or social questions; they were also asked to state whether these prime ministers wanted to make their mark on matters of general governmental organisation. The result was a clear distinction between three levels: at the top was the concern for the general organisation of the government, in the middle was the concern for foreign and economic affairs, and at the bottom was the concern for defence and social affairs. While three-fifths of those interviewed said that heads of governments aimed at exercising influence on general governmental affairs, two-fifths stated that the prime ministers under whom they served aimed at exercising influence in foreign affairs and/ or economic matters and only one-fifth mentioned defence and/or social questions.

The fact that three-fifths of the ministers interviewed mentioned general governmental organisation as an area in which 'their' prime ministers wished to be influential is perhaps not altogether surprising: what is perhaps more surprising is that one-fifth stated that these prime ministers were not involved in this way (and another fifth either did not reply or were not asked the question). What is also rather surprising is that the proportions of prime ministers regarded as involved in economic matters and in foreign affairs should be about the same and therefore that foreign affairs should not be a 'must' for all prime ministers: as a matter of fact, about 30 per cent of the ministers interviewed stated that the prime ministers under whom they served did not attempt to exercise influence in one or other of these fields. Finally, it is also somewhat remarkable that so few prime ministers appeared to wish to exercise influence (one-fifth) on defence or on social questions, with a substantially larger proportion – between a one-third and two-fifths of the respondents – saying that the prime ministers under whom they served did not attempt to exercise influence in these fields.

Table 10.1 Fields of involvement of prime ministers

	Yes		No		No reply		Not asked question	
	N	%	N	%	N	%	N	%
Overall government organisation	245	60	85	21	30	7	50	12
Foreign affairs	159	39	124	30	72	18	55	13
Defence	78	19	159	39	114	28	59	14
Economy	167	41	116	28	71	17	56	14
Social affairs	92	22	137	34	99	24	82	20

While there is thus a three-level hierarchy in terms of fields of involvement of prime ministers, there is also an extent of association between these fields: the two home affairs fields are associated with each other; so are the two external affairs fields.[4] These two types of distinction make it possible to divide prime ministers into four broad types. There are those whose involvement is very limited, since they do not desire to exercise influence in any particular field and at most are concerned with the general organisation of the government. At the other extreme, there are those who are involved in all aspects of the governments that they lead. In between, some are primarily concerned with foreign affairs (and in some cases, defence as well) and can thus be regarded as being more 'traditional'; others are primarily concerned with economic affairs (as well, as in some cases, social affairs as well): they are perhaps more characteristic of the more 'modern' approach to

Table 10.2 Levels of involvement of prime ministers

	N	%
Both foreign affairs and economy (= very involved)	79	19
Foreign affairs only	58	14
Economy only	67	16
Neither (uninvolved)	96	23
Missing	110	27

government, whether they are interventionnist or, on the contrary, want to 'free' the individual from the action of the State. These four types can be labelled as those of 'chairmen', 'activists', foreign-affairs oriented and home affairs-orientated.[5]

The styles of prime ministers

The behaviour of prime ministers depends in part on the substance of the involvement: it also manifests itself by means of a style. Impressionistic evidence strongly suggests that some heads of government are forceful and are anxious to impose their point of view, while others wish to bring about compromises and hope perhaps to reduce conflicts by finding solutions to the disagreements that may exist.

The ministers who were interviewed were asked whether 'their' prime ministers attempted to build a consensus, talked to ministers individually, forced solutions, or took new initiatives. The desire to build a consensus is by far the most prevalent characteristic of Western European prime ministers, according to the ministers who served under them: over two-thirds of the heads of government are said to have practised this mode, against one-sixth who said they had not; one-sixth also said that the prime ministers under whom they served did not talk individually with ministers as against nearly three-fifths who said they did. On the other hand, there were many more respondents who said that 'their' prime ministers did not force solutions or did not take initiatives than there were respondents who viewed the heads of the governments to which they belonged as adopting one or the other of these strong styles: half the respondents stated that the prime ministers under whom they served did not force issues and two-fifths that they did not take new initiatives, as against between a quarter and a third who said that they did.

Positive answers to these questions were not mutually exclusive, however: someone can attempt to build a consensus on some issues while imposing a solution on others. The answers do indeed show that some ministers viewed 'their' prime ministers as having been, so to speak, both men or women of consensus *and* leaders able to impose their views; but there is also an extent to which the two characteristics exclude each other: while about a quarter of the prime ministers were said to have adopted both styles, nearly half were said to have adopted the consensual style only and 7 per cent the forceful style only. Overall,

Table 10.3   Styles of prime ministers

	Yes		No		No reply		Not asked question	
	N	%	N	%	N	%	N	%
Consensual	284	69	67	16	33	8	26	6
Talking individually to ministers	233	57	75	18	71	17	31	8
Taking initiatives	109	27	158	38	111	27	32	8
Forcing issues	122	30	200	49	58	14	30	7

Table 10.4   Types of prime ministerial styles

	N	%
Both consensual and forceful	94	23
Consensual only	185	45
Forceful only	27	7
Neither	17	4
Missing	87	21

as with fields of influence, one can thus construct a typology of styles of prime ministers based on whether these are regarded as having been consensual, forceful, both consensual and forceful, or neither of these.[6]

Variations in prime ministerial influence over time

By and large, respondents feel that the influence of prime ministers does not vary markedly over time: over two-fifths state that it remains the same, while only a fifth hold a contrary view. This does not appear to be – at any rate primarily – a reflection of the fact that some prime ministers do not stay in office for very long periods and thus do not have time, so to speak, to acquire more or less influence: country variations, which we shall examine further in the next section, do not suggest that the influence of prime ministers altered more in those countries in which the heads of government remained in office longer. It should be noted, however, that very few prime ministers remained in office for truly substantial periods (ten years for instance): it is therefore not possible to assess whether there might be changes in influence over very long periods in office.

The fifth of the respondents who stated that the influence of prime ministers varied divide fairly evenly between those who claimed that this influence increased and those who claimed that this influence decreased. In terms of levels of influence, and according to those who were most directly involved, prime ministers thus belong to one of three distinct categories, those whose influence increases, those whose influence remains the same, and those whose influence declines, but the first and last of these categories are relatively small.[7]

The roles of prime ministers

If, instead of looking at the matter from the angle of the prime ministers, we consider it from the angle of the ministers, the latter may want to 'use' 'their' prime minister in order to achieve their own goals. The proportion of those who test what the prime minister feels about an issue before bringing it to cabinet is indeed very large: nearly two-thirds of the interviewees stated that they went to the head of the government before raising a matter as against less than a fifth who said that they did not; this does establish the central position of the prime minister. The point is underlined by the fact that over half the respondents stated that problems that were relatively underexamined at the cabinet meeting tended to be discussed separately by the prime minister and ministers, while only a sixth of the respondents took the opposite view. Finally, nearly two-fifths of the interviewees said that they went to the prime minister in cases of conflict with an important minister, as against slightly over a quarter who said that they did not: this is a substantial proportion even if it is not as large as the proportion of those who use the prime ministerial 'route' to bring matters to the cabinet. As a matter of fact, as might have been expected, the bulk of the ministers who go to 'their' prime minister when they experience a conflict with an important minister also tend to be those who raise with 'their' prime ministers issues that they want to raise subsequently in cabinet, while the converse is not true.[8] Moreover and interestingly, although more said they went to the prime minister in cases of conflict with an important minister than said they went directly to the cabinet in such cases, there is some relationship between these two 'moves': half of those who go to the cabinet in cases of such conflicts also go to the prime minister as against only 40 per cent of those who do not go to the cabinet but go to the prime minister.[9]

The relationship between fields of prime ministerial involvement, prime ministerial styles and prime ministerial roles

In the eyes of the respondents, there is a relationship between the fields of involvement and the style of prime ministers. Thus prime ministers who are characterised by respondents as exercising influence in a particular field tend to be more forceful and take more initiatives. Thus, too, ministers who exercise influence on the economy are more likely than not to force an issue and they are also more likely to take initiatives and less likely to have a consensual approach. This is even more the case of those heads of government who are said to exercise influence on social affairs. The same is true of those ministers who are said to exercise influence in foreign affairs, despite the fact that this field may be regarded as one in which a national consensus is sought. Only those who are said to want to exercise influence on defence matters are more likely to be drawn from among those whose style is consensual, but they are still also more likely to be drawn from among those who force issues and even more among those who take initiatives. These variations are reflected to some extent at the level of the overall relationship between styles and fields of involvement, though the

Table 10.5   Fields of involvement of prime ministers and prime ministerial style (percentages)

Style	Foreign economy	Foreign only	Economy only	Neither	Total
Consensual/forceful	38	23	25	27	29
Consensual	46	70	53	60	57
Forceful	15	2	19	7	10
Neither	1	5	3	6	4
Total	100	100	100	100	100
N	(74)	(53)	(36)	(85)	(248)

Involved in:

differences are not as marked as might have been expected: prime ministers who want to exercise influence in several fields are said to be appreciably less likely to practise a consensual approach only than those who do not have a particular field.

There is no relationship, on the other hand, between prime ministerial roles and the types of fields of influence of prime ministers nor with the style of these prime ministers. Ministers go to heads of government to discuss issues whether or not these heads of government wish to exercise influence in foreign or home affairs; they go to heads of government as much whether these have a consensual or a forceful approach or indeed both or neither. The desire or need to approach the prime minister when there is a problem appears to take place to the same extent whatever the characteristics of this prime minister.

THE BROAD POLITICAL FACTORS ACCOUNTING FOR THE FIELDS OF INVOLVEMENT, THE STYLES AND THE ROLES OF PRIME MINISTERS

If one judges by the responses given by ministers about 'their' heads of government, the characteristics of Western European prime ministers appear to relate clearly and manifestly to the basic distinction between coalitions and single-party governments. They appear related to a somewhat limited extent to the nature of the party or parties forming the cabinet. They appear related in a substantial but rather ill-determined manner to the political culture of the countries concerned.

The single-party/coalition distinction and prime ministerial characteristics

The large apparent impact of the single-party/coalition distinction on characteristics of prime ministerial rule is found, to begin with, in the context of the fields in which prime ministers are said to wish to be involved. As many as two-thirds of the ministers of single-party majority governments state that 'their' prime minister is involved in both home and external affairs, while the corresponding figure for coalition governments is only 10 per cent. Conversely, over a third of the ministers from coalition governments and over two-fifths of the respondents from single-party minority governments state that 'their' prime minister does not wish to exercise influence either in foreign affairs or on the economy, while the corresponding proportion among ministers from single-party majority governments is 12 per cent only. Interestingly, too, ministers from coalition governments mention the involvement of 'their' prime minister in the economy more often than their involvement in foreign affairs (31 *v.* 20 per cent); ministers who served in single-party majority and minority governments rank the two fields in the opposite way.

As a matter of fact, ministers from single-party majority governments describe 'their' prime ministers as more concerned with every field, the difference being very large with respect to foreign affairs, substantial over economic matters and defence, and limited with respect to social affairs, which, as we know, is also the field in which the smallest proportion of prime ministers is said to want to be involved. Moreover, the difference extends even to the general organisation of the government: nearly three-quarters of the ministers from both single-party majority and minority governments state that 'their' prime ministers exercise influence in this respect, as against only a little over half the ministers from coalition governments, a quarter of whom specifically claim that 'their' prime ministers are not concerned with the matter.

Second, there are also substantial differences in style, according to interviewees, between prime ministers from single-party and coalition governments. Prime ministers from coalition governments are regarded by the ministers who serve under them as more likely to be consensual or even to be entirely passive. Twice as many prime ministers from

Table 10.6 Involvement of prime ministers and the single-party coalition distinction (percentages)

	Single-party minority	Single-party majority	Coalition
Both foreign and economy	28	68	11
Foreign	24	15	21
Economy	4	4	31
Neither	44	12	37
Total	100	99	100
N	25	73	199
General organisation of government (% involved)	72	69	54

single-party majority governments are said to have been forceful and only forceful as prime ministers from coalition governments; two-thirds of the prime ministers from coalition governments are said to be consensual and only consensual as against two-fifths of the prime ministers from single-party majority governments. Prime ministers from single-party minority governments constitute an intermediate case: about half – but only half – of them are said to have exclusively a consensual style while the other half are regarded as beeing both consensual and forceful.

In fact, the main difference relates to the proportion of prime ministers who are said to be forceful. A consensual style and a forceful style are not mutually exclusive, as we saw: by and large, the prime ministers from single-party governments, whether majority or minority, are those who tend to adopt both styles, since they are said to be as consensual as prime ministers from coalition governments; indeed, as many as a fifth of the respondents from coalition governments even state that 'their' prime minister did not have a consensual style, a point that was made by only 7 per cent of their colleagues from single-party majority governments about 'their' prime ministers. On the other hand, half the ministers from single party majority governments see 'their' prime minister as adopting (or adopting also) a forceful style or as taking initiatives, while this is said to be the case of 'their' prime minister by only one-fifth of the ministers from coalition governments.

Table 10.7   Style of prime ministers and the single-party/coalition distinction (percentages)

	Single-party minority	Single-party majority	Coalition
Both consensual and forceful	52	43	19
Consensual	48	40	67
Forceful	–	16	6
Neither	–	1	8
Total	100	100	100
N	31	90	199
All consensual	96	71	65
All forceful	48	50	19
Taking initiatives	9	47	21

There is also a substantial difference between coalitions and single-party governments in relation to variations in prime ministerial influence over time. More ministers from single-party majority governments note such variations than do ministers of coalition governments; more of the former also note that these variations go in the direction of an increase in influence of the heads of government. Overall, prime ministers of single-party majority governments are said to be three times more likely to increase their influence over their colleagues than prime ministers of coalitions or indeed of single-party minority governments.

Table 10.8   Change of influence of prime ministers and the single-party/ coalition distinction (percentages)

	Single-party minority	Single-party majority	Coalition
More influence	9	29	9
No change	72	53	42
Less influence	–	14	11
No reply/question not asked	18	4	38
Total	99	100	100

On the other hand, the role of prime ministers does not appear to be influenced by the single-party/coalition distinction. The proportion of ministers who state that they go to 'their' prime minister to discuss cabinet matters is about the same – around two-thirds – in all types of cabinets; indeed, ostensibly, it is in single-party *minority* governments that this referral to the prime minister takes place most often (72 per cent). In fact, the similarity of the roles ascribed to prime ministers by respondents from single-party and from coalition governments contrasts sharply with the marked difference in the extent to which ministers state that they use the cabinet as a whole when there is a problem: only a quarter of the ministers from coalition governments state that they do so (and even fewer ministers from single-party minority cabinets give a similar answer), while this is said to be the case of nearly two-thirds of the ministers from single-party majority governments. Thus ministers go to the same extent to 'their' prime minister when they have a problem, but the cabinet is regarded as having a greater part to play in this respect in single-party majority governments than in coalitions. Prime ministers from single-party majority cabinets may want to exercise influence in more fields, they may also have a more forceful style, but single-party majority cabinets appear to be at the same time more collegial.[10]

Parties in government and prime ministerial characteristics

The type of party or parties that compose the government appears related to an extent to the fields in which prime ministers are concerned. Admittedly, the answers come from the ministers and therefore relate to the parties of these ministers; but some differences are none the less worth noting, for the breadth of involvement varies according to party, indeed to a surprising extent: nearly half (44 per cent) the ministers from christian democrat parties state that the prime ministers under whom they served were not involved in economic matters and in foreign affairs while this is the case of only a third of the liberals, less than a third of the socialists and only 13 per cent of the conservatives. Conversely, conservatives are those who state most that 'their' prime minister is active in both home and external affairs (69 per cent) while only 3 per cent of the christian democrat ministers reply in the same manner. Moreover, as between a desire to influence the economy *or* foreign affairs, ministers from christian democrat parties state that 'their' prime minister tended to choose foreign affairs, while for liberals and conservatives the choice was more on economic questions, and for socialists there was equal choice for each of these fields. Moreover, on all these questions a difference remains, in particular between socialists and christian democrats, when one

Table 10.9   Parties in government and prime ministerial involvement (percentage of positive answers)

	Socialists	Liberals	Christian democrats	Conserv.	Average
Foreign affairs	44	29	30	66	39
Defence	20	20	8	37	19
Economy	28	37	22	71	41
Social affairs	25	19	8	29	22
General organisation of government	63	53	58	65	59

controls for the single-party/coalition distinction.[11] Only in terms of the general organisation of the government does one not find such a 'laid back' character being attributed by ministers from christian democrat parties to the prime ministers under whom they served: there is scarcely any difference between the parties on this point.

Second, there is some apparent association between the party of the respondents and changes in influence of prime ministers over time. Conservatives and socialist ministers are those who state most frequently that the influence of 'their' prime ministers did change over time, christian democrat ministers being those who state least frequently that this is the case of 'their' prime ministers. Here, too, the difference remains when one controls for the single-party/coalition distinction. Conservative and socialist ministers are also those who state most frequently that the change resulted in more influence being exercised by the prime minister, while, in the eyes of christian democrat ministers, a change in the influence of the prime ministers under whom they served was most likely to be in the form of a decline. Thus socialists and conservative ministers can be regarded as 'optimistic' and christian democrat ministers as 'pessimistic' about 'their' prime ministers. This point may be linked to the earlier remark according to which christian democrat ministers attribute to 'their' prime ministers a generally lower profile than do the ministers from other parties.[12]

Meanwhile, however, the style attributed to heads of governments does not appear to be substantially influenced by the parties of the ministers, the only apparent variations being provided by conservative respondents, two-thirds of whom state that the prime ministers under whom they served were 'forceful' as well as, in half these cases, consensual, while the average is under two-fifths; as we shall see later, this difference may be the result to a large extent of the answers given by British ministers, however. In all other respects the style of prime ministers appears to be uninfluenced by party: with respect to reactions to coalition problems, the extent to which prime ministers are said to exercise influence is also almost the same across all the parties.[13]

Finally, the role of prime ministers does not seem to differ either according to the party of the minister concerned. About the same proportion of ministers from all parties state that they discuss matters with 'their' prime minister before bringing them to cabinet, or that matters are discussed by prime ministers and ministers. Socialist and conservative respondents are a little more likely to state that they go to the prime minister when they are in conflict with an important minister, but the difference is small; indeed, variations are also small among the ministers of the various parties in terms of the extent to which ministers raise in cabinet matters on which they have been in conflict with important ministers.

Thus, while party appears to affect the fields in which prime ministers are involved, christian democrat ministers singling out 'their' prime minister as having a more limited concern, the 'party factor' seems not to have an effect on other prime ministerial characteristics. In particular, prime ministers of all parties come to adopt similar styles: this may be in part because the situations that they face tend, on the whole, to be rather similar.

The apparently important but somewhat ill-determined impact of individual country variations

Country variations are large: how far this is a result of specific characteristics of the political culture of the countries concerned is often difficult to assess, however. First, the fields in which prime ministers are said to be involved vary widely from country to country. On average, a quarter of the ministers stated that 'their' prime ministers were influential in both foreign and economic affairs, a third stated that they were influential in neither, while the last two-fifths were divided evenly between the ministers who saw 'their' prime ministers as primarily influential in foreign affairs and those who saw them as primarily influential in economic matters. If we examine the country breakdown, differences are very substantial. No French minister, for instance, is said to have been involved in foreign affairs, a reflection of the fact that, since De Gaulle, French prime ministers have had to concentrate on the home front. Also, for example, the proportion of ministers who viewed their prime minister as relatively uninvolved in *both* foreign and economic affairs is large (over 40 per cent) in Denmark, the Netherlands, Belgium, Austria, and Finland, while this is not the case in Germany, France, Britain, Ireland, Italy, and Norway. There is importance given to foreign affairs in Germany, Italy, Belgium, and Austria, while the stress on economic questions is very large in France and large in Finland and Belgium. Belgium is indeed peculiar in that there is a sharp division between prime ministers who are regarded as oriented towards foreign affairs and prime ministers who are regarded as oriented towards economic questions.

Yet it is not clear that these marked differences are truly the result of differences in political culture. The lack of involvement in foreign affairs of French (and indeed Finnish) prime ministers is structural as much as cultural. What can only be said is that it is useful to examine the way in which the fields of involvement of prime ministers are ranked. Thus, while prime ministers are said to be as concerned on average with foreign affairs as with the economy, the levels of 'popularity' of these two fields vary markedly, as do also the levels of popularity of the other two fields that are examined here, social affairs and defence. Involvement in economic affairs is concentrated in some countries, while involvement in foreign affairs is more evenly spread: economic questions thus come to be rated on a par with foreign affairs overall largely because of the answers given by British and, but less so, French, Irish, and Norwegian respondents; in the other seven cases (Swedish ministers were not asked this question), only 28 per cent of the respondents mentioned economic affairs as being of concern to 'their' prime minister. On the other hand, only three countries (France, Belgium, and Finland) score very low with respect to foreign affairs, while the other countries score between 45 and 90 per cent, the median being 58 per cent.

While the ranking on social affairs is relatively low except, somewhat surprisingly, in Ireland and France, the distribution of replies with respect to prime ministerial concern for defence divides strongly into two groups: in four countries (France, Belgium, Finland, and Austria), there is almost no involvement at all; interestingly, the first three of these four countries are the same as those that score lowest in terms of the involvement of prime ministers in foreign affairs. In the six other countries for which answers were given on this point, involvement in defence matters is substantial and even on average slightly higher than on economic questions for the majority of countries, the median for these six countries being as high as 38 per cent.

The concern of prime ministers for the organisation of governments is also said to differ markedly across countries: in three cases – Germany, Norway, and particularly France – it is very low (40 per cent or less of the ministers mention this involvement); in a further three – Belgium, Italy, and Ireland – it is intermediate (about 60 per cent of the ministers mention this involvement); finally, in Britain, Denmark, Finland, the Netherlands, and Austria, prime ministers are said to be very involved in this matter – with 80 per cent or more of the ministers mentioning it.

The involvement of prime ministers in various fields of government does therefore vary widely from country to country: almost certainly, these variations are a reflection of characteristics of the political culture: perhaps one of the clearest examples in this respect is the high level of involvement of British prime ministers over all the fields of political life while Dutch ministers are said to be relatively less involved. In general, however, the effect of political culture cannot easily be disentangled from the impact of geographical characteristics (such as the size of the country) or from structural factors (such as the institutional configuration), in part because these matters, and especially the latter, can also be viewed as being the product of the political culture.

Prime ministerial style does also provide examples of variations which can be attributed in part or largely to the political culture of the countries concerned. These differences do not seem to affect the proportions of prime ministers who are regarded as passive; but there are substantial cross-country differences in the extent to which prime ministers are said to be consensus-seeking, forceful, or both consensus-seeking and forceful. The proportion of prime ministers said to be consensus-seekers is largest in Scandinavia, except, surprisingly, in Sweden (but probably because many interviewees did not answer this question), in Belgium, Austria, Italy, and Ireland; it is smallest in Germany, Britain, France, Sweden, and the Netherlands. While political culture is probably an important factor in this context, it should be noted that consensus is sought most in the smaller countries (plus Italy – for understandable reasons) and least in the larger countries (plus Sweden, with the reservation already made, and the Netherlands – this last case being perhaps one of the clearest examples of the impact of the political culture of a country on prime ministerial characteristics).

The extent to which a forceful style is practised also varies markedly: it is said to prevail most in Austria, Ireland, Denmark, Britain, and the Netherlands, while almost no respondent from Sweden, Germany, or France stated that it was adopted by 'their' prime minister. How far these variations are the result specifically of cultural elements is difficult to ascertain. The country breakdown does confirm the point made earlier that a forceful style is adopted more commonly when governments are, at least occasionally, of the single-party variety, the Netherlands being the only exception in this respect. France is peculiar in another way: its prime ministers take some initiatives and they discuss matters individually with ministers, but they have neither a consensual nor a forceful style: this is probably because the French cabinet is to a large extent presidential. Whether this is viewed as a cultural or a structural point is a matter for debate, however.

241

Figure 10.1 Fields of influence of prime ministers for country (percentages)

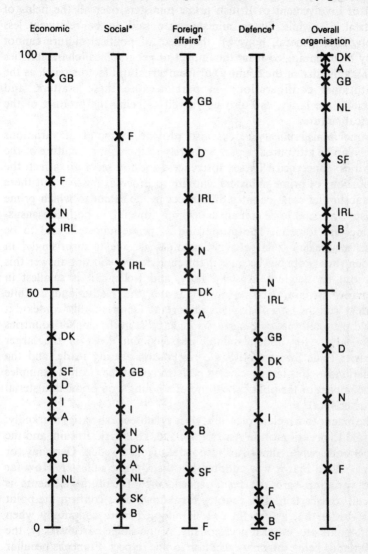

Note: Sweden is not covered

* Germany: not able to cover social affairs.
† Netherlands: no reply on foreign affairs or defence.

Figure 10.2 Style of prime ministers for country (percentages)

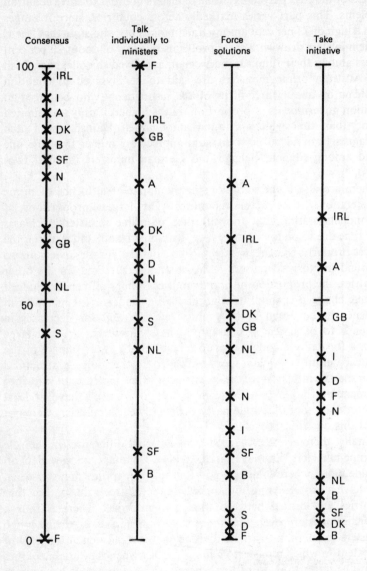

Differences in the style of prime ministers can also be noted in the context of the part played by prime ministers in order to solve coalition problems. This part varies markedly across countries, since it ranges from a high of 73 per cent among Italian ministers who state that 'their' prime ministers dealt with these problems to a low of about 20 per cent or less among their Finnish, Norwegian, and Swedish colleagues. Irish and Austrian prime ministers are said to be involved in coalition problems by about three-fifths of the respondents who belonged to coalition governments, a proportion that is higher, if only to a limited extent, than that which is found among their Danish and Dutch colleagues (around 50 per cent) and appreciably higher than the one found among French, Belgian and German ministers (around two-fifths).[14]

There are also some variations in the apparent influence of prime ministers over time across countries. The largest proportions of respondents stating that the influence of prime ministers increases over time are to be found in France, Britain, Ireland, and Austria; the largest proportions of respondents who hold the converse view are to be found in Norway, as well as in Austria and Ireland. In the other countries, the proportion of prime ministers whose influence is judged to have changed is small, though there is a tendency for increases in influence to be noted in Italy and Denmark and for decreases in influence to be noted in Germany. These differences are not large enough for definite conclusions to be drawn about the impact of the political culture in this respect, however; furthermore, a structural factor may be at play since the countries in which increases of influence are most noted are also those in which governments have at least sometimes been of the single-party variety (Swedish ministers were not asked this question).

Finally, there are also marked cross-national differences in the role of prime ministers between France, Ireland, Denmark, and Sweden, on the one hand, where ministers go often to 'their' prime minister when they have a problem, and Finland where they scarcely do so; the other countries are located between these two extremes. There is thus a tripartite division over the roles that ministers ask 'their' prime ministers to adopt, a tripartite division that is replicated at the level of the extent to which ministers *go to the cabinet* when they are in conflict with an important minister: there might therefore be here a characteristic of the political culture. The main differences in ranking in this context concern Britain, where ministers are likely to go more frequently to the cabinet than to the head of the government to solve

244

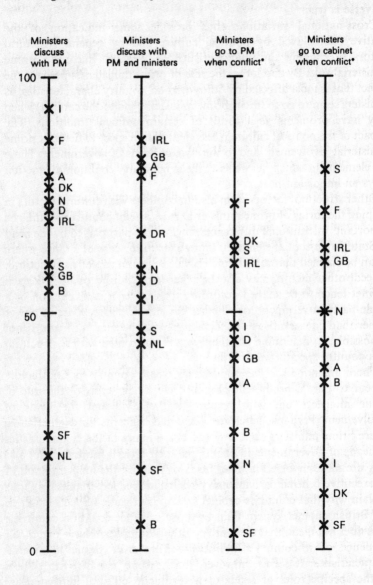

Figure 10.3 Role of prime ministers for country (percentages)

Note: * not able to cover Netherlands.

conflicts with important ministers, and Denmark and Italy, where the converse is true.

Cross-national variations thus provide some indication of the relative part played by political culture and by general structural factors in shaping the characteristics of Western European prime ministerial rule. By and large, the role of prime ministers is perhaps the aspect that is most affected by 'idiosyncratic' country characteristics, as ministers seem to go to 'their' prime ministers (and to the cabinet) when they have problems as a result of certain political traditions. The impact of the political culture is less clear with respect to fields of prime ministerial involvement and to the style of heads of government. These are elements in which, as we saw, the single-party coalition distinction plays an important part.

Other structural factors seem also to compete with cultural factors in shaping the forms of prime ministerial rule. Size of country can thus be important. Institutional differences, such as the part played by the head of State, are essential elements, though, as in the case of France where it can be claimed that this characteristic is cultural as well as structural. Indeed, other factors may also be regarded as mixed or hybrid: each cabinet tends to be shaped according to whether it is a coalition or a single-party government, or whether christian democrats are in power rather than conservatives or socialists: it then becomes difficult, if not impossible, to determine whether we are confronted with a structural or a country-specific cultural factor.

There are none the less some cases where country-specific factors appear to play a prominent part, not merely in terms of the role of prime ministers but with respect to the style and the fields of involvement. Perhaps the clearest example concerns the Netherlands, where prime ministers appear not to share many of the characteristics of heads of governments in coalitions: their style is more forceful and they are more involved in most fields of politics; the long tradition of an executive-centred parliamentary system in the Netherlands may thus explain why that country's cabinet system is in some respects closer to the British cabinet system than to those of other coalition countries. This does not mean that there are no other examples of large and direct influence of a country's political culture over prime ministerial characteristics. It seems, however, that, except perhaps with respect to the specific roles of heads of government, cultural idiosyncrasies have more commonly a diffuse and indirect effect and affect prime ministerial characteristics essentially in combination with structural factors.

FIELDS OF INVOLVEMENT, STYLE, AND ROLE OF PRIME MINISTERS AND CABINET DECISION-MAKING PROCESSES

The fields of involvement, the styles, and the roles of prime ministers are likely to be related to cabinet decision-making processes. To discover the extent of such a relationship, the indicators that can be used are those that helped to assess the centrality of the decisions taken by cabinets, the collective character of these bodies, the extent to which their structure is collegial or hierarchical, and the incidence of conflicts within them.[15]

In general, prime ministerial characteristics do not seem to have any effect on the amount of conflict in cabinets and they seem to have only a small impact on the collective character of these bodies. On the other hand, both the centrality of cabinets and the degree to which these are collegial or hierarchical appear markedly shaped by two of the three sets of prime ministerial characteristics that have been examined in this chapter, the fields of involvement and the style of heads of government.

The lack of relationship between prime ministerial characteristics and the amount of conflict in cabinets

In the eyes of ministers, the amount of conflict in cabinet is not related to any of the characteristics of prime ministers that were analysed in the course of this chapter. Disagreements are no more or no less prevalent whether prime ministers are involved in economic affairs, in foreign affairs, in both, or in neither. They are no more and no less prevalent whether prime ministers are concerned or not with the overall governmental organisation. The style, consensual or forceful, does not appear to have an incidence either, any more than the role that ministers ask 'their' prime ministers to adopt.

These negative findings can be regarded as somewhat surprising: a relationship between levels of conflict and the style of prime ministers or the extent of involvement in political life could have reasonably been assumed. Forceful prime ministers might thus have been expected to provoke more conflict, while consensus-oriented heads of government might have been regarded as likely to endeavour to reduce conflicts. Somewhat comparable comments might have been made about prime ministers concerned with economic matters in contrast to those who are concerned with foreign affairs. Indeed, more 'laid back' prime ministers who let issues go to cabinet might have been expected to allow more conflicts to develop. This is not the case: the origin of conflicts has therefore to be sought in the nature of the problems, in the overall structure of the cabinet system, or in the personality of the members of the cabinet rather than in the characteristics of the involvement, style, or role of prime ministers.

The limited relationship between prime ministerial characteristics and the collective character of the cabinet

Ministers were asked to state whether they or their colleagues acted often, occasionally, or rarely beyond their departmental competence: the answers to this question give an idea of the extent to which cabinets can be regarded as collective. About a third of the respondents stated that acting beyond departmental competence was common in the cabinets to which they belonged, slightly over half said that such a behaviour was occasional, and a very small proportion claimed that it was rare.

There is a relationship, but only a limited one, between the answers to this question and some of the prime ministerial characteristics that have been examined in this chapter. The role of the prime ministers is not related at all: ministers are said to discuss issues with 'their' prime minister or to go to 'their' prime minister when they are in conflict with an important minister to the same extent whether ministers are more or less likely to act beyond their departmental competence and, therefore, whether the cabinet is more or less collective.[16]

There is, on the other hand, some relationship with respect to style of behaviour and to fields of involvement. In terms of style, as might have been expected, consensus-oriented prime ministers are more likely to be found in collective cabinets than prime ministers who are forceful or even than prime ministers who are both forceful and consensus-oriented; ministers who take initiatives are also less likely to be found in collective cabinets. The relationship is not very strong, however: there are many cases of cabinets in which ministers commonly go beyond their departmental sphere in the context of a forceful prime minister.

The extent and type of involvement of prime ministers is also somewhat related to the collective character of the cabinet, but this relationship is not entirely straightforward. Prime ministers who are concerned with all or most fields of government are more likely to be found in collective cabinets in contrast to those who are not involved in either foreign affairs or the economy, but the relationship stops at this point: the level of prime ministerial concern with the general

Table 10.10 Collegiality of the cabinet and style and fields of involvement of prime ministers (percentages)

	Ministers act beyond their competence				
	Often	Occasionally	Never	No reply/ question not asked	Total
Both consensual and forceful	36	61	1	2	100
Consensual	45	47	1	7	100
Forceful	19	77	4	–	100
Neither	29	59	–	12	100
Total	40	54	1	5	100
Both foreign and economy	42	52	3	3	100
Foreign only	45	54	–	1	100
Economy only	19	61	15	5	100
Neither	29	61	2	8	100
Total	35	56	5	4	100

organisation of the government is the same irrespective of the extent to which the cabinet is collective. Moreover, collective cabinets are more likely to be headed by prime ministers who are involved in foreign affairs than by prime ministers interested in the economy. Overall, the relationship between the collective character of the cabinet and prime ministerial characteristics is thus almost U-shaped: the least collective governments are those where prime ministers are little involved as well as those where prime ministers are forceful. A global involvement associated with a stress on consensus on the part of the prime minister is likely to be associated with a collective cabinet.

The sizeable relationship between the centrality of the cabinet and prime ministerial characteristics

As was noted in earlier chapters, ministers were asked whether, in their experience, the cabinet was an arena where issues were debated and could therefore be described as 'central' to decision-making processes. About a third of the interviewees stated that this was always the case, somewhat under half said that this was the case sometimes, and a little over 10 per cent stated that this was not the case.

There is a close association between two of the three aspects of prime ministerial characteristics that we examined in this chapter – namely

the extent and nature of the involvement and the style of behaviour –
and the extent to which the cabinet plays a central part in decision-
making. There is even some relationship with respect to the role of
heads of governments, but it is limited and perhaps purely accidental:
the cabinet is regarded as more central by those ministers who go to the
prime minister either when they are in conflict with an important
minister or when they wish to bring a matter to the cabinet than by
those ministers who either go to the prime minister in both cases or not
at all. This is somewhat peculiar since, as we saw, there is a tendency
for both these answers to be related to each other.[17]

The relationship is more apparent with respect to the extent and
nature of the fields in which prime ministers are concerned. Where
prime ministerial involvement is limited, the centrality of the cabinet is
also limited: little over a quarter of the prime ministers concerned only
with the general organisation of governments belong to cabinets that
are regarded as discussing major issues; the proportion rises to a third
among those prime ministers who are involved in foreign affairs and to
38 per cent among those who are involved in economic matters.

There is also a marked relationship betwen the style of prime
ministers and the centrality of the cabinet, though the direction of the
relationship is perhaps not the one that might have been expected. Only
a third of the respondents who stated that 'their' prime minister was
consensus-oriented also said that the cabinets to which they belonged
were a central arena for issue-debate; the proportion rises to two-fifths
among the interviewees who stated that 'their' prime minister's style
was forceful. In fact, it is among heads of governments who are said to
practise both a consensual and forceful style that one finds the largest
proportion (46 per cent) of ministers stating that the cabinet is always
an arena for issue-debate: the prime ministers whose style is forceful
and only forceful are indeed also more frequently said to belong to
cabinets in which issues are not just not debated occasionally but not
debated at all (seven out of twenty-seven cases as against 15 per cent on
average).

This last figure is too small for any definite conclusion to be drawn,
but it contributes to the general impression that the centrality of the
cabinet is associated with prime ministers who are markedly involved
and who are assertive. It might have been thought that the centrality of
the cabinet tended to increase as the involvement and the 'strength' of
the head of government decreased. This does not seem to be the case:
neither very strong prime ministers nor those who can be regarded as
very weak or 'laid back' are associated with cabinets that debate major

Table 10.11   Centrality of the cabinet and style and fields of involvement of prime ministers (percentages)

| | Cabinet arena for debate | | | | |
	Always	Sometimes	No	No reply/ Question not asked	Total
Both consensual and					
forceful	46	36	13	5	100
Consensual	29	52	14	5	100
Forceful	22	41	26	11	100
Neither	18	53	24	6	101
Total	33	47	15	5	100
Both foreign and economy	34	45	15	7	101
Foreign affairs	27	56	13	5	101
Economy	39	48	8	5	100
Neither	25	43	24	8	100
Total	31	47	15	6	99

issues, in the same way that an orchestra benefits from a moderately strong director and not from one who is too strong or too weak.

The marked relationship between the hierarchical or prime ministerial character of the cabinet and prime ministerial characteristics

Respondents were asked to state whether, in the cabinets to which they belonged, conflicts were solved by means of prime ministerial decisions, thereby suggesting that the cabinet was hierarchical or even 'prime ministerial' instead of being collegial. A third of the respondents stated that such prime ministerial intervention occurred.

There is a definite relationship between these answers and the fact that heads of government are involved in most fields of government, practise a forceful style, and have an active role in response to ministerial requests for advice or help. Not surprisingly perhaps, the weakest association can be found with respect to the role of prime ministers, although one does find some relationship between the extent to which respondents state that they go to 'their' prime ministers when in conflict with an important minister and the extent to which heads of governments are said to impose decisions.

The relationship is substantial with respect to the level and nature of prime ministerial involvement in fields of government and with respect to the style of this involvement. Under a fifth of the prime ministers (18 per cent) who are not involved in foreign affairs and the economy are said to solve cabinet problems by imposing decisions; over half (54 per cent) of the prime ministers who are involved in both these fields are said to solve cabinet problems by imposing decisions. Only a fifth (22 per cent) of the heads of government whose style is consensual (and only 7 per cent of those who are wholly passive) are said to solve cabinet problems by imposing decisions; two-thirds of the prime ministers whose style is forceful and only forceful and 57 per cent of the prime ministers whose style is both forceful and consensual are said to solve problems by imposing decisions.

Table 10.12   Prime ministerial action and role, style, and fields of involvement of prime ministers

	Conflictual problem solved by prime ministerial decision		
	Absolute figures		%
	Yes	No	Yes/no among those giving an answer
Role			
Ministers go to prime minister with problem and when they are in conflict with an important minister	67	58	54
Only go to prime minister with problem	38	53	42
Only go to prime minister if there is a conflict with an important minister	13	11	54
Neither	21	49	30
Style			
Both consensual and forceful	50	38	57
Consensual only	40	143	22
Forceful only	17	10	63
Neither	1	14	7
Fields of involvement			
Both foreign and economy	61	52	54
Foreign only	20	34	37
Economy only	35	26	57
Neither	13	61	18

A hierarchical or 'prime ministerial' cabinet thus tends to be led by a head of government whose style is forceful and whose involvement is broad. The link between a hierarchical structure and both a forceful style and a broad involvement on the part of prime ministers refers to the remark made earlier in this chapter that forcefulness of style and a broad involvement tend to go together: from this combination emerges a greater desire of prime ministers to solve cabinet problems by imposing decisions (and possibly a greater ability to do so). Yet there are also 'prime ministerial' governments in which the head is not forceful and not widely involved in political life while some prime ministers who are forceful and widely involved in political life belong to cabinets that might be collegial as they are not described as hierarchical or 'prime ministerial'. The relationship between strong leadership and a tendency for the cabinet to be hierarchical does exist, but it is not overwhelming; there are also many contemporary Western European governments that are in no sense 'prime ministerial'.

Ultimately, the most important question about prime ministers is whether they do 'make a difference'. It has been suggested by Asquith, the former British Prime Minister, that 'the office of the Prime Minister is what its holder chooses and is able to make of it', while Neustadt points out that '"powers" are no guarantee of power'.[18] Many leadership studies are also concerned with the 'human factor' in politics.[19] One way of attempting to assess variations is to look at the extent to which prime ministers are 'reputed' to have been successful. For this study, experts were asked to state, independently from the ministerial interviews, the part played by the five most important prime ministers in their respective country along a number of given dimensions and to rank these according to their 'strength'.[20] The prime ministers selected at the top of the list in each country were: Hansson (Sweden), Schmidt (Germany), Lubbers (Netherlands), Spaak (Belgium), Thatcher (United Kingdom), Lemass (Ireland), Kreisky (Austria), Kekkonen (Finland) and Gerhardsen (Norway); for France, presidents were named rather than prime ministers and, hardly surprisingly, De Gaulle was at the top of the list. This information was then compared to that of the cabinet ministers interviewed for this study.

There is a substantial difference between the way these prime ministers were rated and the way others were assessed. Top leaders are said to exercise more influence on almost all aspects of government, although they are particularly influential in foreign affairs. They

Table 10.13 'Top' leaders and other prime ministers compared (percentages)

	Top leaders	Other prime ministers
Role		
Going to prime minister	72	58
Going to prime minister in conflict with other ministers	56	36
Style		
Consensual	59	66
Forceful	31	25
Fields of involvement		
Organisation of government	73	52
Foreign affairs	55	34
Economy	52	40

resemble other prime ministers in that they engage in consensus-building, but they are more active than other heads of government: they talk to ministers individually and take more initiatives than the rest of the prime ministers. In terms of their role, they are appealed to slightly more often in the case of conflicts between ministers. Overall, they impose decisions on ministers appreciably more often than other government heads.

As far as the bulk of prime ministers is concerned, the evidence does suggest that, overall, there are both a number of structural differences and a continuum resulting from country specificities and, almost certainly, personality characteristics. The structural distinction that plays the greatest part is that between single-party and coalition cabinets: in single-party cabinets the prime minister clearly enjoys more power and also makes frequent use of it, although, in the main, prime ministers in single-party governments do not use the strongest weapons at their disposal and, for instance, engage in consensus-building to a substantial extent. This task might be easier for them, however, not only because of the relatively homogeneous character of the cabinet, but because other cabinet members know that, if a consensus does not emerge, the prime minister can use other and stronger means. Yet there is also a continuum in that country specificities shape the characteristics of prime ministerial involvement, style, and role, even if they often do so in combination with structural characteristics. Since such a continuum exists, favourable institutional and political conditions can result in some cabinets being very close to being 'prime ministerial'.

Yet strong 'prime ministerial' rule is not characteristic of the majority of Western European cabinets. Many leaders are not deeply involved in important aspects of political life; the majority have a consensual style; ministers are generally inclined to discuss with the prime minister the matters that they wish to raise in cabinet, but in cases of conflicts with important ministers, heads of governments are far from being always involved. The picture of prime ministers imposing their will on reluctant ministers is clearly a marked exaggeration which fits only some cabinets and even these only some of the time.

The analysis that is conducted here does not make it possible to determine how far prime ministers have become or are becoming more 'powerful' by being involved in more matters, by being more often forceful, by adopting a more central role and, ultimately, by imposing more often their decisions on their colleagues. It is possible, indeed likely that such an increase may have taken place, though it must be remembered that many prime ministers of the past have been very powerful, both in the democratic nations of north-western Europe and in the authoritarian empires and kingdoms of central Europe. Whatever evolution there may have been, it remains clear that the decline of cabinet government, if such a decline has taken place, is not a result exclusively, nor perhaps even primarily, of an increase in the power of prime ministers.

Notes

1. See Chapter 3, *passim*.
2. There is a substantial literature on the role of contemporary prime ministers, primarily British. R.H.S. Crossman published his views on 'prime ministerial' cabinets in the Preface he wrote in 1966 to a new edition of Bagehot's *Cabinet Government*. See also J.P. Mackintosh (1977b), *passim*. A more recent definition of 'prime ministerial' government has been given by P. Dunleavy and R.A.W. Rhodes (1990), who have identified three different modes of prime ministerial government: (1) by generally having the ability to decide policy across all issue areas in which the prime minister takes an interest; (2) by deciding key issues which subsequently determine most remaining areas of government policy; (3) 'by defining a governing ethos, "atmosphere" or operating ideology which generates predictable and determinate solutions to most

policy problems, and hence so constrains other ministers' freedom of manoeuvre as to make them simple agents of the premier's will' (p. 8).
3. See the substantial literature on the subject quoted in the bibliography at the end of this volume.
4. The analysis of the relationship between these variables shows that there are two factors, one corresponding to home affairs and the other to external affairs (including defence). The factor loadings are:

	F 1	F 2
Economy	.40111	.83868
Social	.21848	.88901
For. aff.	.42272	.22574
Defence	.89116	.42832

5. This typology is based exclusively on responses to involvement in foreign affairs and economic affairs involvement in order not to have too many missing data. As there is a close relationship between economic and social affairs, on the one hand, as well as between foreign affairs and defence, on the other, and as the proportion of prime ministers singling out social affairs and/or defence is relatively small, a typology including only foreign affairs and the economy provides a satisfactory impression of the proportion of heads of governments falling into each broad category.
6. In this respect, too, there are two factors, corresponding to a consensual and a forceful approach. The factor loadings are:

	F 1	F 2
Consensus	.19333	.80797
Talk to ministers indiv.	.33691	−.72908
Forceful	.84201	.18901
Taking initiatives	.81220	−.30834

7. The figures are the following: no change 180 (44 per cent); increased influence 54 (13 per cent); decreased influence 41 (10 per cent) with 135 respondents (33 percent) not replying or not being asked that question.
8. There is only one factor corresponding to all types of prime ministerial roles. This suggests in particular that the fact of going to the prime minister in case of conflict with an important minister is associated with the more general tendency to go to the prime minister before raising issues in cabinet.
9. The figures are: going to the prime minister and to the cabinet:73; going to neither: 111; going to the prime minister only: 83; going to the cabinet only: 70; missing data: 73.
10. While 36 per cent of the ministers from coalition governments say that they go to the prime minister in cases of conflict with an important minister, as against 42 per cent of the ministers from single-party majority governments, the corresponding proportions of respondents stating that they go to the cabinet in such situations is respectively 27 and 62 per cent.
11. Among the parties the distribution of active ministers is:
soc. 13, lib. 13, chr.dem. 10, cons. 2;
of passive ministers it is:
soc. 18, lib. 16, chr.dem. 21, cons. 2.

Among single-party majority governments the distribution is:
soc. active 31, passive 3; chr. dem, active 0, passive 3.

12. 32 Conservative respondents stated that 'their' prime minister increased in influence, as against 6 who said that he or she declined in influence: the corresponding figures for liberals were 11 and 17, for socialists, 16 and 8, and for christian democrats, 5 and 10. If one controls for the single-party/coalition distinction, the distribution among coalition governments is: soc. more influence, 12, less influence, 6; chr. dem. more influence, 3, less influence, 5.

13. On average, as we saw in Table 10.4, 23 per cent of the ministers stated that 'their' prime minister was both consensual and forceful, 45 per cent that they were consensual only, 7 per cent that they were forceful only, and 4 per cent that they were neither: the proportions were fairly similar for socialists, liberals, and christian democrats, while, for conservatives, they were respectively 33 per cent, 25 per cent, 37 per cent, and 3 per cent.

14. The proportion of ministers from coalition governments stating that 'their' prime minister had influence over coalition problems varied from 13 'yes' answers and no 'no' answers in the Netherlands to 6 'yes' answers and 31 'no' answers in Finland.

15. See Chapter 3, where these four types of variables are analysed in detail.

16. The figures are: discuss issues with prime minister: yes 243, no 126. Go to prime minister in case of conflict with an important minister: yes 148, no 176.

17. The figures are: discuss issues in cabinet always, 105, sometimes 153, never 40.

18. R. Neustadt (1992), p. 10.

19. J. Blondel (1987), *passim* and in particular Chapter 4.

20. P. Gerlich and W. C. Müller (1988).

Part IV
Conclusions: Achievements, Problems and Reforms

11 Decision-Making, Policy Content and Conflict Resolution in Western European Cabinets

Jaakko Nousiainen

Governmental decision-making may be defined as a problem-solving activity on a broad societal scale. The fundamental questions posed by the study of governments are therefore concerned with policy content and policy outcomes, with the issues that become part of the political agenda and are subsequently discussed and decided at various levels of the cabinet system, with the intensity of the actors' involvement, with the extent of their freedom in the policy space, and with the social consequences of decisions taken.

Since the focus of this study is on the role and modes of operation of Western European cabinets, five main points need to be examined. First, to what extent are cabinets free to select and restrict their agenda? How are their activities substantively focused, and which national questions have highest priority?

Second, assuming that one can rank-order governmental business in terms of the social and political significance of issues, what is, in different policy fields, the cut-off point above which issues are dealt with at the level of the authoritative collective decision-making arena and below which they are handled in specialised sectoral arenas? To what extent do cabinets concentrate on broad guidelines or settle specific issues? The government is concerned at one extreme with everyday routines and crisis-fighting and at the other with strategic planning: can entire issue areas be classified along this continuum? Or do other criteria play a part?

Third, while the field and level of importance of issues are thus two discriminating factors, the ideological direction of decisions taken is a third. One tends to distinguish among economic or social policies, for example, according to their partisan colouring; in reality, a distinction between policy *types* irrespective of content may be a better criterion. Wilson and La Spina classify policies according to the degree of diffusion or concentration of the benefits and costs that these policies allocate to their addressees.[1] As it is in the interest of prime ministers and cabinets to avoid highly controversial solutions, the two best combinations seem to be distributive policies with concentrated benefits and diffused costs and general policies with diffused benefits and diffused costs.

Fourth, in what fields are conflicts more widespread? How successfully are these conflicts resolved and how long does it take to obtain such a resolution?

Finally, fifth, to what extent can it be said that cabinet government achieves its aims and really affects in a positive manner the lives of citizens? How far is cabinet government characterised by a particular approach to the resolution of problems, a solution that has often been called 'corporatist' and is based on the idea of attempting to involve, in a consensual manner, as many potential partners as possible?

THE POLICY SPACE OF WESTERN EUROPEAN CABINETS: WHAT DO CABINETS DO?

By policy space we mean here the area within which the collective cabinet makes choices among several policy options. The concept has legal and empirical, positive and negative aspects. The broad framework is provided by the legal arrangements, which stipulate what a government can do and what it must do. The empirical analysis suggests what a cabinet is in reality able to do and what it is willing to do within that defined policy space.

The policy space has three dimensions, a vertical dimension (policy level), a horizontal dimension (policy field), and an ideological dimension (policy type). To operationalise the last two dimensions is relatively straightforward; the first dimension can be operationalised by adopting a hierarchical classification along the lines suggested by Cobb and Elder.[2] One can thus divide poicies into four types, namely (1) routine administrative matters, coming up for regular review; (2) middle level issues that occur periodically, though not always regularly (as budget discussions, administrative reorganisation, tax reform, social security increases or decreases); (3) new issues, typically related to specific situations such as foreign policy initiatives, energy and environmental policies, constitutional reforms, major disturbances in the labour market; some of these issues emerge from the domestic or international environment, while others are created by political actors; (4) strategic innovative decision-making, such as an extensive national planning in wide policy sectors.

Legal requirements and the practical involvement of cabinets in the policy space

The legal regulation of the policy space takes place at two levels: the top level is constituted by the constitutional provisions about the government's tasks in the state structure; under this level are the norms that specify the powers of the cabinet. The most stringent legal and institutional constraints are found in semi-presidential regimes such as France and Finland, since, in both cases, the constitution reserves important powers to the president, who exercises his authority independently to a varying degree.

In terms of formal duties, the British and Swedish cabinets are at opposite extremes: the British cabinet has no legally defined sphere of responsibility; in Sweden, the plenary session of ministers is given by the constitution the responsibility for almost all that is decided at the governmental level since it is stated that 'government matters shall be decided upon at government meetings'. Other Western European countries are located between these two extremes in terms of the respective legal powers of the cabinet and of individual ministers, but, even now, legal rules are vague, although, in general, legislative and budgetary matters must be brought to cabinet meetings for deliberation: there is thus an ill-defined 'grey zone' within which the proper decision-making arena is determined *in casu*, the prime minister and individual ministers having wide discretionary powers as to which new projects they want to see decided collectively.

Finland and Sweden are the countries in which the lines of authority between the different public actors are drawn most accurately and rigidly by law and decree – both vertically and horizontally: in these two countries, all administrative authorities are expected to know which matters fall within their legal competence; uncertainty and demarcation disputes are extremely rare, and entrance into another authority's area requires formal authorisation. Indeed, in these two countries, the cabinet's role is based on the principle that the meeting resolves formally individual administrative 'cases'.

The importance of formal arrangements should not be exaggerated, however; as a matter of fact, Britain and Sweden are close to each other in practice. 'Who decides on everything decides on very little'. The formal session of the Swedish cabinet tends to be little more than a ritual, a decision-making machine that handles about 25 000 issues every year: it is therefore not of interest to know which matters are formally presented for ratification, but which are examined informally. This makes the Swedish cabinet rather similar to the British cabinet.

Two of the most general factors that in practice restrict the agendas are *time constraint* and *institutional inertia*. In terms of time constraints, however, we must remember, as was pointed out in Chapter 4, that, for instance, Dutch ministers spend on average twice as much time as their Finnish colleagues in cabinet meetings. Admittedly, masses of routine matters can be cleared quickly. Meanwhile, there is another aspect to the scarcity of time, namely that governments are often short-lived and that ministers do not see through the solution of long-term problems: it has been argued that two or three years were necessary for ministers to have an impact;[3] furthermore, the time required to draft plans and to reach agreements on the details of these plans is particularly long in coalition governments and yet the duration of these governments is on average somewhat shorter, as we saw in Chapter 3.

For all these reasons, studies of national policy styles suggest that the reactive type is predominant and the anticipatory active type exceptional. Complex organisations react slowly because of their size and because of the established interests of the bureaucracy. When politicians are cross-pressured, they often devise policies that appear to solve the problems: 'The politician must appear to do something, no matter what, as long as he gets the issue off the agenda'.[4] Moreover, following the Kuhnian principle, public policy is elaborated within a certain cognitive framework. Potential solutions are adjusted to the prevailing pattern in different sectors. Truly innovative policies are possible only when preceded by a revision of the dominant paradigm in the field.[5] Changes of cabinet ministers and even of parties may thus lead only to slight changes in policy: thus the participation of communists in seven Finnish governments between 1966 and 1982 did not result in any significant reshaping of established policies in the ministries they controlled.

FILLING THE POLICY SPACE: THE BROAD CABINET AGENDAS

The sources of cabinet agendas: planned items and accidents

The cabinet agenda is based on problems that have become politicised, are objects of conflict among public actors, and become policy issues as a result. This transformation takes place in the party arena, in the electoral arena, in the parliamentary arena, in the bureaucratic arena, and in the corporatist arena before arriving at cabinet level.[6] At this point the agenda has to be drawn and horizontal and vertical aspects of the cabinet's problem-solving mechanisms come into play.

One can distinguish between planned items and items that emerge out of the concrete situation. Government programmes give an idea of the planned activities, but their role as effective agenda sources does vary. In the case of coalitions, there may be detailed negotiations, carefully recorded, which will restrict markedly the policy space of the cabinet;[7] single-party governments, on the other hand, may refer to party documents, primarily the electoral manifesto. In nine of the twelve Western European countries studied here (Belgium, the Netherlands, Germany, Austria, Italy, Denmark, Norway, Sweden, and Finland) new governments always formulate programmes; in Britain, the electoral manifesto of the winning party serves the same purpose; in France and Ireland the practice does vary. The programme is typically presented to parliament for discussion, a programme that, as Figure 11.1 shows, always has a broad scope, whether it is detailed or not. There has been a tendency to shift from brief declarations to long and specific documents, the elaboration of the governmental

Figure 11.1 Structure of government programmes

Specificity		narrow	Scope		broad
	brief manifesto-like		S A	GB IRL	
	somewhat specific	( )	(S)	D	N DK
	detailed and specific		SF F I	NL B	

programme being most developed in countries with a fragmented party system where the coalition-building raises difficult problems.

Yet the extent of specificity decreases sharply as one moves from lower to higher agenda levels. It is possible to negotiate detailed agreements on middle level issues, for example on next year's budget; for new and major issues, on the other hand, only general purposes and goals are likely to be recorded in the final document. The planning process and the identification of the means to achieve the desired ends, which are the real sources of conflicts, take place later in various arenas, depending on the structure of the party–government relationship and on the requirements of the situation.

Moreover, programmatic declarations have different meanings for the various participants. Even when they are detailed and specific, they constitute primarily insurance policies. Party leaders are aware of the fact that the real settlement of the issue will take place later: by including many types of issues within the government agreement, they seek a tentative assurance that they will have a voice in that settlement.[8] Parts of the programmes tend to be pseudo-agendas: they reflect the hopes of the participants rather than realistic expectations; their aim is to reduce the frustrations of a variety of groups.

The cabinet agenda can never be entirely fixed on the basis of programmes, however: new problems, goals, and solutions are continuously introduced. Thus the real agenda of most cabinets is filled with recurrent middle level issues and with new issues that are below the 'high policy' level. One thing leads to another, and initiatives and impulses coming from many sides are joined together in a complicated preparation process.

Policy orientations reflect in particular the objective requirements of the problems at hand as well as the standpoints of the decision-makers; they also depend on situational and personal factors: the 'events approach' to cabinet research has identified the role of situations.[9] 'Cabinet behaviour is disorderly. . . . Some cabinets come into existence with well-defined policy proposals which are sweeping in their potential for social change and which are swiftly promulgated into law, while others seem content to accomplish little in the way of major reform. Still others seem beset with conflict and controversy, while some encounter little adversity.'[10]

Meanwhile, personal factors enter the picture. Some policy sectors may be given priority because a particular prime minister is interested and appoints the right ministers, while nothing appears to happen over other large areas. A study of West German coalitions thus indicated that the direct linkage between party programme and cabinet policy was largely explained by the occupancy of cabinet portfolios.[11]

Single-party cabinets and coalitions differ from each other significantly with respect to the manner in which inputs are processed into agenda items. In single-party cabinets there is a direct link between party preferences, the main points of the government declaration, and the actual cabinet agenda, although the detailed specification and operationalisation of programmatic demands may take place either in the party organisation or in the cabinet. In the case of coalitions the link is not direct; there also has to be joint bargaining to reconcile conflicting goals. Thus the compromises reached may be such that the origin of a measure is no longer identifiable.

The cabinet's position depends in part on whether the government programme has been imposed from outside, or whether the ministers have actively participated in drafting it; but it is also important to know where the day-to-day bargaining system is located, specifically, within the cabinet machinery, whether it takes place in an inner cabinet or in a cabinet committee, on the one hand, or in institutionalised meetings of organisational leaders. The first two formulas leave ministers with wide room of manoeuvre, the last means that the entire cabinet is a dependent agent. Hence a paradox: the more the parties penetrate the government in terms of ministerial recruitment, the more the government becomes functionally detached from its makers. There are also other background features: in a strongly conflictual political culture and/or when equal parties compete for power, a party's ministerial group is an advanced base fighting against several enemies. Party objectives can only be reached partially: ministers are under supervision, as they might be inclined to make excessive concessions in the name of peace in the coalition and in the preservation of their own positions. In more consensual conditions, the top party leaders are likely to enter the government themselves to pursue long-term national policies, rather than fight for some vital group interests.

CABINET DECISION-MAKING

The vertical determination of collective agendas: the cut-off point below and above which matters are not discussed in cabinet

As far as the basic governmental structure is concerned, the collective agendas of single-party cabinets can be expected to be restricted above a given point, administrative routines and many middle level issues being left to individual ministers to decide, though these ministers may submit such matters at their discretion to the collective body. Decisions on high-level policies depend on the governmental power structure: collegial cabinets discuss these together, while prime ministerial and oligarchical cabinets do so in small groups of influential ministers. In this case the main function of the cabinet meeting is to satisfy the psychological needs of members.

In coalitions formed by parties that are equally strong, as the partners keep a close watch on each other, the cut-off point below which matters come to the effective agenda is likely to be lower: relatively minor matters – for example, appointments at a junior level – may be political and become the object of a 'give-and-take' among the parties. Routine administrative and many middle level issues are thus emphasised in the day-to-day governmental process; the style of decision-making becomes essentially incrementalist and strategic decision-making may escape from the cabinet as such and be handled by an oligarchical coalition committee, although, even in this case, all ministers are probably able to take part indirectly in the decisions in their party groups. Meanwhile, the cut-off point above which matters are not discussed is often also lowered: indeed, the more competitive and conflictual the coalition, the stronger the propensity of the agenda to slide downward, as conflictual high policy issues are left aside for the sake of preserving harmony among cabinet partners. Initial governmental agreements often exclude these issues from the agenda.

The same situation occurs in minority governments, especially when these are temporary. Their agenda is not likely to include high-level questions; the weaker the parliamentary support, the more this will be the case: non-partisan caretaker cabinets tend to restrict their activities to routine administrative matters, and to those recurrent middle level issues that need to be settled absolutely.

The distinction between 'central' and 'dependent' cabinets does apply here, as 'dependent' cabinets implement decisions made by party leaders outside the cabinet system in terms of new issues and strategic policy-making, while cabinets that are central formulate these themselves. The point arises in all types of governments, since, as we saw in Chapter 3, there is little difference in this respect between the evaluations of those who had served in single party governments, whether of the majority or of the minority type, and those who had served in coalitions. The same conclusion can be drawn for countries that experienced governments of both types, except in Austria where ministers from single-party governments state far more often than ministers from coalition governments that the cabinet is always an important arena for discussions on major policies. The country differences are those that appear most substantial, with respondents from Belgium, Finland, France, Ireland, and Norway stressing the role of the cabinet meeting, while respondents from Britain, Denmark, Germany, Italy, and the Netherlands see it only occasionally as a policy-shaping arena. One must distinguish, however, between ministerial dependence and cabinet dependence: individual ministers may be forced to keep close contact with leading party organs, but the cabinet as a whole may remain a place where compromises and adjustments are made. This situation may lead to less than rational solutions or indeed even to immobilism, however.

Ministerial interviews provide information about variations among cabinets in terms of the vertical dimension of agenda-building. As was already indicated in Chapter 3, there is a greater tendency for ministers to affect each other's actions in single-party governments than in coalitions, although the difference is relatively small: in coalitions, parties often endeavour to 'colonise' the departments under their control and are keen not to let cabinet partners interfere in their policies. Indeed, ministers in coalition governments are less concerned to settle matters in discussions with some other ministers – in this case, with ministers from their own party – than ministers in single-party governments. This is probably because, as we noted earlier, the collective agenda tends to be stretched vertically in coalitions; primarily innovative and politically sensitive issues must in all circumstances be brought to plenary sessions, the ministers being left without much choice for individual action.

There are limitations to this trend, however. First, the decision-making styles of the ministers of the two types of government do not differ from each other in countries that have been ruled both by single-party governments and by coalitions, Austria, Denmark, Ireland, Norway and Sweden. Second, the fact that ministers are subordinated does not mean that departmental issues go automatically to the cabinet meeting; the effective handling often takes place somewhere in-between, primarily in a more or less private discussion with the prime minister or some other ministers. Even cabinet committees, let alone the full cabinet, are less frequently resorted to than these informal arenas. In coalitions there is again less willingness – or need – to place matters in front of the whole team.

The horizontal agenda: the fields covered by cabinets

Other things being equal, single-party governments are likely to be concerned primarily with policy areas that are closely connected with their *raison d'être*, and in particular with their basic ideology, their interest group linkages, and their electoral tactics. When a party is large, however, differences from one to another are likely to be slight. Overall, compact majorities appear best suited to pursue extensive and nationally important general policies;[12] in heterogeneous Centre-left and Centre-right – as well as exceptionally Left-right – coalitions, on the other hand, the inputs of all partners must be taken into consideration. The collective agenda will thus cover extensively the political field, the dominant profile being a mixture of general and distributive policies.

Minority governments probably prefer to avoid conflictual issues, as confrontations with a majority in parliament may endanger their very existence. The substance of these questions varies according to situations and political systems, however. Problems in which the national interest is at stake and that call for consensual decision-making, such as foreign policy and defence issues, are also avoided by minority governments. Minority governments depending on support coming from different parties will tend to favour distributive policies at the middle level of the overall policy space.

Cabinets that are central transform inputs from various sources into collective decisions inside the cabinet system, while the policy space of dependent cabinets is increasingly reduced as one moves from more peripheral issues to core areas of partisan commitment. Cabinets that are central can expand the agenda and cover many general policies; dependent cabinets are forced to concentrate on distributive policies in the interest areas of participant parties.

FROM CONFLICT TO CONSENSUS

In 1988, the Finnish State Council handled in eighty-one formal plenary sessions a total of 4472 agenda items (the figures from the two previous years were 4649 and 5060). A final decision was reached on 2143 items; the rest – about half of all the issues considered – were presented as the cabinet's recommendation to the presidential session for final resolution: in the majority of these cases, the effective decision was also made by the cabinet.[13]

The four ministries with the highest number of agenda items – foreign affairs, finance, education and culture, and transport – were responsible for 50 per cent of all cabinet business; on the other hand, the four most 'inactive' or most independent departments – labour, defence, interior, and environment – were responsible for only 13 per cent.

If these items are in turn subdivided 'vertically' in terms of their importance, 31 per cent concerned legislation, other parliamentary business, and government decrees, 2 per cent each national planning, 'decisions in principle', and the more important aspects of foreign relations. Thus a little more than one-third of all the issues presented at cabinet meetings related to general policy questions while almost two-thirds concerned individual and routine administrative decisions: in this last group, personnel management and matters involving various government committees formed the largest single category (29 per cent of all items).

In other cabinets, the numbers of matters to be decided was much smaller. It would seem that each of these cabinets had to deal approximately, during the 1980s, every year and on the basis of about forty-five meetings a year, with 500 to 700 items of a middle or high level character demanding genuine political deliberation; alongside these, perhaps 300 to 600 undisputed matters had to be decided on. This is on the understanding that, by the 1980s, too, in most countries, middle-to-high level issues were no longer discussed at length in the full cabinet as a whole but that, as we saw in Chapter 4, the most important deliberations had come to take place in formal committees and in informal meetings of ministers.

Conflictual questions, as they have been reported in the press, give an idea of the matters that occupied the time of national cabinets. These conflicts do not occur only over major issues, as the number of middle level problems that give rise to disagreements shows; they touch on the whole range of the agenda, although they are a little more concerned with foreign and economic policies than with other questions. In the larger countries, foreign and defence issues are both conflictual policy-making areas and agenda items of high policy value; they are of minor importance in Ireland, Belgium, Finland, and Sweden. Interestingly, this country division corresponds to the one that we found in the previous chapter to obtain with respect to the fields of involvement of prime ministers across Western Europe. In the Swedish cabinet, social issues, such as welfare schemes, employment, housing and environment, are raised more often than in other countries. In the

Table 11.1 Political field of cabinet conflicts (percentages)

Policy area	A Austria	B Belgium	DK Denmark	SF Finland	F France	D Germany	I Italy	IRL Ireland	NL Netherlands	S Sweden	GB Britain
Foreign affairs, defence	13	5	13	2	12	21	5	10	12	4	13
Justice, general administration	19	11	12	24	8	38	10	6	11	–	11
Finance, management of the economy	13	17	22	22	16	31	33	42	35	20	21
Material production	21	11	8	18	15	–	7	20	10	28	23
Social affairs	21	8	20	17	13	3	12	16	19	36	16
Cultural problems	–	38	4	3	6	–	12	2	4	4	9
Miscellaneous and general political	15	11	19	13	29	7	21	6	10	8	8
Total	102	101	98	99	99	100	100	102	101	100	101
N	39	37	230	294	81	29	42	159	159	25	188

Belgian cabinet, the language and nationality problem is the most burning issue, with almost 40 per cent of all conflicts revolving around this question. Administrative matters play a large part in Germany and Finland: civil service appointments have often been conflictual in these two countries.

In general, the policy problems of Western European cabinets in the 1970s and 1980s were predominantly related to public finance, the management of the national economy, and material production – industry, commerce, transport, energy. Only in Finland have agricultural questions often been conflictual in cabinet, probably because of the central part played by the Agrarian party in the coalitions of that country; elsewhere in Western Europe, agriculture appears as a conflictual issue only at the European Community level.

In three countries, data have been collected in such a way as to make it possible to consider variations over time and across types of cabinets. In Britain, there were strong differences between major issues in the Labour and Conservative cabinets. For the Labour cabinets of 1974–9 the problematic areas were industrial policy and European affairs; for the Conservative government of 1979–83, national defence, energy issues and regional development, as well as to an extent social policy, featured most prominently within the cabinet. In the Netherlands, on the other hand, there were few differences between cabinets of the 1972–80 period and those of the 1981–7 period in terms of problematic issues, except that financial problems seem to have caused more concern to the cabinets of the second period than to their predecessors. The behaviour of two large Centre-left coalitions of 1966–8 and 1984–5 in Finland varied markedly: the second cabinet had three times as many conflicts as the first; the strained relations between the social democrats and the centre party in the 1980s were reflected in quarrels about appointments.

NATIONAL DECISION STYLES AND THE RESOLUTION OF CONFLICTS IN CABINETS

This last point indicates that there may be substantial variations in the intensity of conflicts in cabinets. In general, it may be hypothesised that conflicts arising between ministers belonging to the same party are the least serious, that conflicts between ministers from different parties are more serious, while the most fundamental are those in which the prime minister (as well as the president in France and Finland) are involved.

Table 11.2 Actor profiles of cabinet conflicts (percentages)

Ministers involved	A Austria	B Belgium	DK Denmark	SF Finland	F France	D Germany	IRL Ireland	I Italy	NL Netherlands	S Sweden	GB Britain
Ministers of the same party	26	–	26	4	14	14	12	19	18	–	87
Same party, different factions	–	5	2	–	7	3	5	1	–	4	1
Different parties, individual	8	24	3	19	11	28	12	42	39	20	–
Different parties, party members	20	68	23	53	16	24	31	28	22	60	–
PM v. minister, same party	38	–	3	–	19	17	31	–	5	16	13
PM v. minister, other party	8	3	3	5	10	14	7	6	3	–	–
Minister or PM v. parliament	–	–	–	5	24	–	–	1	–	–	–
Other actors	–	–	39	13	–	–	2	2	13	–	–
Total	100	100	99	99	101	100	100	101	100	100	101
N	39	37	230	294	81	29	42	159	158	25	188

The origin and nature of conflicts

There are indeed substantial variations in the persons involved in conflicts as well as in the actors in these conflicts. By and large, prime ministers are not markedly involved when the coalitions are complex. Thus one finds the Austrian and German chancellors and the French prime minister being parties in many conflicts, but not heads of government in Finland, Italy, Belgium, and the Netherlands, where coalitions are built with difficulty and cut across the ideological divide. As we saw in the previous chapter, the main task of these prime ministers is to reduce internal tension; they have also to be able to exercise an arbitration role; if, in these types of coalitions, the prime minister openly takes a stand in a cabinet dispute, this means that tension is high and that the cabinet is close to collapsing. The actors in the conflicts are thus typically ministers belonging to different parties. As the political undertones of conflicts vary, however, it is not possible to distinguish firmly between partisan and departmental conflicts in these coalitions; indeed, even in the single-party British cabinets, where almost 90 per cent of the reported conflicts are based on divergent departmental interests, factional divisions based on ideological distinctions are not wholly ruled out.

The solution of conflicts

Governments cannot survive long in an atmosphere poisoned by incessant conflicts: it is therefore important that these conflicts be resolved quickly. As a matter of fact, about two-thirds of these are ended within one month, the most conspicuous deviant case being that of the Netherlands, where the number of accidental and quickly resolved conflicts is small and the share of persistent conflicts is high, these persistent conflicts tending to occur primarily in the fields of public economy and of social and health policy. In French and British cabinets, persistent conflicts take place in the fields of public finance, the political management of the economy, and industrial policy. Overall, as might have been expected, interparty conflicts tend to last longer than intraparty conflicts, irrespective of the type of problem.

The ultimate outcome of a conflict, in the case of a total deadlock, is the resignation of the government or of one of the coalition parties. Of the twenty-six total resignations covered by the analysis of conflicts undertaken for this study, the main causes were general governmental policy (seven cases), the management of the economy (six cases), and

Table 11.3   Solution of cabinet conflicts (percentages)

Final outcome	A	B	DK	SF	F	D	IRL	I	NL	S	GB
Total resignation	–	24	2	1	9	–	–	2	3	–	–
Individual resignation	5	8	4	–	19	17	15	–	3	–	–
Compromise	22	46	37	41	42	35	23	80	35	24	20
Problem frozen	8	3	2	7	17	3	13	10	13	40	11
Someone wins without resignations	60	8	45	48	11	45	30	8	26	16	66
Other solution	5	11	11	2	3	–	20	–	21	20	3
Total	100	100	101	99	101	100	101	100	101	100	100
N	37	37	230	217	81	29	40	140	136	25	183

financial issues (four cases); four out of nine resignations in Belgium (but only four of them) were connected with the language question.

Less dramatic is the case of individual minister resignations. These occur rarely in Belgian, Dutch, Finnish and Italian governments: this is perhaps because, on minor matters, the minister may accept defeat, whereas more important issues are raised at the interparty level and a compromise has then to be negotiated to keep the coalition alive. Such occurrences are rare also in Austria, despite the fact that conflicts are relatively frequent in that country: chancellors impose their solution and losing ministers comply. On the other hand, the high frequency of ministerial resignations in some countries may be related to the strong position of the prime minister (or prime minister and president) in these countries: whether a party to or an umpire in the conflict, the head of the government is the ultimate decision-maker, and the only solution for a losing but uncompromising minister is to give up his or her portfolio. However, there are limits to this power, even in France: the prime ministers of that country may impose their will upon the ministers from their own party, but they must often negotiate compromises with representatives of other parties in order to preserve the unity of the parliamentary majority.[14] On the other hand, in Britain, someone normally wins without further complications. There are well-publicised exceptions, however, and ministers are also often eased out subsequently in periodic reshuffles. Meanwhile, as was

Table 11.4   Arenas of conflict solution (percentages)

Arena	A	B	DK	SF	F	D	IRL	I	NL	S	GB
Cabinet	30	49	26	66	63	24	71	44	41	80	45
Cabinet committee	–	14	2	5	–	3	2	29	6	–	38
Parliament	3	5	23	10	5	–	2	6	3	–	2
Party/parties	30	22	26	7	6	14	5	6	1	–	–
Cabinet and party/parties	35	8	12	10	26	3	5	11	22	20	1
Other	3	3	12	2	–	55	15	4	27	–	14
Total	101	101	101	100	100	99	100	100	100	100	100
N	37	37	230	217	81	29	40	114	143	25	107

pointed out in Chapter 3, the level of tension in British cabinets is said by respondents to be relatively low.

Conflicts can be solved both inside and outside the cabinet proper. In Britain and Sweden, about 80 per cent of the conflicts – and in Ireland slightly less – are settled within the cabinet, either at the full meeting or in a committee. These are countries where the government is based frequently or always on a single party: this mode is presumably best suited to an integrated structure of agenda management. The cabinet is the working committee of the party: there is no clear institutional distinction between party and government. In Britain, conflictual matters are usually delegated to cabinet committees. There is also an emphasis on the cabinet arena in Italy, Belgium, and Finland, despite the fact that these countries have fragmented party systems; this is a result of the fact that the cabinet is detached from background groups in its everyday operations, and that there is no other institutional arena for settling disputes occurring on these issues. As we saw in Chapter 7, party leaders do not meet outside the cabinet in Finland, while party presidents are sometimes in the cabinet in Belgium, and the Italian party structure is typically too factional to provide clear and continuous extra-cabinet leadership.

In Austria, Germany, and France, the decision-making profile is different. In Austria, the grip of party organisations is so strong that most disputes, irrespective of their content, are sent to the parties or to a joint group of cabinet and party members; as we saw, the chancellor is also very influential. The influence of the chancellor is equally large in Germany, where half the conflicts are solved by the head of the government alone. In France, the cabinet meeting appears to play a somewhat larger part in solving conflicts, but it is not clear how often the solution is based in reality on a decision of the prime minister or of the president of the Republic taken in the context of the cabinet meeting.

In France and Finland in particular, a large proportion of conflicts are said to be concerned with 'general' governmental matters. In coalitions, these matters threaten the existence of the government, and consequently their resolution often depends on party decisions; on the other hand, disputes on fiscal policy are normally settled inside the cabinet, as are questions of an administrative character or middle level issues that are on the cabinet agenda.

TYPES AND STYLES OF POLICY-MAKING

The most fundamental question, however, is whether governments achieve their goals, not so much in terms of technical efficiency (that is to say in terms of the relation between resources used and outcomes produced), but in terms of their ability to achieve a large proportion of the expected outcomes. This means also determining whether parliamentary governments have some room for manoeuvre to make choices among several policy options.

One of the main concerns of policy analysis research during the past two decades has been to find explanations for national policy outcomes, and primarily for macro-economic performance; these explanations have been sought in terms of the political composition of governments, of the interaction models between interest groups, of the political weight of competing social classes in capitalist states, and of the socio-economic structure of society. Research designs have been varied, the testing has been difficult, and the results somewhat inconsistent. Of these attempts, perhaps the easiest to test have been those that have linked policy outcomes to the partisan composition of governments.

Such a link between party programmes, government declarations, and outputs must be expected to be clearest in single-party majority cabinets, since these have the greatest opportunity to do what they said they wanted to do. Much is expected of ministers, as election pledges are 'on the table' as soon as the winning party enters into office. A study of Britain and Canada confirms that cabinets in both countries have a generally high record of success in implementing their intended policies, assuming that they have a secure parliamentary majority and a full session at their disposal.[15] Over the 1945–78 period, the British cabinet implemented on average 64 per cent of intended policies and the Canadian cabinet implemented an even higher proportion, although this does not necessarily mean that governmental policies were particularly innovative or far-reaching.

The case of coalitions is different since negotiation and conciliation processes are likely to interplay across the whole life-span of the cabinet. Two opposite hypotheses can be put forward as to what might occur: there may be immobilism with policy 'underproduction' or intense action with policy-'overproduction'. The first hypothesis is based on the assumption that the governmental agenda is restricted by negotiation and conciliation problems, with the effect that issues on which there is a zero-sum game among the coalition partners are excluded. Policies will be reduced to the highest common denominator – typically rather low; indeed, the greater the ideological, social and political heterogeneity of the coalition, the more questions of high policy are likely to be omitted from the effective agenda. Yet it may be that party elites can by-pass the difficulty by offering payoffs to each participant. While, in the first case, the coalition will produce less, in the second, it will produce more than would be the case in a single party cabinet.

Both the policy overproduction and the policy underproduction hypotheses have been supported by empirical evidence from various European countries. According to Schmidt's interpretation, the economic environment is the crucial independent variable. 'In periods of economic prosperity it is easy to give a great deal to a great many people. Hence the ideological and social heterogeneity of the coalition is not a crucial obstacle.'[16] The decision-making arrangement is totally different in periods of economic crisis. 'The room for manoeuvre on the part of the government and of the coalition partners becomes narrower, economic conflicts tend to become more intense, and if large-scale deficit spending is excluded, it is no longer possible to distribute increments'.[17] For political reasons the attitudes of coalition partners are uncompromising and come closer to their core ideological goals. Fewer general policies are adopted and the implementation of distributive policies becomes more difficult: all partners fear ending up as losers, remaining attentive and hostile. The Italian experience lends support to the assertion that politically weak and dependent coalitions, whose life is largely coloured by power conflicts among coalition parties, tend generally to carry through piecemeal but extensive distributive policies by giving something to everyone. 'Instead of legislating about general situations and broad interests, governments tend to meet particularistic demands and to regulate small groups.'[18]

The room for manoeuvre of minority governments is also varied, as these differ from one another markedly in terms of parliamentary support, the number of participant bodies, and the location of the cabinet on the ideological spectrum. These governments need extra support in parliament: if this comes from one or more parties that are not willing to defeat the cabinet, the room for manoeuvre can be relatively large.[19] Minority governments are strongest where they occupy a centre position and are facing opposition from both Left and Right: they might then be able to preserve a distinctive profile for a substantial period. In the Danish case, when votes in parliament are analysed, policy elasticity is found to be extremely high, as the government accepts defeat to a surprisingly large extent.[20] As a result, most parties thus appear to be effective policy-makers; in some cases, even the normal roles of government and opposition are reversed. However, such a pattern is possible only in consensual political systems in which minority governments are not merely transitional solutions; contrary to the 'immobilist' hypothesis, there is then a considerable expansion of the governmental policy space and of the scope of outputs.

Figure 11.2   Policy styles and roles of governments

		Governmental strategy	
		active problem-solving	reactive problem-solving
Actor relationships	consensual	A. Policy coordination	B. Policy ratification
	pluralist–competitive	C. Policy direction	D. Policy adoption

Broad decision-making styles – is corporatism the cabinet style *par excellence*?

If the government's approach to social problem-solving and the structure of organised interest intermediation are both taken into account, four ideal-types emerge.[21] Two of these, (A) and (B), correspond to a 'corporatist' formulation of policies, based on an integrated structure of organised interests and on the government's willingness to 'deal' with interests, to be accommodating, and to look for a consensus. The difference between the two cells is based on whether the government plays an active part or has a more reactive and adaptive attitude towards new issues. The other two types are cases of State intervention, one of which (C) is dynamic, while the other (D) is static.

In relation to economic matters, there are clear differences in predominant decision-making modes across countries. These can be broadly characterized as corporatist *v.* pluralistic or consensual *v.* competitive. The extent to which each of these modes is effective is not clear. 'Different methods and different ways of using the same basic method often give different results, and tend in any case to leave room for varying interpretations as well as for unexplained residuals.'[22] In the 1970s and early 1980s, it was usually believed that a consensual policy style, involving the participation of labour unions and of organised business in policy formation, and in which leadership was coalescent rather than competitive, was a significantly positive factor of economic performance, despite the fact that bargaining might be time-consuming and decision-making rather rigid. Subsequently, however, there has been less agreement on this point.

Therborn found little evidence to suggest that corporatism matters in terms of economic outcomes, although there seems to be a positive relationship in the case of Scandinavia.[23] Overall, however, at any rate as far as general system stability is concerned, consensus democracy seems superior to majoritarian democracy for plural societies.[24]

Moreover, there may not be only one predominant policy-making mode in a country over all the policy-making areas; differences between policy sectors may even have tended to increase. As the innovative policies of the 1950s and 1960s became 'normal' public functions, the focus of activities shifted from the collective cabinet in the direction of ministries: this can be expected to have resulted in the formation of autonomous and self-contained policy communities with their own clientele relationships, their machinery of preparation of decisions, and their decision-making modes.

Long-term trends in policy-making styles are also affected by situational factors. The traditional bureaucratic 'policy adoption style' (D) presupposes a low level of State activity, a low degree of organisation, a large amount of political illiteracy, and a hierarchical structure of authority. Cabinet ministers are informed on a weekly basis of routine measures; they acquiesce easily to policies since few alternatives are open to them. As resources and expectations grow, the government becomes more active, relies on a more rational preparation of proposals, and resorts to stronger measures – regulative and distributive – to direct social and political development. The importance of the cabinet in setting agendas and deciding on priorities becomes significant: final policy decisions are the result of a complex interplay between different levels of the cabinet system.

The mobilisation and organisation of the citizenry forces the cabinet to be ready to accept forms of negotiation and coordination: consensus grows at the expense of imposition. Policy stagnation, as a result of increasing welfare provisions and/or a decline in economic growth, leads to segmentation, to negative relationships and to the reduction of the cabinet's role merely to ratify decisions taken elsewhere. Such an evolution appears to have been completed in several Western European countries by the end of the 1970s.

At this point, three alternative paths are open. The circle may be closed by a return to imposition politics as 'it is extremely difficult to negotiate sacrifices'. Or the search for new solutions may stimulate the policy direction rôle of the cabinet, as some developments in the Thatcher cabinets suggest. Or the negotiation mode may be preserved and even emphasised where corporatism is strong, though, as organised groups are increasingly protective of their interests, decisions are taken more *ad hoc* in a difficult bargaining process.

A comparative analysis on the ways in which Western European democracies responded to the economic crisis of the mid-1970s is revealing.[25] The crisis brought about a change in the general pattern of policy-making insofar as, in practice, most countries ultimately moved from a pattern of rather reactive and consensual politics to one of innovation and conflict (the second path). This change occurred principally in Britain, but also in Belgium and Denmark. Other countries, such as Sweden, the Netherlands, and Austria, tried to maintain consensus even though they were also moving towards policy innovation. The division roughly corresponded to the distinction between the more corporatist and the more pluralistic systems. The extent of corporatism was also related to the time-lag: the least corporatist states moved first and the most corporatist states last. Yet the true economic consequences of those policy changes remain difficult to assess on a comparative basis.

The policies that cabinets implement are the result both of the inputs which, by a variety of channels, society presses on the government and of the action of cabinet members who operate within structures that differ appreciably from country to country. Thus the policy space is in substantial part predetermined by programmes and by circumstances. Yet the cabinets are the bodies that take the decisions concerning these issues and, as a result, they can legitimately be regarded as being in charge, although cabinet composition and cabinet rules markedly reduce the room for manoeuvre. In the context of this complex set of arrangements, the basic originality of cabinets, namely the collective and collegial character of these bodies, as well as their central decision-making position, is sometimes lost sight of and indeed even regarded as abandoned. This conclusion is partly true, although it is not certain that cabinets were fully collegial and collective in the past. Moreover, in the end, the policy outcomes of many, and probably of the majority of cabinets most of the time, have a consensual and a corporatist character, as if the nature of the decision process was reflected in the content of the decisions taken. It is not possible to demonstrate that the group character of the cabinet process and consensual outcomes are closely linked, let alone that one influences the other; it is none the less worth noting that cabinet decision-making in Western Europe has, by and large, a consensual nature and that when, occasionally, a particular cabinet moves away from this mode of behaviour, there is eventually a return to a more consensual approach.

Notes

1. J. Q. Wilson (1980). A. La Spina (1990), *passim*.
2. R. W. Cobb and C. D. Elder (1972), pp. 85–9.
3. R. Rose (1971), pp. 393–414.
4. G. Gustafsson and J. Richardson (1989), p. 417.
5. P. Ahonen (1986), pp. 309–11.
6. G. Sjöblom (1986), pp. 94–5.
7. For Belgium, see L. de Winter (1989), p. 726.
8. D. Truman (1964), p. 285.
9. E. C. Browne and D. W. Gleiber (1986), p. 93.
10. Ibid., p. 299.

282   *Decision-Making, Policy and Conflict Resolution*

11. R.I. Hoffebert and H.D. Klingemann (1990), pp. 277–304.
12. A. La Spina (1990), pp. 12–16.
13. Data provided by Cabinet Information Office.
14. J.-L. Thiébault (1989), pp. 93–6.
15. I. Budge, D. Robertson, and D. Hearl (1987), Ch. 1.
16. M. Schmidt (1983), pp. 51–2.
17. Ibid., p. 54.
18. M. Cotta (1988), p. 135.
19. K. Strom (1990), Ch. 4.
20. E. Damgaard and P. Svensson (1989), *passim*.
21. J. Richardson (1982), p. 13. K. Schubert (1988), pp. 176–8.
22. G. Therborn (1987), p. 260.
23. Ibid., pp. 260–74.
24. J. Pekkarinen, M. Pohjola, and B. Rowthorn (1991), *passim*.
25. E. Damgaard, P. Gerlich, and J.J. Richardson (1989), pp. 184–91.

12 Evaluating Cabinet Decision-Making

Svein Eriksen

The cabinet is a multi-purpose body. Its main activities are coordination, innovation, and management. *Coordination* is a manifest requirement, but it is often difficult to achieve, given the multiplicity and complexity of the governmental tasks. *Innovation* is regarded as one of the tasks of cabinets, since these are deemed to be instruments of social change: a new government often means a new beginning. The view that the cabinet is an innovating agent is connected to the fact that in most Western European countries the cabinet has a virtual monopoly of initiation of legislation. All major political reforms are prepared in the ministries and presented to parliament after discussion in cabinet. The idea that a change of cabinet also means a break is helped by party political rhetoric, especially at election time, when party leaders claim that a new era is about to begin.

Meanwhile, ministers are departmental heads and therefore *managers*. The involvement of the cabinet in this respect is limited but it exists, partly because some decisions have legally or constitutionally to be approved by the cabinet and partly because some matters are considered important in their own right. It is often emphasised that the structure, processes, and personnel of the public service are significant determinants of cabinet performance: thus all cabinets have to face questions of public sector staffing and organisation.

There is a complex relationship between coordination, innovation, and management. These three types of activities may be conflicting or be mutually reinforcing; indeed, cabinets may not be able to sustain all three equally efficiently and trade-offs have to be made. Political circumstances and the aptitude of ministers are among the factors shaping the decision-making behaviour of cabinets and helping to decide whether the emphasis (if any) is on coordination, innovation, or management.

AN OVERALL ASSESSMENT OF CABINET PERFORMANCE

Western European ministers are generally satisfied with cabinet performance, as we saw in Chapter 8. Overall, as we noted, 62 per cent of the ministers interviewed were satisfied or very satisfied, while only 27 per cent were dissatisfied or very dissatisfied.

There are cross-country variations, however. In six countries, Norway, Denmark, Finland, the Netherlands, Austria, and Germany, the proportion of ministers who were satisfied or very satisfied with cabinet decision-making was more than twice as large as the number of those who were dissatisfied. In Britain, Ireland, Belgium, and Italy, the satisfied were in a majority, but the proportion of dissatisfied was a large minority. It is worth noting, as was pointed out in Chapter 8, that this last group is composed of the more 'parliamentary' among Western European countries. Finally, in France alone is there a majority of ministers dissatisfied, while in Sweden only a tiny minority responded and claimed that they were dissatisfied.

There are also variations within each country. Thus, in Austria, members of the Kreisky cabinet were all satisfied and those who were very satisfied were almost as numerous as those who were only satisfied (five *v.* six). The assessment of Klaus's second cabinet and of Sinowatz's

Table 12.1   Level of satisfaction of ministers with the cabinet process per country (percentages)

	Very satisfied	Satisfied	Dissatisfied	Very dissatisfied	No reply/ not asked
Sweden				5	95
Norway	19	64	–	3	14
Finland	21	43	19	6	–
Denmark	20	53	10	7	–
Britain	3	60	32	5	–
Ireland	18	33	42	3	–
France	5	32	35	5	22
Belgium	4	50	29	8	8
Netherlands	16	48	32	–	4
Germany	12	83	4	–	–
Austria	27	53	13	–	7
Italy	10	40	30	5	15
Overall	14	48	23	4	11

cabinet was more guarded (three satisfied and one dissatisfied in each case). In Finland, Sorsa's first and sixth cabinets were less praised (two satisfied, one dissatisfied, and one very dissatisfied for each cabinet) than Koivisto's second cabinet (two very satisfied and one satisfied). In France, Mauroy's first two cabinets were evaluated negatively (two satisfied, six dissatisfied, and two very dissatisfied), while three members of Pompidou's, Couve de Murville's and Chaban Delmas' cabinets said they were either very satisfied (one minister) or satisfied (two). In Norway, Willoch's two cabinets and Brundtlandt's 1981 cabinet received the highest marks, while the cabinets of Bratteli, Korvald, and Nordli were judged less positively and the cabinet of Borten most negatively of all, but the numbers are small and differences should therefore be interpreted with caution.

We examined in Chapter 8 the characteristics of, and some of the reasons for, the assessment given by ministers of their satisfaction or dissatisfaction. In general, satisfaction appears related to some extent, though only to some extent, to three main aspects of cabinets, namely when:

(1) major issues are thoroughly debated in the cabinet meeting;
(2) disagreements are solved by consensus;
(3) the prime minister exercises influence by consensus, by forcing issues, or by shaping the external context of the work of the cabinet.

On the other hand, dissatisfaction is also associated to some extent, though only to some extent, with cabinets in which:

(1) major issues are not thoroughly debated at full meetings but are examined informally among ministers, in cabinet committees, or during discussions between the prime minister and a group of ministers;
(2) disagreements are not primarily solved in the full meeting but, instead, are solved in cabinet committees or by the prime minister and a group of ministers;
(3) the prime minister exercises influence by talking to ministers individually.

Meanwhile, we also saw in Chapter 8 that the evaluation of cabinet performance varies according to the roles that these ministers perform in cabinet. The generalists or 'all-rounders' – that is to say, those who discuss regularly matters outside their departmental area – are significantly more satisfied than ministers who stick to their portfolio, a trend that applies to eleven of the twelve countries studied here and which was examined in some detail in Chapter 8: the one exception is the Netherlands, where ministers preoccupied with their own ministry are slightly more satisfied than those who attempt to exercise influence on a broader front. This means, as we noted, that, on the whole, overall cabinet life does not truly satisfy the specialists. On the other hand, since 'all-rounders' are likely to be more concerned with the overall direction of cabinet business than their more departmentally oriented colleagues, it might be concluded that cabinets perform their tasks of coordination relatively well and that such coordination may occur at the expense of ministers fighting for their departments.[1]

Table 12.2   Minister's evaluation of cabinet decision-making by making role conception (percentages)

Ministers' involvement outside department		*Level of satisfaction*		
		Very satisfied and satisfied	*Dissatisfied and very satisfied*	*Total*
	Often	84	16	100
	Sometimes	70	30	100
	Never	63	37	100

Overall, as we also saw in Chapter 8, the difference in levels of satisfaction between ministers in single-party cabinets and ministers in coalitions is small, but it does exist: the fact that ministers in coalition governments are a little more dissatisfied would seem linked to the weaknesses often associated with this kind of government, namely delays, non-decisions, and a cumbersome way of handling business; this is particularly the case in Belgium. Indeed, the *type* of coalition does appear to influence the evaluations made by the ministers and thus provide an indication of the way the cabinet works. The number of parties in the coalition, the ideological distance between these parties, and the relative strength of the components seem significant. In Belgium, the lowest ratings go to cabinets associating christian democrats and socialists: decision-making in these cabinets appears to be particularly difficult, the government being politically hetero-geneous and the two sides being roughly of equal strength and thus able to block each other's initiatives.

As was pointed out in Chapter 8, political ideology does make some difference, but only a slight one, with non-socialist ministers being more satisfied than socialists. Indeed, the true difference may be even smaller: this seems of course at first sight to suggest that ministers wishing to bring about change find it perhaps difficult to initiate and implement political reforms through the cabinet system; but the trend is found only in Britain, Belgium, and France, while there is no difference at all in this respect in the other countries. In each of these cases, moreover, special circumstances may explain the high levels of dissatisfaction. In Britain, Left-wing Labour ministers are most critical, their dissatisfaction being mainly related to their status as a small minority and their feeling of frustration about their apparent impotence. The discontent of Belgian socialists may be related to the strong position of the christian democrats both in the political system and in the civil service. The dissatisfaction of French socialist ministers may be partly a result of the fact that prime minister Mauroy's notion of how cabinet discussions should be conducted ran counter to established traditions and partly to the opinions of a number of his colleagues within the socialist government.[2]

CABINET PERFORMANCE, THE NATURE OF THE CABINET MEETING AND COMMITTEE PROLIFERATION

Cabinet government is government by committee. This affects both the way business is handled and the nature of the decisions that are arrived at. When cabinet members are appointed, efforts are made to obtain a blend of newcomers and veterans, of generalists and specialists, and of a range of political opinion. The collective and interactive nature of cabinet decision-making may be assumed to produce decisions that are 'multi-valued, consensual, stable, and systematically assessed'.[3] By contrast, a more hierarchical system of decision-making will probably reflect more closely the idiosyncratic views of one or a few top leaders. On the other hand, the collective nature of cabinet government may also result in inefficiency. Bodies of this kind are not noted for their ability to settle conflicts and to initiate and carry out swift and decisive action; they are more famous for the passive way in which they take decisions and the irritation that they create. Weak response to policy crisis may thus be one of the main pathological characteristics of cabinet government.

A cabinet is not normally a group of like-minded colleagues, but an assembly of rival departmental heads. As ministers have to bargain with one another, free and open argument may be difficult. Decisions arrived at sometimes appear to be compromises enshrined in a language that is not always intelligible to those who are entrusted with their implementation. Norwegian permanent secretaries have complained that, when concerned with matters involving the conflicting interests of two or more departments, cabinet decisions may be hard to interpret.[4] Belgian ministers note that the imprecise nature of cabinet minutes leads to uncertainties and quarrels over interpretation.

The size of the cabinet is sometimes cited as a problem, particularly in Belgium, but occasionally also in France, Britain, and the Netherlands, especially when the agenda is long, complex, and controversial decisions have to be taken quickly. However, the requirement of keeping the size of cabinets below the point at which these become unmanageable must be balanced against the need for cabinets to be large enough to include the interests that have to be coordinated. Over the last century, political and economic forces have exercised an increasing pressure to enlarge cabinets: what is therefore surprising is that the size of these bodies in Western Europe has not grown more than it has. This suggests some success in balancing considerations of size with demands for representation.

Most cabinets have a limited influence as deliberative bodies, as we saw in the previous chapters. Many decisions are referred to other arenas such as cabinet committees, bi- or multi-lateral ministerial meetings, or discussions between the prime minister and other cabinet members. This transfer of business may lead to more efficient decision-making, but problems arise as a result.

The role and working mode of the cabinet committees have been the object of some discussion. In Britain, for instance, it is pointed out that, while cabinet committees may improve the efficiency of the cabinet machine, they are also too numerous; they do not relate to any overall strategy, but tend to handle issues as these arise or as the prime minister sees fit.[5] A number of British ministers argue that the selective circulation of committee papers makes it difficult for them to be fully informed of the cabinet's general strategy. In the Netherlands, the decision-making capability of the cabinet committees is reduced by the fact that they are too large and do not have sufficient authority.[6] In the grand coalitions of Austria, the great number of cabinet committees was considered to be a sign of immobilism rather than a potential for efficient coordination.[7] In Finland, the proliferation of committees has resulted in a duplication of agendas and a heavy burden on ministers' time.[8] Similarly, Belgian ministers complain that meetings of cabinet committees are too numerous and too lengthy and that the existence of inner cabinets results in delays and non-decisions. French cabinet committees are said to have become so numerous that they have effectively undermined the role of the cabinet meeting.[9] In Denmark, the chairmen of committees in charge of sector coordination seem to have no strong incentive to bring their own affairs to discussion in the committees if they can avoid it.[10]

COORDINATION

A glance at the literature on cabinet reform suggests that problems of coordination have been a central and in some countries, such as Britain, Italy, and the Netherlands, *the* central – consideration in efforts to reform cabinet decision-making. A study of power in Norway concluded that the ability of public authorities to act in concert had been weakened.[11] Belgian ministers complain that the multi-party character of the cabinet leads to an excessive preoccupation with party political problems, with political inertia and distrust, and with contradictory statements from ministers belonging to different parties.

Problems of cohesion and coordination at the 'centre' of government have been studied in some countries on the assumption that lack of central coordination was one of the main reasons why public expenditure had come to be out of control in the second half of the 1970s. Indeed, the agenda and the environment of cabinets changed in five ways which have had a marked impact on the ability to achieve coordination. First, the vast expansion of the public sector increased the interrelatedness of governmental policies and activities: issues such as environmental protection and regional development cut across established departmental boundaries. Second, the size and complexity of the public sector result in the government pursuing inconsistent goals. Third, modern communications, extensive media coverage, and the democratic institutions themselves force decision-makers to react increasingly faster: this means that only limited attention can be given to the overall cohesiveness of policies; yet decisions have to be taken. Fourth, an increased emphasis on coordination between ministries and interest groups may make general governmental coordination more difficult: the cabinet is under pressure to accept agreements that the line ministries have negotiated with tough and resourceful groups. Fifth, modern technology is also responsible in that acute problems, let alone disasters, in nuclear and chemical industries, in space research, in petroleum production, are difficult to handle. Cabinets have to take decisions involving a number of governmental bodies; questions are of great technical complexity and there is disagreement and even conflict among the ministers concerned. Chernobyl and the Rhine spills are examples of decision-making situations of this type. Moreover, problems of coordination are probably felt more acutely in times of stagnation when policy change, and hence policy harmonisation, may necessitate a substantial and painful reallocation of resources. Cohesion is more easily achieved when the main task of policy-makers is to distribute resources in the context of a growing economy.

Moreover, in the French case, the dual executive leadership of president and prime minister leads to division at the top. Overall, most ministers probably look at coordination with mixed feelings. They applaud it as a general principle but avoid achieving it in practice; they then complain if it is too severe, especially if it comes from the minister of finance.

INNOVATION

There are two aspects to the question of innovation in the context of cabinet decision-making. One concerns the implementation of election programmes: the other relates to the ability of the cabinet to elaborate policies that are novel.

There is no conclusive evidence on the extent to which cabinets can decide and implement ideologically based reforms. The correlation between politics and policy is contingent on a number of factors, such as country, time period, and the policy area, as both single-country and cross-national studies have shown. Thus cabinets have been criticised for not being able to implement promised or expected reforms, the Thatcher cabinets being notable exceptions in this context.[12]

There was widespread optimism about the problem-solving capacity of governments until the early 1970s: the financial resources and the technical knowledge seemed sufficient. Socialists and social democrats looked to an active State as the final arbiter of economic life and as the distributor of wealth. These views were largely abandoned in the 1970s when economies took a sharp shift downwards: the problem-solving capacity of governments seemed then less than self-evident and a 'revolution of falling expectations' set in. Hence the tendency to scale back the public sector either by abolishing public activities altogether or transferring them to the private sector. This is a clear indication of a reduced confidence in the problem-solving capacity of governments.

A number of factors seem to limit the innovating capacity of cabinets. First, in most Western European countries probably, bargaining, mutual adjustment, and consensus-formation are the prevailing policy-making style. This leads to reactive policies and to a bias towards defending the *status quo*. Second, the 'free' parts of the budget are limited. Cabinets inherit the decisions of their predecessors; laws and regulations specifying the nature and level of social benefits cannot be repealed without violating implicit or explicit contracts with citizens.[13] Third, cabinets often give low priority to policy innovation. In Denmark it has been argued that the primary objective of recent cabinets has been to survive and not to carry through specific policies.[14] In the Netherlands and in the British Labour party the point has been made that ministers have become isolated from party opinion. Fourth, the policy intentions of political parties are often platitudinous and inconsistent; they cannot easily be translated into legislation and programmes of action.[15] Fifth, public administration has become too large, complex, departmentalised, and rigid, while the tenure of ministers is often too short to allow for effective control.[16] Political leadership takes generally the form of framework decisions, implemented according to the discretion of civil servants, sometimes after negotiations with interest organisations. Sixth, the nature of the cabinet meeting itself does not stimulate in general innovative and long-range policy-making. There is not much correlation between how important an issue is and how much time is spent on it in cabinet. The cabinet is felt to be overloaded with a mass of technical decisions and ministers have little time to consider strategies and to clarify objectives. Lack of time and an overloaded cabinet agenda are common complaints in Belgium, the Netherlands, Sweden, Finland, and Ireland.[17] Several British ministers have also pointed out that too little time is spent on general strategy and policy planning and that there is a lack of information on sensitive, non-departmental issues coming to the cabinet.

MANAGEMENT

Differences in historical background and especially in patterns of ministerial recruitment in Western Europe suggest that the stress on managerial skills varies markedly. In some countries, for instance in Austria, the Netherlands, and Finland, the cabinet has only gradually evolved from being a body of top civil servants to being party-based. Ministers in these countries are therefore likely to tend towards specialisation and to be more administratively minded than where bureaucratic traditions are weaker. In Britain, for instance, where the cabinet has a large proportion of 'amateurs', only a minority of ministers seem concerned with administrative matters.[18]

In both Britain and Belgium, the lack of administrative experience of ministers is a source of some criticism: the need to draw cabinet members from parliament in Britain does restrict the pool of eligible candidates:[19] alleged scandals in the British ministry of defence have thus been related to the minister's insufficient familiarity with public management.[20] Belgium cabinet members are not selected because of their managerial competence, but for political reasons: this leads to administrative drawbacks, especially in budgetary and personnel policies. These weaknesses are said to be increased by the existence of a large personal staff (a ministerial *cabinet*), which functions as a screen between ministers and civil servants.

Some cabinets include a minister in charge of administrative matters, but these have rarely a central position in the government. The corresponding departments are often unpopular in the civil service; they are remote from substantive decisions and therefore tend to lose battles with the programme ministries.[21] Admittedly, in the 1980s, a number of governments developed comprehensive policies of administrative reform. Some cabinets even tried to give the issue considerable importance:[22] actual results have not been very impressive, however. Indeed, these efforts have been dismissed by some as symbolic and as corresponding to situations in which cabinets can avoid harsh substantive policy decisions by taking refuge in matters of reorganisation.[23]

Effective institutional change is difficult to achieve for many reasons and cabinets cannot therefore be expected to push administrative reforms vigorously and persistently. First, there is no fully developed theory of institutional change and the effects of reforms are uncertain.[24] Moreover, attempts to alter the administrative structure often generate severe conflicts. Such battles 'are likely to be fought with some motivation, less inhibition, and greater skills than is true of either conflicts over the substance of public policy or of competition between personal interests'.[25] The conclusion can thus be drawn that administrative change is not worth the time, effort, and discomfort involved. Third, institutional change is unlikely to have marked effects unless top administrators are also changed. Overall, substantive issues are generally of greater interest to ministers than to civil servants: such proposals can then be shelved in order to secure support on other matters.[26]

AREAS OF CABINET REFORM

Attempts to improve the quality of decision-making may include a wide variety of measures, based on two basic strategies, 'top down' and 'bottom up', although each strategy incorporates some elements of the other.

Top down approaches

The top down approach is often associated with a call to strengthen the centre of government. It has a distinctly rationalistic or technocratic flavour and evokes the image of firm leadership with clear-cut and long-term goals to be implemented through an administrative chain of command and not based on agreements between conflicting groups. Such an approach is attractive to all reformist governments: this was particularly the case of those that were in power in the 1960s and 1970s. The White Paper on the 'Reorganisation of Government' published by the Heath government in 1970 represents a high point in such attempts at achieving centralised rationality. Specifically, the top down approach typically includes such measures as the strengthening of the position of the prime minister, the appointment of superministers, and the introduction of comprehensive planning arrangements.

Strengthening the centre

During the 1970s, a number of countries adopted measures designed to enhance the strategic capacity of cabinets. The most discussed reform was that which led to the setting up of the Central Policy Review Staff (CPRS) in Britain by the Heath government in 1970, a body that was abolished by Margaret Thatcher in 1983. The aim of the CPRS was to counter the tendency of parties in power to lose sight of the priorities listed in their manifestoes and to become immersed in day-to-day administration. At about the same time, coordination and long-term planning were enhanced in Germany in the early 1970s by the setting up of the planning division of the chancellor's office and procedures designed to determine priorities were also introduced. We noted in Chapter 6 that there was an increase in the size of prime ministers' offices in most countries during the postwar period, although we also saw that the increase was too limited to affect the balance of power between centre and periphery in the cabinet system.

Proposals were made in Italy and the Netherlands to enhance the constitutional and political position of the prime minister, but little was achieved in practice. The idea of setting up a prime minister's department was also suggested in Britain, the aim being to oversee the government's global strategy and to integrate policy and politics into a single whole.[27] It has even been suggested that the cabinet should be remodelled on the American pattern, with collective responsibility being abandoned and the prime minister being solely in charge of policy.[28]

Coordination of government sectors: the introduction of superministers
Another attempted reform has consisted in creating posts of superministers. There are two main versions of the idea, one being to appoint ministers in charge of truly coordinating departments, the other being to give some ministers the task of supervising a number of their colleagues in charge of individual departments. While the first formula gives the superminister effective power, the second leaves the coordinator with limited influence, as he or she has a small staff and basically only a secretariat: the 'top down' character is thus more marked in the first arrangement than in the second. One of the most radical attempts to achieve comprehensive coordination was that which led to the setting up of giant departments in Britain in the early 1970s. These departments, which have since then for the most part been dismantled, were the result of amalgamations and were designed 'to propose and implement a single strategy for clearly defined and accepted objectives'.[29] In Italy, a number of proposals were made to set up superministries, but none of these was implemented, although, during the fourth Rumor government, an informal merger of three economic ministries did take place.[30]

Further distinctions have to be made, moreover, between arrangements that give superministers a supervisory role only. They may have some powers to issue directives or in effect only be chairmen of cabinet committees; they may coordinate whole departments or extend their jurisdiction to parts of departments only. Various combinations of these arrangements have indeed been tried. In Britain, superministers without portfolio were appointed in the Douglas-Home and Wilson cabinets. In France, a minister in charge of coordinating the economic departments was appointed during the second Pompidou cabinet; coordinating ministers were also appointed when the Socialist party came to power in 1981. In Sweden, coordinating ministers have been appointed from time to time; indeed, in 1990, the departments were reorganised into three main groups, each of which was headed by a coordinating minister. In the Netherlands, the Vonhoff committee suggested that departments should be grouped into five major policy areas, one minister in each sector being responsible for coordination in that sector: the cabinet did not endorse these proposals, however, as they were regarded as violating the principle of ministerial equality.[31] In Italy, a suggestion was made in 1976 to create four posts of ministers with coordinating responsibilities for the economy, education, defence, and justice; but the idea was not implemented: the only move in this direction occurred during the fourth Moro cabinet, when the deputy prime minister was given the task of coordinating the governmental economic programme.

Improving procedures for planning and budgeting

In the late 1960s and in the 1970s, national planning was emphasised in most Western European countries, on the assumption that this move would help to improve the policy formation process, since an endeavour would be made to anticipate future problems and not merely to react to current issues; decision-makers would be able to examine various courses of action open to them, evaluate the consequences of each of these, and choose the one that appeared to be the best.

This philosophy found its institutional expression in a number of ways, for instance through the setting up of planning units, the introduction of long-term plans and budgets, the use of new procedures for budgeting (PPBS, zero-based) and for policy analysis (PAR and Rayner scrutinies in Britain, 'turnusgennengange' in Denmark, 'omradegjennomganger' in Norway, and 'heroverwergingen' in the Netherlands, a programme designed to help with the reassessment of policies).

Although not all the innovations mentioned in this chapter have been thoroughly evaluated and therefore a truly comprehensive conclusion cannot be drawn, many objectives of the 'top down' inspired reforms have clearly not been met. Some of the institutional novelties of the 1960s and 1970s were abandoned, while the enthusiasm for planning was replaced by substantial scepticism and even cynicism.

Various explanations have been offered for the limited success of the reforms. The institutional arrangements for coordination and budgetary steering have been criticised for being based on technocratic assumptions that did not take into account some basic realities of political life. Procedural reforms may clarify policy options and the consequences of different courses of action, but they do not simplify decision-making when what is at stake is to overcome opposition in public opinion, among pressure groups, and within professional institutions.

Bottom up approaches

Bottom up approaches are based on a more realistic assessment of political life. The emphasis is on decentralisation with sub-units enjoying considerable autonomy to innovate and harmonise policies. Conflicts and inconsistencies are tackled as they occur and coordination takes place through bargaining and mutual adjustment, not through the imposition of a plan decided centrally. Consultation, bargaining, and the setting up of parallel procedures and channels to handle problems are thus the mechanisms that characterise bottom up approaches.

There are indeed examples of ministries and of cabinet positions set up to stimulate 'creative tension' within the governmental apparatus: thus Harold Wilson established the Department of Economic Affairs and the Ministry of Technology, at least in part, in order to counterbalance the treasury.[32] In coalition cabinets, mechanisms of interparty accommodation have been introduced: in the Austrian grand coalitions of the two major parties, for instance, the ministers of one party have been assisted by junior ministers belonging to the other party; in Finland, policy harmonisation is achieved by appointing two ministers to the same department.

Proposals have also been made in order to increase the deliberative role of the cabinet: thus, in Belgium and Finland, decisions on minor matters were delegated to individual ministers in order to leave the cabinet free to concentrate on the most important and most controversial issues; in Sweden, it has been suggested that the present constitutional principle of collective responsibility be replaced by a system of individual ministerial accountability for minor matters: these proposals have not been adopted so far, however.

It may indeed be difficult for governments to follow a bottom up approach generally and carefully, as such a strategy evokes the image of inefficient compromises and assumes that social change develops at a slow and steady pace. When conditions change rapidly and profoundly, a conceptual shake-up may be required. A fundamental rethinking of governmental strategies did occur in the 1980s and took the form of an emphasis on privatisation and on deregulation, on the grounds that the vast expansion of the public sector had made coordination and governance difficult, if not impossible, and that the result had been policy contradictions, delays, indeterminacy and, consequently, inefficiency and a waste of resources. The solution to these problems was said to require scaling back the public sector by abolishing activities altogether or by transferring them to the private market: such a campaign was launched, of course, in Britain; it had echoes also in the Netherlands, in Denmark, and even in Iceland, though little was done in practice except in Britain.

THE LACK OF CABINET REFORM AS SUCH

Although 'crisis' suggestions were thus advanced, hardly any Western European government has launched truly comprehensive and effective programmes designed to improve *cabinet decision-making* over the last three decades. Ideas have been aired; attempts have been made, notably in Britain. Yet the number and range of reforms actually implemented have been very small. In Sweden, the cabinet machinery is not considered an instrument that the cabinet of the day can arrange or rearrange in order to suit its policy aims.[33] Cabinet reforms tend therefore to occur gradually and *ad hoc*, often as side effects of changes at lower administrative levels. It was argued in 1971 that cabinet reform had been one of the great unstudied questions of the previous decade:[34] the same point can be made in the 1990s.

This state of affairs may be a result of scepticism as to whether problems of cabinet decision-making can be solved by institutional reforms of the cabinet. Lack of coordination or innovation are not matters that can be handled by introducing measures solely concerning the cabinet machine; the efficiency of cabinets is affected by the political culture and in particular by social and political fragmentation. Organisational and procedural changes seem unable to achieve little more than some tinkering at the edges. Meanwhile, on the other hand, resistance to reform is strong, perhaps for symbolic reasons, as changes in the cabinet arrangements touch the very centre of the political machine. Since these changes may be regarded as potentially tilting the balance of political power, opposition is likely to be strong on the part of politicians accustomed to the *status quo* or actors not likely to benefit from the changes.

The pressure for reform will continue to be slight so long as ministers remain broadly satisfied with cabinet decision-making. Problems of coordination, innovation, or management are rarely at the top of preoccupations, since, as we noted, 'all rounders' are reasonably satisfied, while departmentally oriented ministers may not believe that a solution can be found. Such a high level of satisfaction among the practitioners is somewhat surprising given the large number of criticisms that are voiced in the specialised literature: the titles of books and articles published in the mid and late 1970s suggested that the system was about to break down.[35]

Perhaps the literature was unduly alarmist. Perhaps ministers, who are responsible for the way the cabinet system works, are reluctant to reveal deficiencies that may be associated with their own shortcomings or weaknesses and that they might have been able to remedy, but left uncorrected. Perhaps, too, ministerial responses about cabinet life constitute primarily an assessment of the interaction taking place among cabinet members within and in connection with the cabinet meeting: the wider, structural setting in which the cabinet is embedded may not therefore have been commented upon.

In fact, ministers may not even be fully aware of the import of some of the problems discussed in the literature. For a variety of reasons, a number of cabinets give low priority to policy innovation and to managerial questions: when this is the case, ministers cannot be expected to view the lack of political reform as a serious problem or to be particularly sensitive to administrative questions. Furthermore, ministers have in general to concentrate so much of their time and energy on their department that they cannot be expected to have a major commitment to matters of coordination; indeed they are anxious not to be 'coordinated' in too severe a manner.

On the other hand, problems of modern governments may have been treated in a somewhat lopsided way in the literature. An emphasis on problems of coordination seems to suggest that most public activities are uncoordinated: this is not the case. What is at stake is not the existence but the extent of coordination. Meanwhile, the assessment of the ability of governments to solve social problems seems to vary cyclically. Optimism was the mood of the 1960s, pessimism was the hallmark of the late 1970s and of the 1980s. In the 1990s, the strong doubts about the extent to which governments can be controlled seem to have given way once more to more optimism. Some studies of the late 1970s appear inordinately gloomy, with the stress on 'ungovernability' being widely used to describe the plight of cabinets, especially in Britain: the expression had almost entirely disappeared from the literature by the early 1990s.

The fact that the cabinet system has undergone few *formal* changes does not mean that it has been static. A key feature of this system is its flexibility: by means of *informal* adjustments in the way of handling business, the system has adapted to changing circumstances: the setting up of committees is a manifest example of such a change. More formalised and rigid arrangements might have made it far more difficult to gear the cabinet machinery to the needs of the time. The ministers' lack of enthusiasm for cabinet reform may thus reflect an inclination to preserve that flexibility as well as the overall responsiveness of cabinet organisation to changing governmental and political requirements.

Notes

1. See Chapter 8. It is important to remember that all ministers want more technical knowledge.
2. J. L. Thiébault (1988), p. 86.
3. P. Dunleavy and R. A. W. Rhodes (1990), p. 19.
4. S. Eriksen (1988b).
5. C. Seymour-Ure (1970–1), pp. 196–207.
6. R. B. Andeweg (1985), p. 152.
7. P. Gerlich and W. C. Müller (1988), p. 148.
8. L. Westerlund (1990).
9. J.-L. Thiébault (1988), p. 101.
10. J. G. Christensen (1985), p. 136.
11. NOU 1982:3 Makturedningens sluttrapport.
12. D. Steel and D. Heald (1984), pp. 13–14.
13. R. Rose (1980), p. 11.
14. G. Rye Olsen (1990).
15. R. Rose (1969). P. Haungs (1973). W. C. Müller and W. Philipp (1987).
16. J. P. Olsen (1988), p. 10. H. Döring in R. S. Katz (ed) (1987). W. Müller and W. Philipp (1987).
17. J. Van Putten (1982), p. 191. T. Larsson (1988b).
18. B. Headey (1974).
19. R. Rose (1971), p. 400.
20. B. Headey (1974), p. 278.
21. J. M. Lee (1982). R. A. Chapman (1983). J. P. Olsen (1988).

22. J. G. Christensen (1990).
23. J. P. Olsen (1988). G. Rye Olsen (1990).
24. J. March and J. P. Olsen (1983). J. Salomon (1981).
25. F. Scharpf (1985), p. 8.
26. J. March and J. P. Olsen (1983).
27. J. Hoskyns (1983), p. 147.
28. C. Seymour-Ure (1970–1).
29. Government White Paper, Cmnd. 4506 (1970), p. 5.
30. S. Bartolini (1982), p. 210.
31. R. Andeweg (1988a), p. 144.
32. C. Pollitt (1984).
33. T. Larsson (1990), p. 182.
34. C. Seymour-Ure (1970–71), p. 204.
35. See for instance W. Parsons (1982).

13   Conclusion

Jaakko Nousiainen and Jean Blondel

Cabinet decision-making is small-group decision-making. The system is therefore structurally and functionally more flexible than parliamentary or bureaucratic decision-making. Cabinets can shift their focus of interest and vary their agenda-formation process horizontally and vertically according to both short- and long-term developments.

Overall, cabinet decision-making seems to be more affected by general characteristics than by specific structural variables. First, even if events analysis shows that national governments have differing policy problems and peculiar ways of solving them, overall agenda profiles are similar. Second, national traditions and the structure of the governmental system provide a stable framework: the cabinet seems more constrained by this framework than by variations in the party structure or by the ideological complexion of the cabinet; personalities play a part, but it seems that even strong leaders do not truly alter patterns of cabinet decision-making.

Formally, the decision-making poles of the cabinet are the full meeting, on the one hand, and individual ministers, on the other; in practice, there are increasingly intermediate elements, such as ministerial committees, various *ad hoc* working groups and other coordination mechanisms, cabinet committees being almost everywhere one of the most important and most institutionalised elements of this chain.

A varying number of issues reach the cabinet meeting. At one extreme, all ministers are well informed about these problems, formulate solutions, and accept joint responsibility for the decisions taken; at the other extreme, there is purely formal decision-making, which may become symbolic as is the process by which the Queen gives royal assent to bills and orders in council in Britain. Between these two extremes are situations in which a process of ratification takes place that legitimises decisions taken elsewhere but still gives the participants an opportunity to intervene at the last moment and ultimately even a veto power.

The British cabinet constitutes a special case among Western European cabinets, as it discusses a selection of topical questions rather than formally deciding on many matters and it solves interdepartmental conflicts rather than systematically planning and leading governmental policies. It is free to debate any problem, but the scope of its agenda is in quantitative terms narrower than that of other Western European cabinets. Characteristically, the policy space of the British cabinet is defined primarily in negative terms in the Standing Orders: these state what should *not* be brought to the meeting. More positively, the business of the cabinet is devoted, in the main, to questions involving the collective responsibility of the government, and to questions on which there is a conflict of interest between departments. The share of partially collective decision-making is large, and as cabinet committees have the power to take decisions without referring to the full meeting, ratification problems do not loom very large.

In Germany and France, the cabinet has a formally stronger position; its legal powers are more extensive than in Britain, but in both countries strong constraints prevent it from becoming a major policy-maker and a truly 'working cabinet'. In Germany the dualism of the executive power is constitutionally entrenched: 'The Federal Chancellor shall determine, and be responsible for, the general policy guidelines. Within the limits set by these guidelines, each Federal Minister shall conduct the affairs of his department autonomously and on his own responsibility.'[1] The emphasis is thus on the federal chancellor as a power leader and on individual ministers as autonomous task leaders. The arrangement leaves no room for an independent role for the collective cabinet to shape general policies or solve more specific problems. In practice, decisions relate to the upper level of the governmental agenda, but even there the tendency is towards ratification: thus the cabinet gives a final political check to the general lines of governmental policy.[2]

The collective profile of the French government is still lower, indeed hardly visible. The cabinet is primarily a functional arena for the president of the Republic and the prime minister; ministers resemble loyal civil servants more than political co-actors. This is despite the fact that many ministers interviewed stressed the importance of the cabinet as an arena for issue debate. Ministers may initiate policies, but if there is conflict the decision rests with the president or the prime minister, while an extensive network of interdepartmental committees takes the arbitration function away from the cabinet. The main role of the cabinet meeting is thus to disseminate information: the French cabinet operates typically on the basis of a number of ministerial statements on aspects of foreign and domestic policy and on departmental initiatives, each of these statements being followed by a summing up by the president or the prime minister.

Austria and Italy are in the next category, despite the fact that the context of the government's functioning differs sharply in these two countries. The collective cabinet's decision-making sphere is larger in Austria because of a legal and bureaucratic tradition; in Italy it is because of heterogeneous coalitions. Yet strong constraints, both internal and external, restrict cabinet involvement at the 'upper' parts of the agenda: the Austrian cabinet operates in a highly organised political setting, surrounded by strong institutions, while in Italy the prevailing weaknesses of the decision-making centre leaves scope for the interplay of a variety of external bodies.

As the data used in this study show, a description of the Austrian governmental policy as a chancellor rule is not ill-founded, but party organisations are also actively involved in the settlement of politically sensitive issues. Routine matters are typically settled by formal procedures, while real decision-making in conflictual high-level policies has tended to slide outside the cabinet system to smaller intra-party or inter-party bodies. Strong corporatism in the form of group consultation also sets the tone of executive decision-making in the country.

The picture is more complex in Italy. Traditionally, party leaders refuse cabinet positions and remain outside the government, but the party system is not strong enough to ensure that arbitration mechanisms will be permanently located outside the cabinet in the party summits: thus the main point where conflicts are solved between the coalition partners is the cabinet or its committees. Yet, although the cabinet meeting cannot be ignored in decision-making, 'the government as a collective body has perhaps been far less in control or at the centre of the policy-making process than in other European countries'.[3] In a polycentric system the political preparation of issues and the elaboration of compromises is performed in many arenas where there is interaction between many kinds of actors, from parliament to the bureaucracy, interest groups and parties. The government participates through individual ministers or party groups rather than as a separate entity. The cabinet meeting is thus likely to remain of secondary importance for the discussion of strategic policies; it is a legitimiser rather than a policy-maker. It participates extensively but not intensively in decision-making.

In the remaining seven cases – Scandinavia, Ireland, Belgium, and the Netherlands – cabinets have remained closer to the original model of a parliamentary executive. Indeed, in four of these countries, ministers state emphatically that major policy issues are regularly debated in cabinet. This group consists of relatively small countries where agenda items are less numerous and problems of governance, in most cases, less complex. The cabinet has escaped the process of disintegration and, even now, attempts to combine political and administrative leadership, from broad policy lines to day-to-day routines. It cannot handle all parts of the extensive agenda with the same intensity, but the breadth of its formal field of activity provides at least an opportunity for a systematic selection of issues to be discussed and for an extensive supervision of the political-administrative machine. The entire policy-making area is visible and is under its control. These cabinets can thus be described as being truly collective.

The central character of collective government is based either on tradition (Ireland, the Netherlands, and Sweden), on coalition needs (Belgium), or on both. In the Finnish case, these factors reinforce each other; in Sweden, Norway, and even more in Denmark, single-party governments have been so frequent that there has been a move towards the departmentalisation of decisions. This point is reflected in the judgements passed by Danish ministers on the role of the cabinet meeting: some two-thirds considered it to be an important arena for issue debate only sometimes, while the other third hardly gave it any importance at all. In Ireland, the principle of collective responsibility is so strong that moves towards the departmentalisation of the cabinet have effectively been blocked and no cabinet committees have been set up, while committees were introduced in Sweden at the beginning of the 1990s only.

Coalition governments in Scandinavia and in the Netherlands are characterised by a cabinet-centred policy-making style and not by party-centred decision-making. Party leaders accept portfolios and the interparty bargaining system is built inside the cabinet, not in party summits: the multi-party system and the sophisticated corporatism of these countries generate complex arrangements, however, as all important groupings – parties, interest organisations, and public agencies – have a veto power and no major policy can succeed without their support. The cabinet thus becomes the centre of societal coordination, arbitration, and decision-making. The process of interest aggregation takes place to a large extent within the government system but in consultation with the major economic groups. A similar development takes place in Belgium, where the grip of the 'partitocracy' appears to have weakened in recent years.[4]

Yet these cabinets govern together only up to a point, as a distinction needs to be made between the administrative and the political agendas. Ministers do not have enough time to discuss routine matters seriously: these are normally merely legitimised by the cabinet, although there still remains a residual veto power of members of the cabinet and this veto power can be of some importance in view of the demands made occasionally by the parties in the administrative field.

Because of the smaller size of the cabinet in some of the smaller countries, more serious consideration can be given to 'upper level' issues: yet strategic policy planning and the settling of major disputes tend even there to be transferred to sub-groups of the cabinet, such as the inner circle of a single-party cabinet, meetings of coalition leaders, or some of the permanent cabinet committees.

A study of Finnish governments showed that the unofficial preparatory meeting of the full cabinet was an arena where middle level issues could be handled, where policy alternatives could be weighed, and where conflicts between parties could be solved.[5] In general, the ministers interviewed felt that the cabinet was ill-suited to discuss general policy lines. In the fields of foreign and economic policy, in particular, decisions on broad principles are made in the relevant cabinet committee, where ministers sit as representatives of their party groups, and only go to the cabinet for ratification.

Large numbers of routine issues are handled in weekly administrative sittings in less than an hour: the fact that these decisions are not delegated to individual ministries indicates that this arena is not without its significance in preserving the collective tradition. Information is spread widely and party political control inside the cabinet is increased.

We began this study by stressing the tension existing between the collective and collegial ideology of parliamentary countries, on the one hand, and the need for efficient government and therefore for a more ministerial structure, on the other. We also began this study by stressing the existence of a major divide between single-party governments and coalitions. Perhaps the ultimate conclusion is the somewhat optimistic point that modern cabinet government in Western Europe constitutes, by and large, a synthesis between, or an amalgam of, the two poles of each of the two divides, the divide between the coalition-cum-collegial *v.* hierarchical government and the divide between single-party *v.* coalition government.

The analysis of the distinction between single-party government and coalitions did show that there were some important areas where these distinctions seemed to have an apparent effect, but it also showed that there were many areas where this effect was limited or even non-existent. For example, while ministers are more departmentally inclined in coalition governments, this is only a trend; while prime ministers are more likely to be forceful in single party government, this, too, is only a trend; meanwhile, rules and precedents tend to cut right across the single-party/coalition divide, and cabinets are only regarded as somewhat more central in one type of government than in the other.

This situation seems to be a result, in part at least, of two quite different sets of causes. First, as was shown in detail in Chapter 3, there are many types of coalitions and what appears in the first instance to be a dichotomy is in reality a continuous dimension. Governments are not only of the single-party or of the coalition type: they have, in a sense, more or less of a coalition character, as coalitions can be more or less extreme, more or less ideologically diverse, and composed of partners who are more or less equal. The dimensional nature of this distinction stems also from the fact that some countries – indeed a near-majority of the Western European countries – oscillate between single-party and coalition governments, with the result that various traditions and practices develop over and above the single-party/coalition divide.

Yet the distinction between single-party and coalitions is not unimportant: quite the contrary, when the point is combined with the question of the tension arising between the requirements of collegial and collective *v.* efficient decision-making, the true impact of the single-party/coalition distinction does emerge. For, in reality, the ideology of collective and collegial government stems from the same root as that which leads to coalition government, while the practical need for more hierarchical structures is what leads not just to single-party government as such, but to all the accommodations and arrangements that have emerged in both single-party and coalition governments. This applies when these arrangements take the segmentation form that results from committee developments or the fragmentation form that is a result of ministerial autonomy. Thus it is probably the case that cabinet government has to transcend or overcome the tension between collegial and collective government, on the one hand, and hierarchical government, on the other; and that it has to do so to an extent by oscillating between coalition and single-party government, by taking elements of both, sometimes simultaneously, sometimes in succession. Cabinet government, in order to function, has to adopt many of the characteristics of single-party rule; but, to be acceptable, it has to take some of the clothes of coalitions.

Parliamentary cabinets have three main tasks: they are concerned with innovation, with coordination, and with management. The increase in the problems facing governments and the acceleration of the rhythm of politics have led in many cases to a reformulation, rather than a real disappearance of the old cabinet idea. While the cabinet probably does not form a truly consistent whole anywhere, it remains a system at the centre of which is a group of men and women who, whether they wish it or not, have to govern together. There is still continuous interaction among the different levels of the cabinet system, although the intensity of the involvement of the cabinet itself does vary markedly.

Cabinets certainly matter for policy, although not in the traditional sense of being the manifest – and even less the exclusive – decision-makers. Their base has become broad since what they do is related to the entire community. As political decision-making has become dispersed throughout society, governments are subjected to increasing pressures from many directions, from supporting and opposing groups, from bureaucratic bodies, big business, organised interests, and the international environment. This is the reason why, in the end, the cabinet remains a group and is a collective and collegial reflection of at least a large segment of the national forces. In this sense, cabinet government still entails governing together. The cabinet is where the action is: it performs tasks that no one else performs, in that it keeps this conglomerate together and steers it in the direction of a somewhat vaguely perceived national interest.

Notes

1. Constitution of the Federal Republic of Germany, art. 65.
2. F. Müller-Rommel (1988a), p. 166.
3. M. Cotta (1988), p. 137.
4. A.-P. Frognier (1988b), pp. 77–8.
5. J. Nousiainen (1990), *passim*.

Appendix I: The Ministerial Survey

The ministerial survey on which this study is based was undertaken especially for this research project in nine countries, Britain, Ireland, Norway, Denmark, Finland, France, Belgium, Germany, and Italy, while the results of analogous surveys having taken place or being in the process of taking place in three other countries (Sweden, the Netherlands, and Austria) were analysed jointly whenever possible.[1] The survey was undertaken by members of the team of each country or by close associates. Each team member was free to conduct the interview in the way that was felt the most appropriate; it was indeed understood that most members would wish to elaborate country studies that could well have a different emphasis. However, in order to achieve uniformity at the cross-national level, members of the team drew together a schedule composed essentially of closed questions, which they were asked to fill in immediately after having conducted each interview. In some cases, questions could not be asked, for instance because time had run out or because it appeared impossible to return to some ground already covered. In the case of the two countries where interviews had already taken place, the Netherlands and Sweden, the two scholars concerned, R. Andeweg and T. Larsson, agreed to return to the records of the interviews that they had conducted and to fill in the common questionnaire; naturally enough, not all the questions of the common questionnaire had been asked of ministers in these two countries: there are therefore a number of points – rather small in number – which could not be covered. Perhaps the main area that was not covered in these two countries – as well as in Finland – was that of the part played by prime ministerial staffs: Chapter 6 is therefore based on interviews in nine countries only. In the case of Austria, the national study was not so advanced that the common questions could not be asked.

A distinction was made in filling in the questionnaire between a 'no reply' answer – which resulted from a refusal to answer a particular point – and a 'not able to cover' answer – which stemmed from the fact that the minister was not asked the question at all, for the kind of reasons mentioned earlier. In most cases, throughout this volume, the two categories are presented as 'missing data', the distinction being made only when it appears necessary.

The ministers interviewed tend to be ex-cabinet ministers rather than members of the government at the time. This choice was dictated both by reasons of practical availability and of political opportunity. Especially in the large countries, responses to such a sensitive set of questions as the ones being asked in this survey were appreciably more likely to be frank and straightforward on the part of ex-ministers than on the part of ministers in office. As what was sought here was not substantive information about particular policies but general judgements about proceedings in and around cabinet, the fact of interviewing ex-ministers was in no way a handicap. The only problem that could arise in some cases was that of the balance among the political parties, for instance when one party had been out of office for a long time before forming the administration that was in power when the survey took place. This might have affected to an extent both France and Germany: fortunately, however, enough ministers in the coalition in office had left the government before interviews took place and the problem turned out not to be serious.

Overall, 410 interviews were completed. The country breakdown of these interviews is given below, these figures constituting about half of the total universe of ex-cabinet ministers either alive or sufficiently well to be interviewed, a proportion that had been the original target. There were only a small number of refusals. The ministers interviewed were promised confidentiality: this is respected throughout this volume and, indeed, in the data themselves. However, the party of the minister and the nature of the coalition, if any, to which the minister belonged, is known.

We wish once more to thank most warmly all those who agreed to be interviewed and who gave such clear and specific answers: without these, the present study could not have been carried out. We wish also to recall our thanks to all those who were involved in the collection and preparation of the data.

The numbers of ministers interviewed per country were the following:

Austria	30
Belgium	49
Britain	40
Denmark	28
Finland	47
France	37
Germany	24
Ireland	33
Italy	26
The Netherlands	25
Norway	36
Sweden	35

The common schedule that was elaborated in order to build the data base for the ministerial survey is shown overleaf.

Notes

1. A similar survey was undertaken in parallel to cover members of the European Commission. It is hoped that the results of the analysis will be published, separately, in the near future.
2. The answers that are numbered are in most cases given a choice between 'yes' and 'no'. In addition, for all variables, special codes are provided for 'no reply', 'not able to cover', and 'not applicable'.

MINISTERIAL QUESTIONNAIRE AND DATA[2]

Country ....

Full name ....

01 In matters relating to your department,   (not coded)
what kinds of decisions did you not feel able
to take on your own?

    a) For what reasons?

        1 innovative
        2 politically hot
        3 cost large
        4 coordination
        5 other

    b) If you wanted/had to bring an issue to
cabinet, what strategy would you follow?

        1 agreement with other
           ministers
        2 cabinet committee
        3 discussion with PM
        4 cabinet secretariat
        5 directly to cabinet
        6 other

02 In your opinion, was the cabinet a place where
major issues were thoroughly debated?

      – yes always
      – yes sometimes
      – no

    a) If in more than one cabinet:
In this respect did you feel that there were
differences among cabinets to which you
belonged?

      – yes
      – no

    b) If yes, second cabinet:

      – more debate
      – less debate
      – same as one

       If yes, third cabinet:

      – as first cabinet
      – as second cabinet
      – more debate
      – less debate

    c) If you feel that matters were not fully
discussed in cabinet, where do you think
discussions that discussions mostly took
place?

        1 informal ministerial
        2 cabinet committees
        3 PM and ministers
        4 parties
        5 bureaucracy
        6 interest groups
        7 other

d) Let us return to discussions in cabinet. In your experience, were there instances of substantial disagreement amongst cabinet members?
  - frequent
  - occasional
  - rare
  - never

e) If in more than one cabinet, were there differences with respect to disagreements in the cabinets to which you belonged?
  - yes
  - no

f) If yes: was the second cabinet
  - more conflictual?
  - less conflictual?

g) If yes: how were these disagreements solved?
  1 consensus
  2 PM imposes
  3 referred to cabinet committee
  4 referred to discussions between PM and a minister
  5 referred to discussions between PM and ministers
  6 referred back to sponsoring department
  7 referred to discussion among ministers
  8 votes
  9 other (specify)

h) How satisfied are you on the whole with the cabinet decision-making process?
  - very satisfied
  - satisfied
  - dissatisfied
  - very dissatisfied

i) What were the points which seemed to you in need of reform?
  (not coded)

03 And now to come to your own role, did you yourself go out of your departmental area in cabinet discussions?
  - yes often
  - yes sometimes
  - never

a) In general was it common for ministers to participate in discussions not related to their departmental matters?
  - yes common
  - yes occasional
  - never

04 What ministers seem to you to be more important? Rank the two most important ministers.
  (not coded)

a) Why?

1   substance of ministry
2   status
3   seniority of minister
4   official post, e.g. deputy PM
5   party position
6   other

b) (if minister of finance not mentioned) and what about the minister of finance? why not?

–   too junior in party
–   too 'new' minister
–   other

c) If you had a conflict with these important ministers what would you do?

1   drop the issue
2   go to PM
3   go to cabinet
4   other

05 As regards the PM (under whom the minister has served the longest) would you say he or she was

–   very influential?
–   somewhat influential?
–   not very influential?

a) On what types of matters was he or she most influential?

1   overall governmental organisation
2   special 'domain'
3   economy
4   social affairs
5   foreign affairs
6   defence
7   your department
8   coalition problems
9   all these areas
10 others

b) In what ways did he or she exercise influence?

1   consensus
2   talking to ministers individually
3   forcing the issue
4   taking new initiatives
5   shaping the external context
6   other

c)   Did this mode of behaviour change   – yes
     during the PM's tenure?   – no

d)   If yes: in what way?   – more influence
                                                – less influence

06   Did you feel that the PM's office (staff and   – yes
     secretariat) played a considerable part in the   – somewhat
     policy process?   – no

     a)   On what matters?   (not coded)

     b)   How did the office act?   1   preparation of the
                                                     agenda
                                                 2   control of policy
                                                     suggestions
                                                 3   advising the PM
                                                     politically
                                                 4   developing own
                                                     policy suggestions
                                                     for cabinet

07   Which of the following would you consider to
     have been particularly useful for your activity
     as minister?

     1   prior knowledge of the subject matter of
         your department?
     2   your technical capacity or your
         knowledge as an administrator?
     3   your experience as an MP?
     4   your experience as a junior minister?

     a)   Considering your prior training and   – yes
          experience, would you have been happier – no
          in another departmental position?

     b)   If yes: then which?   (not coded)

08   Roughly speaking, as minister what
     proportion of your time did you allocate to
     the following?

     1   being in your office
     2   outside on cabinet work
     3   outside on other political business   (not coded)

09   In the matter of minister–civil servant   1   good collaboration
     relationships, what kind of rapport did you   2   overselling by civil
     establish with the officials in your dept.?   servants

3 blocking by civil
  servants
4 mutual blocking
5 other

10 What kind of party meetings did you attend?
– none
– some official
– some unofficial, e.g.
  faction
– both official and
  unofficial
  active in party life
– to some extent active
  in party life

a) If unofficial, specify which

(not coded)

b) What kind of relationship existed between ministers and the top party executive?

1 close cooperation
2 competition
3 infrequent contact
4 almost no contact

c) What kind of relationship existed between ministers and the parliamentary party (Fraktion)?

1 close cooperation
2 competition
3 infrequent contact
4 almost no contact

d) If you were a minister in a coalition:

What sort of contact existed between the coalition partners, both inside and outside government, to influence government policy?

– party summits
– informal
  collaboration
– informal competition
– no contact
– formal collaboration

e) What differences in decision-making, if any, were there between the coalitions to which you belonged?

– some
– very little
– none

f) If some: in what way for the 2nd coalition?

1 party summits
2 informal
  collaboration
3 informal competition
4 no contact

If some: in what way for the 3rd coalition?

1 party summits
2 informal
  collaboration

g) If some: what were the reasons for these
    differences?

3   informal competition
4   no contact

–   PM
–   parties
–   PM and parties
–   other

11 How did you brief yourself on cabinet
    matters?

1   cabinet secretariat
2   your officials
3   your personal staff
4   your own party
5   outside policy
    adviser
6   other

a) What about the media? Did they
    influence your decisions regarding:

1   topics for cabinet
    discussions
2   amount of time given
    to cabinet discussion
3   presentation of
    cabinet decisions
4   substance of cabinet
    decision

b) Which media were most influential?

–   press
–   radio
–   television
–   agency material
–   press and radio

12 Party of minister (15 party types)

13 Cabinet number (first)

14 Cabinet type

–   single minority
–   single near majority
–   single majority
–   coalition
–   no party

15 Number of parties in government

16 Parties in government (51 coalition types)

17 Parties in government (reduced to 20 coalition
    types)

18 to 27: Repeat 13 to 17 twice for second and
    third cabinet

Appendix II: The Newspaper Survey

Alongside the ministerial study and in order to complement it, an analysis of newspaper reports on cabinet conflicts was undertaken in eleven of the twelve countries: for technical manpower reasons, the analysis could not be carried out in Norway. The coverage was done on a sample basis, the period or periods being selected by the members of each team on the grounds of particular political relevance and in order to discover, for instance, whether there were contrasts among different governments. From the start, the data were considered to be only an adjunct to the main ministerial study, as it was unclear how far the reporting of cabinet conflicts in newspapers was homogeneous over time and space. The results turned out to be rather encouraging, but it was felt unwise to give to the findings of the newspaper survey too much emphasis in the body of the volume.

The sources of information consisted of major national newspapers and the overall time-span comprised the years from 1961 to 1987, but specific periods studied have varied from country to country. The analysis covered a continuous period with respect to Austria (1968–87), Belgium (1961–87), Denmark (1965–87), France (1971–85), Germany (1969–82), Ireland (1968–86), Italy (1972–87), the Netherlands (1963–87), and the United Kingdom (1970–83). In Finland only the years 1966–8 (Paasio I government), 1972 (Paasio II), 1975–7 (Liinammaa, Miettunen II and Miettunen III), and 1983–7 (Sorsa VI) were examined and in Sweden the periods selected for analysis were the months of January, May and October at five-year intervals starting in 1965 and ending in 1980.

The concept of cabinet conflict was defined broadly, encompassing 'any situation in which cabinet members differ in opinion, preference, interest or activity'. Every newspaper item that explicitly mentioned such a situation was included in the sample.

Qualitative data were analysed and classified along the following dimensions: cabinet in question, year when first reported, duration of the conflict, actor profile, content of the conflict, ultimate outcome, and arena of solution.

The conflicts mentioned in the press were analysed on the basis of a common schedule drawn up by the members of the team. This schedule does not of course give more than a partial flavour of the conflicts but at least some broad comparisons can be made, as can be seen in particular in Chapter 11.

This common schedule was the following:

Conflict Data

1) Country
   – Sweden
   – Denmark

316

- Germany
- Netherlands
- Belgium
- France
- Great Britain
- Ireland
- Italy
- Austria
- Finland

2) Conflict number

3) Cabinet number

4) Year conflict first reported

5) Duration in months
   - 0 to 1 month
   - 1 to 2 months
   - 2 to 3 months
   - 3 to 4 months
   - 4 to 5 months
   - 5 to 6 months
   - 6 to 7 months
   - 7 to 8 months
   - 8 to 9 months
   - 9 to 10 months
   - 10 to 11 months
   - 11 to 12 months

6) Actor dimension
   - PM against minister(s) of same party
   - PM against minister(s) of other party(ies)
   - ministers of same party against each other
   - ministers of same party but of different factions
   - ministers of different parties acting as individuals
   - ministers of different parties acting as party members
   - minister(s) or PM against parliament
   - other

7) Solution dimension
   - total resignation
   - resignation of some
   - compromise
   - problem frozen
   - someone wins without resignation
   - other

8) Solution place
   - cabinet
   - parliament

- party or parties
- cabinet and party or parties
- cabinet committee
- other

9) Political field of conflict (30 different fields of choice)

10) Minister of finance involved
- yes
- no

Bibliography

This bibliography lists only the general or comparative volumes on cabinet processes as well as the most important country studies that have appeared in recent years. For a more detailed coverage of each country, the best approach is to look in turn at the bibliographies appearing at the end of the classical country texts mentioned here. Moreover, this bibliography mentions only the biographies and autobiographies that have had a significant impact on cabinet studies (e.g. the Crossman *Diaries*) or those that give a particular slant to the role of ministers or prime ministers in cabinet (e.g. O. Ruin's study of Tage Erlander).

GENERAL AND COMPARATIVE WORKS

Aberbach, J.D., Putnam, R.D. and Rockman, B.A. (1981) *Bureaucrats and Politicians in Western Democracies* Cambridge, Mass.: Harvard Univ. Press.

Arter, D. (1984), *The Nordic Parliaments. A Comparative Analysis* New York: St. Martin's Press.

Bakema, W.E. (1991), 'The ministerial career', in Blondel, J. and Thiébault, J.L. (eds.), *Government Ministers in Western Europe*, London: Macmillan, pp. 70–98.

Barber, J.D. (1968), *The Lawmakers*, New Haven, CT.: Yale University Press.

Baylis, T.A. (1989), *Governing by Committee. Collegial Leadership in Advanced Societies*, Albany: State Univ. of New York Press.

Blondel, J. (1980), *World Leaders. Heads of Government in the Postwar Period*, London: Sage.

Blondel, J. (1982), *The Organisation of Governments. A Comparative Analysis of Governmental Structures*, London: Sage.

Blondel, J. (1984), 'Dual leadership in the Contemporary World', in Kavanagh, D and Peele, G., *Comparative Government and Politics*, London: Heinemann, pp. 73–91.

Blondel, J. (1985), *Government Ministers in the Contemporary World*, London: Sage.

Blondel, J. (1987), *Political Leadership*, London: Sage.

Blondel, J. (1991), 'Ministers of Finance in Western Europe: A Special Career?', *EUI Working Papers SPS* n. 91/11, Florence: European University Institute.

Blondel, J. and Müller-Rommel, F. (eds.) (1988), *Cabinets in Western Europe*, London: Macmillan.

Blondel, J. and Thiébault, J.-L. (eds.) (1991), *The Profession of Government Minister in Western Europe*, London: Macmillan.

Budge, I., and Keman, H. (1990), *Parties and Democracy. Coalition Formation and Government Functioning in Twenty States*, Oxford: Oxford Univ. Press.

319

Budge, I., Robertson, D., and Hearl, D. (eds.) (1987), *Ideology, Strategy and Party Change: Spatial Analysis of Post-War Election Programmes in 19 Democracies*, Cambridge: Cambridge Univ. Press.

Bunce, V. (1981), *Do New Leaders Make a Difference? Executive Succession and Public Policy under Capitalism and Socialism*, Princeton: Princeton Univ. Press.

Burch, M. (1990), 'Power in the Cabinet System', *Talking Politics*, Vol. 2 (3), pp. 102–8.

Campbell, C. (1983), *Governments under Stress. Political Executives and Key Bureaucrats in Washington, London and Ottawa*, Toronto: Univ. of Toronto Press.

Campbell. C. (1987), 'Canada' in Plowden, W. (ed.), *Advising the Rulers*, Oxford: Basil Blackwell, pp. 124–42.

Campbell, J. C. (1977), *Contemporary Japanese Budget Politics*, Berkeley, Ca: Univ. of California Press.

Castles, F. G., and Wildenmann, R. (eds.) (1986), *The Future of Party Government. Visions and Realities of Party Government*, Berlin/New York: De Gruyter.

Cobb, R. W. and Elder, C. (1972), *Participation in American Politics*, Boston: Allyn & Bacon.

Damgaard, E., Gerlich, P., and Richardson, J. J. (eds.) (1989), *The Politics of Economic Crisis*, Aldershot: Avebury.

De Winter, L. (1991), 'Party and Parliamentary Pathways to the Cabinet', in Blondel, J. and Thiébault, J.-L. (eds.), *The Profession of Government Minister in Western Europe*, London: Macmillan.

Dodd, L. C. (1976), *Coalitions in Parliamentary Government*, Princeton, N.J.: Princeton Univ. Press.

Finer, S. E. (ed.) (1975), *Adversary Politics and Electoral Reform*, London: A. Wigram.

Frognier, A. P. (1991), 'Elite circulation in Cabinet government', in Blondel, J. and Thiébault, J. L. (eds), *The Profession of Government Minister in Western Europe*, London: Macmillan, pp. 121–35.

Gustafsson, G., and Richardson, J. J. (1979),'Concepts of Rationality and the Policy Process', *European Journal of Political Research*, Vol. 7 (4), pp. 415–36.

Herman, V., and Pope, J. (1973), 'Minority Governments in Western Democracies', *British Journal of Political Science*, (Apr.), Vol. 3 (2), pp. 191–212.

Herman, V., and Alt, J. E. (eds.) (1975), *Cabinet Studies: A Reader*, London: Macmillan.

Hood, C. (1986), *Administrative Analysis*, Brighton: Wheatsheaf.

Jones, G. W. (ed.) (1991), *West European Prime Ministers*, London: Frank Cass.

Katz, R. S. (1986), 'Party Government: A Rationalistic Conception', in Castles, F. G., and Wildenmann, R. (eds.), *Visions and Realities of Party Government*, Berlin/New York: De Gruyter.

Katz, R. S. (1987), (ed.) *Party Governments: European and American Experiences*, Berlin/New York: De Gruyter.

King, A., (1975), 'Executives', in Greenstein, F.I. and Polsby, N.W. (eds.), *Handbook of Political Science*, Vol. 5: *Governmental and Institutions Processes*, Reading, Mass.: Addison-Wesley.

La Spina, A. (1990), 'Some Reflections on Cabinets and Policy-Making: Types of Policy, Features of Cabinet, and Their Consequences for Policy Outputs', *EUI Working Papers SPS*, n. 90/5, Florence: European Univ. Institute.

Laver, M., and Shepsle, K.A. (1990), 'Government Coalitions and Intraparty Politics', *British Journal of Political Science*, Vol. 20, pp. 489–507.

Lembruch, G., and Schmitter, P.C. (eds.) (1982), *Patterns of Corporatist Policy-Making*, London: Sage.

Lijphart, A. (1968), *The Politics of Accommodation*, Berkeley: Univ. of California Press.

Lijphart, A. (1984), *Democracies: Patterns of Majoritarian and Consensus Government in Twenty-one Countries*, New Haven, Conn.: Yale Univ. Press.

Luebbert, G.M. (1986), *Comparative Democracy: Policymaking and Governing Coalitions in Europe and Israel*, New York: Columbia Univ. Press.

Machin, H. (1987) 'Advice in Economic and Foreign Policy', in Plowden, W. (ed.), *Advising the Rulers*, Oxford: Basil Blackwell, pp. 158–69.

Mackie, T.T., and Hogwood, B.W. (eds.) (1985), *Unlocking the Cabinet. Cabinets Structure in Comparative Perspective*, London: Sage.

March, J., and Olsen, J.P. (1983), 'Organizing Political Life: What Administrative Reorganization Tells us about Government', *American Political Science Review*, Vol. 77 (2), pp. 281–96.

Müller, W.C. and Philipp, W. (1988), 'Prime Ministers and other Government Heads', in Blondel, J. and Thiébault, J.-L. (eds.), *The Profession of Government Minister in Western Europe*, London: Macmillan.

Neustadt, R.E. (1992), *Presidential Power*, new edition, New York: John Wiley.

Norton, P. (ed.) (1990), *Parliaments in Western Europe*, London: Frank Cass.

Olsen, J.P. (1988), 'The Modernisation of Public Administration in the Nordic Countries', *Hallinon Tutkismus* (Administrative Questions), pp. 2–17.

Parsons, W. (1982), 'Politics without Promises', *Parliamentary Affairs*, Vol. 35, pp. 421–35.

Pekkarinen, J., Pohjola, M., and Rowthorn, B. (1991), *Social Corporatism – A Superior Economic System*, Tokyo: UN University.

Pfeffer, J. (1981) (ed.), *Power in Organisations*, London: Pitman.

Plowden, W. (ed.) (1987), *Advising the Rulers*, Oxford: Basil Blackwell.

Pridham, G. (ed.) (1986), *Coalitional Behaviour in Theory and Practice: an Inductive Model for Western Europe*, Cambridge: Cambridge Univ. Press.

Richardson, J. (ed.) (1982), *Policy Styles in Western Europe*, London: George Allen & Unwin.

Riker, W.H. (1962), *The Theory of Political Coalitions*, New Haven, CT.: Yale Univ. Press.

Rose, R. (1971), 'The Making of Cabinet Ministers', *British Journal of Political Science*, Vol. 1, pp. 393–414.

Rose, R. (ed.) (1980), *Challenge to Governance. Studies in Overloaded Polities*, London: Sage.

Rose, R. (1984), *Understanding Big Government*, London and Los Angeles: Sage.

Rose, R. (1987), *Ministries and Ministers. A Functional Analysis*, Oxford: Oxford Univ. Press.

Rose, R., and Suleiman, E. N. (eds.) (1980), *Presidents and Prime Ministers*, Washington, D.C.: American Enterprise Institute.

Salomon, J. (1981), 'The Goals of Reorganization', *Administration and Society*, Vol. 12, pp. 471–500.

Sarangi, P. (1986), 'Determinants of Policy Change: A Cross-National Analysis', *European Journal of Political Research*, Vol. 14, pp. 23–44.

Scharpf, F. (1985), 'Policy Failure and Institutional Reforms: Why Should Form follow Function?', *International Political Science Association* paper.

Schattschneider, E. E. (1942), *Party Government*, New York: Holt, Rinehart and Winston.

Schubert, K. (1988), *Interessenvermittlung und staatiche Regulation*, Opladen: Westdeutscher Verlag.

Seymour-Ure, C. (1970–1), 'The "Disintegration" of the Cabinet and the Neglected Question of Cabinet Reform', *Parliamentary Affairs*, Vol. 24 (2), pp. 196–207.

Sjöblom, G. (1986), 'Problems and Problem Solutions in Politics', in Castles, F. G. and Wildenmann, R. (eds.), *Visions and Realities of Party Government*, Berlin/New York: De Gruyter.

Steiner, J. and Dorff, R. H. (1980), *A Theory of Political Decision Modes*, Chapel Hill: Univ. of North Carolina Press.

Strom, K. (1984), 'Minority Governments in Parliamentary Democracies', *Comp. Pol. Stud.*, Vol. 17 (2), pp. 199–228.

Strom, K. (1986), 'Deferred Gratification and Minority Government in Scandinavia', *Legislative Studies Quarterly*, Vol. 11 (4), pp. 583–605.

Strom, K. (1990), *Minority Government and Majority Rule*, Cambridge: Cambridge Univ. Press.

Therborn, G. (1987), 'Does Corporatism Really Matter? The Economic Crisis and Issues of Political Theory', *Journal of Public Policy*, Vol. 7, pp. 259–84.

Thiébault, J.-L. (1989) 'Jalons pour une analyse des conflits gouvernementaux', in Cahiers du CRAPS (Center de Recherchoes Administratives Politiques et Sociales), n. 7, *Les Gouvernements*, Université de Lille II, pp. 20–48.

Thiébault, J.-L. (1990) 'Les hiérarchies gouvernementales en Europe Occidentale', in Cahiers du CRAPS (Centre de Recherches Administratives, Politiques et Sociales), n. 10, *Les Gouvernments*, Université de Lille II. pp. 9–32.

Toniolo, G. (ed.) (1988), *Central Banks' Independence in Historical Perspective*, Berlin: De Gruyter.

Truman, D. (1964), The Governmental Process, New York: Knopf.

Weller, P. (1985), *First among Equals. Prime Ministers in Westminster Systems*, Sydney: George Allen & Unwin.

Weller, P. (1987), Types of Administration, in Plowden, W. (ed.) *Advising the Rulers*, Oxford: Basil Blackwell, pp. 149–57.

Wilson, J. Q. (ed.) (1980), *The Politics of Regulation*, New York: Basic Books.

COUNTRY WORKS

Austria

Berchtold, K. (1974), 'Die Regierung', in Fischer, H. (ed.), *Das politische System Österreichs*, Vienna: Europaverlag.

Bleier-Bissinger, H. (1988), *Bundeskanzler Dr. Alfons Gorbach und seine Zeit*, Graz: Strahalm.

Gerlich, P., and Müller, W.C. (1988), 'Austria: Routine and Ritual', in Blondel, J., and Müller-Rommel, F. (eds.), *Cabinets in Western Europe*, London: Macmillan.

Gerlich, P., Müller W.C., and Philipp, W. (1988), 'Potentials and Limitations of Executive Leadership: The Austrian Cabinet since 1945', *European Journal of Political Research*, Vol. 16 (2), pp. 191–206.

Müller, W.C., (1988), 'Die neue große Koalition in Österreich', *Österreichische Zeitschrift für Politikwissenschaft*, Vol. 17, pp. 321–47.

Müller, W.C. (1990), 'Changing Executive-Legislative Relations in Austria', paper presented at the *ECPR Joint Session of Workshops*, Bochum.

Müller, W.C. (1991), 'Regierung und Kabinettsystem', in Dachs, H. *et al.* (eds.), *Handbuch des politischen Systems Österreichs*, Vienna: Manz.

Müller, W.C. (1992), 'Austrian Governmental Institutions: Do They Matter?', *West European Politics*, Vol. 15 (1), pp. 99–131.

Müller, W.C. (1993), 'Models of Government and the Austrian Cabinet', in Laver, M., and Shepsle, K. (eds.), *Cabinet Ministers and Parliamentary Government*, New York: Cambridge Univ. Press.

Müller, W.C. and Philipp, W. (1987), 'Parteienregierung und Regierungsparteien in Osterreich', *Österreichische Zeitschrift für Politikwissenshaft* (1987), Vol. 16, pp. 277–302.

Müller, W.C., Philipp, W. and Steininger, B. (1987), 'Sozialstruktur und Karrieren österreichischer Regierungsmitglieder (1945–1987)', *Österreichisches Jahrbuch für Politik*, pp. 143–63.

Nassmacher, K.-H. (1968), *Das Österreichische Regierungssystem*, Cologne: Westdeutscher Verlag.

Pelinka, A., and Welan, M. *Demokratie und Verfassung in Österreich* (1971), Vienna: Europaverlag.

Welan, M. and Neisser, H. (1971), *Der Bundeskanzler im österreichischen Verfassungsgefüge*, Wien: Hollinek.

Weissensteiner, F. and Weinzierl, E. (eds.) (1983), *Die Österreichischen Bundeskanzler. Leben und Werk*, Vienna: Österreichischer Bundesverlag.

Belgium

Dewachter, M., and Das, E. (1991), *Politiek in Belgie. Geprofileerde machtsverhoudingen*, Leuven: ACCO.

De Winter, L. (1989), 'Parties and Policy in Belgium', *European Journal of Political Research*, Vol. 17 (6), pp. 707–30.

Frognier, A.-P. (1988a), 'The Mixed Nature of Belgian Cabinets between Majority Rule and Consociationalism', *European Journal of Political Research*, Vol. 16 (2), pp. 207–28.

Frognier, A.-P. (1988b), 'Belgium: A Complex Cabinet in a Fragmented Polity', in Blondel, J. and Müller-Rommel, F. (eds.), *Cabinets in Western Europe*, London: Macmillan.

Britain

Allison, G. T. (1971), *The Essence of Decision: Explaining the Cuban Missile Crisis*, Boston: Little, Brown.

Amery, L. S. (1936), *Thoughts on the Constitution*, Oxford: Oxford University Press (new edition 1964).

Bagehot, W. [1867] (1964), *The English Constitution*, London: Watts & Co.

Barber, J. (1991), *The Prime Minister since 1945*, Oxford: Basil Blackwell.

Barnett, J. (1982), *Inside the Treasury*, London: Andre Deutsch.

Benn, T., (1990), *Against the Tide: Diaries 1973–6*, London: Heinemann.

Blackstone, T. and Plowden, W. (1988), *Inside the Think Tank*, London: Heinemann.

Bruce-Gardyne, J. (1986), *Ministers and Mandarins*, London: Macmillan.

Burch, M. (1987), 'The Demise of Cabinet Government', in Robins, L. (ed.), *Political Institutions of Britain*, London: Longman.

Burch, M. (1988, a), 'The British Cabinet: A Residual Executive', *Parliamentary Affairs*, Vol. 41(1), pp. 34–48.

Burch, M. (1988), 'The United Kingdom', in Blondel, J. and Müller-Rommel, F., *Cabinets in Western Europe*, London: Macmillan.

Burch, M. (1990), 'Who Organises What? The Cabinet System and the Flow of Business', *Manchester Papers in Politics*, n. 3.

Cabinet Office, (1992), *Questions of Procedure for Ministers*, London.

Castle, B. (1984), *The Castle Diaries: 1964–70*, London: Weidenfeld and Nicolson.

Chapman, R. A. (1983), 'The Rise and Fall of the CSD', *Policy and Politics*, Vol. 11, pp. 41–61.

Clarke, M. (1992), *A Question of Leadership*, Harmondsworth: Penguin Books.

Cockerell, M. *et al.*, (1985), *Sources Close to the Prime Minister*, London: Macmillan.

Coombes, D. and Walkland, S. A. (eds) (1980), *Parliament and Economic Affairs in Britain*, London: Heinemann.

Crossman, R. H. S. (1972), *Inside View: Three Lectures on Prime Ministerial Government*, London: Jonathan Cape.

Crossman, R. H. S. (1963), Preface to *The English Constitution*, reprinted in King, A. (ed.), *The British Prime Minister* (2nd ed., 1985), London: Macmillan.

Crossman, R. H. S. (1975, 1976, 1977), *The Diaries of a Cabinet Minister*, Vol. 1: *Minister of Housing 1964–66* (1975) Vol. 2: *Lord President of the Council and Leader of the House of Commons 1966–68* (1976), Vol. 3: *Secretary of State for Social Services 1968-70* (1977), London: Hamish Hamilton and Jonathan Cape.

Dell, E. (1991), *A Hard Pounding: Politics and Economic Crisis, 1974–76*, Oxford: Oxford Univ. Press.

De Smith, S. A. (1981), *Constitutional and Administrative Law* (4th ed.), Harmondsworth: Penguin Books.

Donoughue, B. (1985), 'The Conduct of Economic Policy', in King, A. (ed.). *The British Prime Minister*, London: Macmillan, pp. 47–71.

Donoughue, B. (1987), *Prime Minister: The Conduct of Policy Under Harold Wilson and James Callaghan*, London: Jonathan Cape.

Donoughue, B. (1988), 'The Prime Minister's Diary', *Contemporary Record*, Vol. 2 (2).

Döring, H. (1987), 'Party Government in Britain – Recent Conspicuous Constraints', in Katz, R. S. (ed.), *Party Governments: European and American Experiences*, Berlin: De Gruyter.

Dunleavy, P. (1990), 'Re-interpreting the Westland Affair: Theories of the State and Core Executive Decision-Making', *Public Administration*, Vol. 68 (1).

Dunleavy, P. and Rhodes, R. A. W. (eds.) (1990), 'Special Issue: The Core Executive', *Public Administration*, Vol. 68 (1).

Franks, Lord (1986), *Falkland Islands Review: Report of a Committee of Privy Counsellors*, London: Sphere.

Gamble, A. M. and Walkland, S. A. (1984), *The British Party System and Economic Policy 1945–1983*, Oxford: Clarendon Press.

Hall, P., Land, H., Parker, R. and Webb, R. A. (1975), *Change, Choice and Conflict in Social Policy*, London: Heinemann.

Harris, R. (1990), *Good and Faithful Servant*, London: Faber and Faber.

Headey, B. (1974), *British Cabinet Ministers: The Role of Politicians in Executive Office*, London: George Allen and Unwin.

Heclo, H. and Wildavsky, A. (1974), *The Private Government of Public Money* (2nd ed., 1981), London: Macmillan.

Henderson, N. (1984), *The Private Office*, London: Weidenfeld and Nicolson.

Hennessey, P. (1985), 'The Quality of Cabinet Government in Britain', *Policy Studies*, Vol. 6, pp. 15–45.

Hennessey, P. (1986), *Cabinet*, Oxford: Basil Blackwell.

Hennessey, P., (1989), *Whitehall*, London: Secker and Warburg.

Hogwood, B. and Mackie, T. T. (1985), 'The United Kingdom: Decision Sifting in a Secret Garden', in Hogwood, B. and Mackie, T. T. (eds.), *Unlocking the Cabinet: Cabinet Structures in Comparative Perspective*, London: Sage, pp. 36–60.

Holmes, M. (1982), *Political Pressure and Economic Policy. British Government 1970–74*, London: Butterworth.

Hoskyns, Sir J. (1983), 'Whitehall and Westminister: An Outsider's View', *Parliamentary Affairs*, Vol. 36 (2), pp. 137–47.

Ingham, B. (1991), *Kill the Messenger*, London: Fontana.

James, S. (1986), 'The Central Policy Review Staff', *Political Studies*, Vol. 34 (3), pp. 423–40.

James, S. (1992), *British Cabinet Government: The Role of Politicians in Elective Offices*, London: Routledge.

Jenkins, S. (1984), 'The Star Chamber, PESC and the Cabinet', *Political Quarterly*, Vol. 56 (1).

Jones, G. W. (1983), 'Prime Minister's Departments Really Create Problems', *Public Administration*, Vol. 61, pp. 79–84.

Jones, G. W. (1985), 'The Prime Minister's Office under Margaret Thatcher', in King, A. (ed.), *The British Prime Minister* (2nd ed.), London: Macmillan.

Kellner, P., and Crowther-Hunt, Lord (1977), *The Civil Servants*, London: Macdonald.

King, A. (ed.) (1985) *The British Prime Minister* (2nd ed.), London: Macmillan.

King, A. (1991), 'The British Prime Ministership in the Age of the Career Politician', *West European Political*, Vol. 14 (2).

Klein, R. and Lewis, J. (1977), 'Advice and Dissent in British Government: The Case of the Special Advisers', *Policy and Politics*, Vol. 6, pp. 1–25.

Lee, M. (1990), 'The Ethos of the Cabinet Office', *Public Administration*, Vol. 68 (2).

Mackintosh, J. P. (1977a) *The Government and Politics of Britain* (4th ed.), London: Hutchinson.

Mackintosh, J. P. (1977b) *The British Cabinet* (3rd ed.), London: Stevens.

Mackintosh, J. P. (ed.), (1977c), *British Prime Ministers in the Twentieth Century*, London: Weidenfeld and Nicolson.

Madgwick, P. (1991), *British Government: The Central Executive Territory*, Oxford: Philip Allan.

Mosley, R. K. (1969), *The Story of the Cabinet Office*, London: Routledge and Kegan Paul.

Neustadt, R. E. (1985), 'White House and Whitehall' in King, A., ed. *The British Prime Minister*, London: Macmillan, pp. 155–74.

Parkinson, C. N. (1971), *The Law of Decay*, Boston: Houghton Mifflin.

Pliatsky, L. (1982), *Getting and Spending: Public Expenditure, Employment and Inflation*, Oxford: Blackwell.

Plowden, W. (ed.) (1987), *Advising the Rulers*, Oxford: Basil Blackwell.

Pollitt, C. (1984), *Manipulating the Machine. Changing the Pattern of Ministerial Departments 1960–1983*, London: George Allen and Unwin.

Ponting, (1986), C. *Whitehall: Tragedy and Farce. The Inside Story of How Whitehall Really Works*, London: Hamish Hamilton.

Prime Minister and the Minister for the Civil Service, (1970), *The Reorganization of Central Government*, Cmnd. 4506, London: HMSO.

Rose, R. (1980), 'British Government: The Job at the Top', in Rose, R. and Suleiman, E. N. (eds.), *Presidents and Prime Ministers*, Washington: American Enterprise Institute.

Rose, R. (1986), 'British MPs: More Bark than Bite?', in Suleiman, E. (ed.), *Parliaments and Parliamentarians in Democratic Politics*, New York: Holmes & Meier.

Rush, M. (1984), *The Cabinet and Policy Formation*, London: Longman.

Seldon, A. (1990), 'The Cabinet Office and Coordination', *Public Administration*, Vol. 68 (1), pp. 103–20.

Sexton, M. (1979), *Illusions of Power: The Fate of Reform Government*, London: George Allen and Unwin.

Seymour-Ure, C. (1989), 'Prime Minister's Press Secretary: The Office since 1945', *Contemporary Record*, Vol. 3 (1).

Steel, D. and Heald, D. (1984), 'The New Agenda', in Steel, D. and Heald, D. (eds.), *Privatizing Public Enterprises*, London: Royal Institute of Public Administration.

Theakston, K. (1987), *Junior Ministers in British Government*, Oxford: Basil Blackwell.

Walker, P. G. (1972), *The Cabinet*, Glasgow: Fontana.

Wass, D. (1984), *Government and the Governed*, London: Routledge.
Weller, P. (1983), 'Do Prime Minister's Departments Really Create Problems?',
   Public Administration, Vol. 61 (1), pp. 59–78.
Weller, P. (1985), *First Among Equals: Prime Ministers in Westminster Systems*,
   London: George Allen and Unwin.
Willetts, D. (1987), 'The Role of the Prime Minister's Policy Unit', *Public
   Administration*, Vol. 65 (4), pp. 443–54.
Williams, M. (1972), *Inside Number Ten*, London: Weidenfeld and Nicolson.
Wilson, S.S. (1975), *The Cabinet Office to 1945*, London: HMSO.

Denmark

Christensen, J.G. (1990) 'En dansk administiations politik for go'erne',
   Nordisk Administrativt Tidsskrift, no. 1, pp. 63–78.
Christensen, J.G. (1985), 'In Search of Unity: Cabinet Committees in
   Denmark', in Mackie, T.T. and Hogwood, B.W. (eds.), *Unlocking the
   Cabinet. Cabinet Structures in Comparative Perspectives*, London: Sage.
Damgaard, E., and Svensson, P. (1989), 'Who Governs? Parties and Policies in
   Denmark', *European Journal of Political Research*, Vol. 17, pp. 731–45.
Damgaard, E. (1990), 'Danish Experiments in Parliamentary Government',
   paper presented at the *Joint Workshops of the ECPR*, Bochum.
Rye Olsen, G. (1990), 'Modernisering og afbureaukratisering i 1980'ernes
   Danmark', *Nordisk Administrativt Tidsskrift*, 2.
Schou, T.L. (1988), 'Denmark', in Blondel, J. and Müller-Rommel, F. (eds.),
   Cabinets in Western Europe, London: Macmillan.
Thomas, A.H. (1982), 'Denmark: Coalitions and Minority Governments', in
   Brown, E.C. and Dreijmanlis, J. (eds.), *Government Coalitions in Western
   Democracies*, London: Longman.
Vahr, J. (1991), 'The Prime Minister and His Staff: The Case of Denmark',
   Paper for the *Joint Workshops of the ECPR*, Essex.

Finland

Ahonen, G. (1986), 'Do Policies Develop like Scientific Paradigms? On
   Occupational Safety and Health Legislation in Finland', *European Journal of
   Political Research*, Vol. 14, pp. 305–19.
Blåfield, A., and Vuoristo, P. (1985), *Kalevi Sorsan suuri rooli*, Helsinki:
   Kirjayhtymä.
Karjalainen, A. and Tarkka, J. (1989), *Presidentin ministeri. Ahti Karjalaisen
   ura Urho Kekkosen Suomessa*, Helsinki: Otava.
Nousiainen, J. (1990) *Suomen presidentit valtiollisina johtajia K.J. Stählbergista
   Mauno Koivistoon*, Porvoo-Helsinki: WSOY.
Nousiainen, J., (1988a) 'Finland' in Blondel, J., and Mïller-Rommel, F. (eds.),
   Cabinets in Western Europe, London: Macmillan.
Nousianen, J. (1988b), 'Bureaucratic Tradition, Semi-Presidential Rule and
   Parliamentary Government: The case of Finland', *European Journal of
   Political Research*, Vol. 16 (2), pp. 229–49.
Nousiainen, J. (1992), *Politiikan huipulla: Ministerit ja ministeristöt Suomen
   parlamentaarisessa järjestelmässä*, Poorvoo-Helsinki: WSOY.

Suomi, J. (1990), *Kuningastie. Urho Kekkonen 1950–1956*, Helsinki: Otava.
Tiihonen, S. (1990), *Hallitusvalta. Valtioneuvosto itsenäisen Suomen toimeen-panovallan käyttäjänä*, Helsinki: Valtion Painatuskeskus.
Virolainen, J. (1969), *Pääministerinä Suomessa*, Helsinki: Otava.
Westerlund, L. (1990), *De politiska sekreterarna i Finland. Regeringens informella samordningsmekanism*, Abo: Abo Academy Press.

France

Avril, P. (1987), *La Vème République. Histoire politique et constitutionnelle*, Paris: Presses Universitaires de France.
Browne, E. C., and Gleiber, D. W., (1986), 'Cabinet Stability in the French Fourth Republic', in Pridham, G. (ed.), *Coalitional Behaviour in Theory and Practice: An Inductive Model for Western Europe*, Cambridge: Cambridge Univ. Press.
Dogan, M. (1989), Chapter on France, pp. 19–44 in Dogan, M. (ed.), *Pathways to Power: Selecting Rulers in Pluralist Democracies*, Boulder, Co.: Westview Press.
Elgie, R. and Machin, H. (1991), 'France: The Limits to Prime-Ministerial Government in a Semi-Presidential System', *West European Politics*, Vol. 14 (2), pp. 62–78.
Fournier, J. (1987), *Le travail gouvernemental*, Paris: Presses de la Fondation Nationale des Sciences Politiques.
Gouaud, C. (1989), 'Le Conseil des Ministres sous la Cinquième République', *Rev. du Droit Pub. et de la Sc. Political*, (2), pp. 423–96.
Lord, G. (1973), *The French Budgetary Process*, Berkeley, Ca: University of California Press.
Py, R. (1985), *Le secrétariat général du gouvernement*, Paris: La Documentation Française.
Quermone, J. L. (1987), *Le governement de la France sous la Cinquième République*, Paris: Dalloz.
Suleiman, E. N. (1980), 'Presidential Government in France', in Rose, R. and Suleiman, E. N. (eds.), *Presidents and Prime Ministers*, Washington, D.C.: American Enterprise Institute.
Thiébault, J.-L. (1988), 'France: Cabinet Decision-Making under the Fifth Republic', in Blondel, J. and Müller-Rommel, F. (eds.), *Cabinets in Western Europe*, London: Macmillan.

Germany

Hoffebert, R. I., and Klingemann, H. D. (1990), 'The Policy Impact of Party Programs and Government Declarations in the Federal Republic of Germany', *European Journal of Political Research*, Vol. 18, pp. 277–304.
Haungs, P. (1973), 'Die Bundes republik – en Parteienstaat?', *Zeitschrift für parlamentsfragen*, Heft 4, pp. 502–24.
Johnson, N. (1983), *State and Government in the Federal Republic of Germany*, Oxford: Pergamon Press.

Mayntz, R. (1980), 'Executive Leadership in Germany: Dispersion of Power or Kanzlerdemokratie?', in Rose, R. and Suleiman, E. N. (eds.), *Presidents and Prime Ministers*, Washington, D.C.: American Enterprise Institution.

Mayntz, R. (1987), 'West Germany', in Plowden, W. (ed.), *Advising the Rulers*, Oxford: Basil Blackwell.

Mayntz, R. and Scharpf, F. (1975), *Policy-Making in the German Federal Bureaucracy*, Amsterdam: Elsevier.

Müller-Rommel, F. 'Federal Republic of Germany: A System of Chancellor Government', in Blondel, J. and Müller-Rommel, F. (eds.), *Cabinets in Western Europe*, (1988a), London: Macmillan.

Müller-Rommel, F. (1988b), 'The Centre of Government in West Germany', *European Journal of Political Research*, Vol. 16 (2), pp. 171–90.

Müller-Rommel, F. (1992), 'The Chancellor and his Staff: From Adenauer to Kohl', in Padgett, S. (ed.), *The Development of the German Chancellorship*, London: Hurst Publisher.

Niclauss, K. (1988), *Kanzlerdemokratie. Bonner Regierungspraxis von Konrad Adenauer bis Helmut Kohl*, Stuttgart: Kohlhammer.

Rudzio, W. (1983), *Das politische System der Bundesrepublik Deutschland*, Oplanden: Leske und Budrich.

Saalteff, T. (1990), 'Efficient but Powerless? West Germany's Bundestag after 40 years' *Eur. Cons. for Pol. Research* paper.

Scharpf, F.W. (1987), 'Grenzen der institutionellen Reform', *Jahrbuch zur Staats- und Verwaltungswissenschaft*, Vol. 1, pp. 111–51.

Schmidt, M.G. (1983), 'Two Logics of Coalition Policy: The West German Case', in Bogdanor, V. (ed.), *Coalition Government in Western Europe*, London: Heinemann.

Smith, G. (1991), 'The Resources of a German Chancellor', *West European Politics*, vol. 14 (2), pp. 48–61.

Ireland

Farrell, B. (1971), *Chairman or Chief? The Role of the Taoiseach in Irish Government*, Dublin: Gill & Macmillan.

Farrell, B. (1987), 'Government Formation and Ministerial Selection', *Ireland at the Polls 1981–1987*, Durham, NC: Duke Univ. Press.

Farrell, B. (1988), 'Ireland. The Irish Cabinet System: More British than the British Themselves', in Blondel, J. and Müller-Rommel, F. (eds.), *Cabinets in Western Europe*, London: Macmillan, pp. 33–46.

Italy

Bartolini, S. (1982), 'The Politics of Institutional Reform in Italy', *West European Politics*, Vol. 5 (3).

Cassese, S. (1980), 'Is There a Government in Italy?', in Rose, R. and Suleiman, E. N. (eds.), *Presidents and Prime Ministers*, Washington D.C.: American Enterprise Institute.

Cotta, M. (1987), 'Il sotto-sistema Governo-Parlamento', *Riv. It. di Sc. Political*, Vol. 17, pp. 241–83.

Cotta, M. (1988), 'Italy: A Fragmented Government', in Blondel, J. and
    Müller-Rommel, F. (eds.), *Cabinets in Western Europe*, London: Macmillan.
Dogan, M. (1989), 'How to Become a Minister in Italy?', in Dogan M. (ed.),
    Pathways to Power, Boulder, Co.: Westview Press, pp. 99–140.
Hine, D. and Finocchi, R. (1991), 'The Italian Prime Minister', *West European
    Politics*, Vol. 14 (2), pp. 79–96.
Ruggeri, A. (1981), *Il consiglio dei ministri nella costituzione*, Milan: Giuffé.
Spagna Musso, E. (1979), *Costituzione e struttura del governo*, Padua: Cedem.

Netherlands

Andeweg, R. B. (1985), 'The Netherlands: Cabinet Committees in a Coalition
    Cabinet', in Mackie, T. and Hogwood, B., *Unlocking the Cabinet*, London:
    Sage.
Andeweg, R. B. *et al.*, (1980), 'Government Formation in the Netherlands', in
    Griffiths, R. T. (ed.), *The Economy and Politics of the Netherlands since 1945*,
    The Hague: Nijhoff Publishers.
Andeweg, R. B. (1988b), 'The Netherlands: Coalition Cabinets in Changing
    Circumstances', in Blondel, J. and Müller-Rommel, F. (eds.), *Cabinets in
    Western Europe*, London: Macmillan.
Andeweg, R. B. (1988), 'Centrifugal Forces and Collective Decision-Making:
    the Case of the Dutch Cabinet', *European Journal of Political Research*, Vol.
    16 (2), pp. 125–51.
Andeweg, R. B. (1991), 'The Dutch Prime Minister: Not Just Chairman, Not
    Yet Chief?', *West European Politics*, Vol. 14 (2), pp. 116–32.
Bakema, W. E. and Secker, I. P. (1988), 'Ministerial Expertise and the Dutch
    Case', *European Journal of Political Research*, Vol. 16 (2), pp. 153–70.
Van Putten, J. (1982), 'Policy Styles in the Netherlands', in Richardson, J. (ed.),
    Policy Styles in Western Europe, London: George Allen and Unwin.
Rehwinkel, J. P. (1991), *De Minister-president*, Zwolle: Tjeen Willink.

Norway

Eriksen, S. (1988a), *Herrskap og tjenere. Om Samarbetet mellan politiker og
    tjenestemenn i departementene*, Oslo: Tano.
Eriksen, S. (1988b), 'Norway: Ministerial Autonomy and Collective Respon-
    sibility', in Blondel, J. and Müller-Rommel, F. (eds.), *Cabinets in Western
    Europe*, London: Macmillan.
Olsen, J. P. (1980), 'Governing Norway: Segmentation, Anticipation and
    Consensus Formation', in Rose, R., and Suleiman, E. N. (eds.), *Presidents
    and Prime Ministers*, Washington: American Enterprise Institute.

Sweden

Isberg, M. (1982), 'The First Decade of the Unicameral Riksdag: The Role of
    the Swedish Parliament in the 1970s', *Forkningsrapporter*, no. 1, Stockholm:
    University of Stockholm.
Larsson, T. (1986) *Regeringen och dess kansli*. Stockholm.

Larsson, T. (1988a), Forändringar i och problem med den svenska regeringens och regeringskansliets organisation sedan 1840', *Nordisk Administrativt Tidsskrift*, 2.

Larsson, T. (1990), 'Regeringens och regeringskansliet organisationsstruktur, berednings-og beslutformer under 150 år', *Att styra riket* (commission set up to study the history of Swedish governments from 1840 to 1990).

Larsson, T. (1988), 'Sweden: The New Constitution. An Old Practice Adjusted', in Blondel, J. and Müller-Rommel, F. (eds.), *Cabinets in Western Europe*, London: Macmillan.

Ruin, O. (1990), *Tage Erlander*, Pittsburgh: Univ. of Pittsburgh Press.

Stenbäck, P. (1981), *Regeringens ekonomisk-politiska utskott. Funktion och problematik*, Föredrag vid Ekonomiska Samfundets möte den 7 maj, 1981.

Vinde, P., and Petri, G. (1978), *Swedish Government Administration: An Introduction*, Lund: Prisma/The Swedish Institute.

Index

Western European countries covered by this volume are not specifically mentioned in the index. See specific entries for country characteristics.